Château Cuisine

ANNE WILLAN

CHÂTEAU CUISINE

PHOTOGRAPHY BY
CHRISTOPHER BAKER

IN ASSOCIATION WITH
FRIENDS OF VIEILLES MAISONS FRANÇAISES

CONRAN OCTOPUS

NOTE

Basic recipes included in the glossary are cross-referenced with page numbers, whereas glossary tips and techniques are indicated with an asterisk.

First published in 1992 by
Conran Octopus Limited
37 Shelton Street
London WC2H 9HN

Both metric and imperial quantities are given in the recipes. Use either all metric or all imperial, as the two are not interchangeable.

Designer – Paul Welti
Project Editors – Louise Simpson and Denise Bates
Editor – Norma MacMillan
Editorial Assistant – Josephine Mead
Production – Julia Golding
Food Photography Stylist – Caroline Champenois
Map Artist – Rodney Paull

British Library Cataloguing in Publication Data
Willan, Anne
Chateau Cuisine
1. Title
641.5

ISBN 1 85029 393 7

Typeset by Servis Filmsetting Ltd
Printed in Hong Kong

Contents

FOREWORD

Château d'Ainay-le-Vieil, a magnificent fortress with nine imposing turrets, is owned by Princesse Georges-Henri de la Tour d'Auvergne and her five brothers and sisters (right).

The elegant drawing room at Château du Fëy, home of La Varenne cooking school (title page).

Anne Willan takes full advantage of the glorious produce at her local market in Burgundy (copyright page).

It is often said that the history of a society can be traced through the recipes of its people. In France, a country renowned for its crops and livestock as well as its fish and wild game, it was often the kitchens of the châteaux that gathered and retained the traditional recipes of the region. Here these recipes were then influenced by the exotic spices and methods that came from the East and by the strange fruits and vegetables from the New World. These imports enhanced the produce of the great châteaux, and brought out the full flavours of their native fish, meat and game.

In a land of such indisputable gourmands and gourmets, history and gastronomy have developed hand in hand. Henri IV owes his popularity to his Sunday Chicken, which he promised to all his people, and the *grand chef* Vatel is best remembered for committing suicide when the dinner he had prepared for Louis XIV was not ready on time. Many other celebrities have given their name to delicious recipes and are still commemorated on our menus today.

Gastronomy and the fine arts are more closely linked in France than in any other country. Paintings, porcelain, glassware, sculpture and even interior design all bear witness to the historic importance of food in our culture. Even the word *cuisine* refers not only to the kitchen as a workplace, but signifies the entire art of cooking for the French. Right from the beginning, the kitchen was a hallowed area of the château, often carefully planned and equipped, as today, with mechanical wonders, not to mention a battery of copper pots and earthenware. The recipes that our cooks created have always been a subtle synthesis of different tastes, influenced by geography and climate, by fashion, religious belief and folklore.

I myself spent a privileged childhood in a medieval château, which has been in my family for more than 500 years. We spent a happy time there, living in step with the seasons amongst a continuous throng of cousins, and playing under the canopy of the trees or up in the huge old lofts. Like so many other old families, we knew how to live in the present, but the house acted as a touchstone with the past, withstanding the hustle and bustle of the outside world.

The hold of such houses on our lives and our emotions is also keenly felt by everyone who has so kindly opened their doors to us. And it is to those people that I would like to express my sincere thanks for their warm welcome and the generous sharing of their personal recipes and family traditions.

The mission of Friends of Vieilles Maisons Françaises is to help preserve the architectural heritage of France. We at FVMF have joined enthusiastically in creating this very special book, which brings you a personal glimpse of more than 30 châteaux and country houses, of the families who live in them, and of their cooking. Through *Château Cuisine* we hope you will enjoy not just the richness of French cooking, but also the splendid architecture, which bridges the centuries from the Middle Ages through the Renaissance and right up to the present day.

Princesse Georges-Henri de la Tour d'Auvergne
President, Friends of Vieilles Maisons Françaises
Château d'Ainay, February 1992.

Château Cuisine has been published in collaboration with Friends of Vieilles Maisons Françaises, an international non-profit association dedicated to preserving France's architectural heritage, notably through mobilising international support for restoration of historic monuments. If you would like more information about FVMF, please contact Friends of Vieilles Maisons Françaises

91 rue du Faubourg Saint-Honoré
Suite 31,
75008 Paris.

INTRODUCTION

Château d'Anjony with its gracious interiors and beautiful antiques is also a family home (right).

Surely no two words are more evocative of the civilisation and culture of France than château and cuisine. Both are universal terms, needing no translation. And for me, working on *Château Cuisine* has proved to be a double pleasure, involving two of my favourite subjects: history and fine food.

Early on, my husband and I had the good fortune to meet Friends of Vieilles Maisons Françaises, the international foundation based in New York. Through Burks Hamner, Vice Chairman of FVMF's Southern California chapter, we met Princesse Georges-Henri de la Tour d'Auvergne, President of FVMF, and her associate, Simone Monneron, in Paris. From start to finish, this book has depended on their joint dedication and great enthusiasm more than I can say.

The four of us rapidly agreed on the ground rules for *Château Cuisine*: each château, whether large or small, great monument or family *manoir*, must be privately owned and inhabited. The properties would cover a wide range of styles and geographical settings. And most importantly, the owners must share our own love of good food. We defined five regions – the Île de France and the Loire valley, with their great palaces of leisure; the romantic north, land of mist and sea; the heart of France – Burgundy and the Berry in particular; châteaux, often fortresses, with a mountain background; and of course, châteaux in the sun.

Missing from our grand design was a photographer. The imaginative pictures of Christopher Baker speak for themselves – his creative eye and camera are a château's best friend. Jane Sigal's contribution as roving researcher, recipe editor, and project coordinator is less visible, yet has also been vital to the progress of this book. My associates at FVMF join me in expressing our deep appreciation to them both.

What has emerged is a personal portrait of thirty four châteaux. Times change, and we now live in a world where owners must be highly inventive to make their property habitable and economic. Talking to the châtelains who have so generously given of their time, I've been constantly delighted by the diverse ways great old buildings are being brought to life, whether by opening to the public, by accepting overnight guests, or by launching a restaurant in the outbuildings. Few châteaux now depend in the old way on the surrounding land, though some are vineyard properties, particularly in the south. For every owner, a château is a way of life; in the words of the Duchesse de Chevreuse at Dampierre, 'to leave is unimaginable'.

What a pleasure, too, the hundred recipes in *Château Cuisine* have been. No sign of dreary old classics, but plenty of surprises with dishes which transfer extraordinarily well from page to plate – reassuring proof, if any were needed, of continuing French expertise in the kitchen. Appropriately, it was the Princesse de Poix, a niece of that great gourmet, Talleyrand, who declared that '*le signe distinctif d'une femme bien née, c'est de se connaître en cuisine*'. ('The distinguishing mark of every well-bred woman is to know her way in cuisine'). Two Empires, five Republics and several foreign occupations later, this lapidary judgement still stands. As Henrik de Monpezat, the French-born Prince Consort of Denmark, told me, 'I take pride in keeping a good table'. Now I've come to appreciate that he was speaking for all his fellow châtelains.

Anne Willan

Anne Willan

Château du Feÿ, February 1992.

CHÂTEAUX

# of Leisure

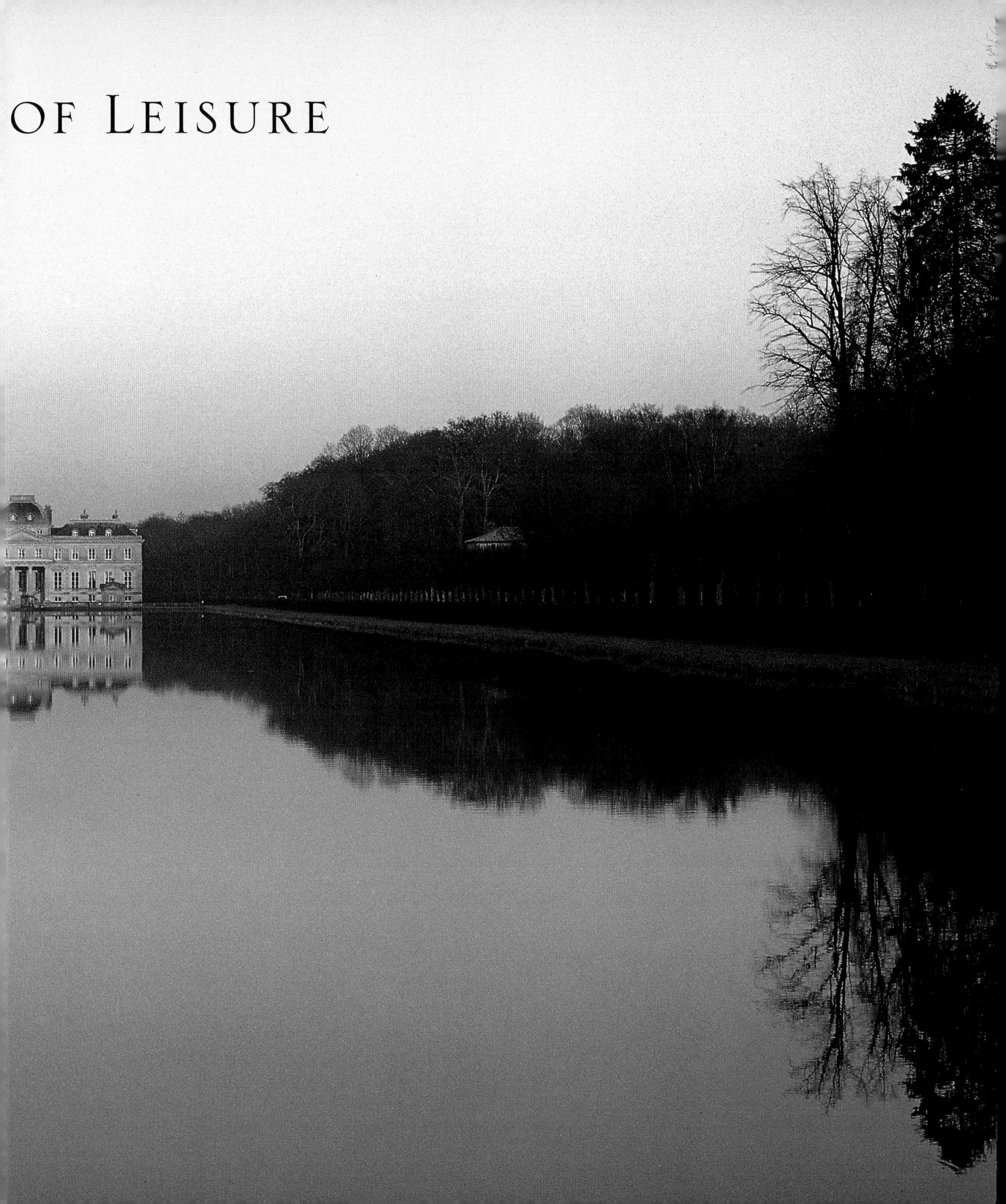

Château du Marais

The concept of the country retreat, or '*résidence secondaire*' is by no means a new one. Paris is ringed with châteaux built for the leisure of their metropolitan owners. Versailles began as a hunting lodge, and Henri II designed Anet for the enjoyment of his mistress, Diane de Poitiers. The Château du Marais is a latecomer as a pleasure dome, having been constructed as recently as 1778 by a wealthy government treasurer-general called Le Maistre. It was clearly his intent to entertain on a grand scale — hence the stately pillars and vast *cour d'honneur* for the reception of carriages. The artificial lake, over 500 metres long, reflects its surroundings so perfectly it is known as 'the mirror'.

The property quickly passed from Le Maistre to a young widow, Madame de la Briche, who organised country festivals for the peasantry. 'We set large tables in the parkland alleys,' she recorded in her diary. 'The only expenses for a charming day, full of gaiety and goodwill, were the cakes and spice breads, the wine, and the violinists for dancing.' Her generosity was happily rewarded, for Le Marais was left untouched during the Revolution.

The magnificent gardens of the Château du Marais, with their spring cloak of daffodils (right), stretch down to the imposing 'mirror' lake (previous page).

In the early 19th century, Château du Marais was a favourite meeting place of the French literary and political establishment. The restoration of the property began in earnest under Anna Gould, the American railroad heiress who married the Duc de Talleyrand-Périgord in 1908.

Happily, the tradition of receptions and literary salons at Le Marais lasted another 50 years, so much so that in the 1830s the château was called 'the most solid structure of the monarchy'. Guests included statesmen such as Talleyrand and the novelists Madame de Staël and Prosper Mérimée. Another literary giant of the age, François-René de Chateaubriand, described Madame de la Briche as 'an excellent woman, never short of good luck'.

Since the time of Madame de la Briche, Le Marais has been a château owned and appreciated by women. It passed to her daughter and granddaughter, and then at the end of the century to the most famous châtelaine of all, the American railroad heiress, Anna Gould, who started a programme of restoration. In 1908 she married Hélie de Talleyrand-Périgord, who was a duke not once but three times over – Duc de Talleyrand, Duc de Dino and Duc de Sagan. The first person to hold all three titles was a colourful personality, Dorothea of Courland, who was Talleyrand's niece by marriage and also one of his many mistresses.

Under the American duchess, the Château du Marais again became an exclusive haven for Europe's nobility: her granddaughter, known as the Duchesse de Sagan, is the present owner. She shares with her three children the task of maintaining the château and its outbuildings, which include an orangery, a museum devoted to family history and a functioning water mill, besides 25 hectares of parkland. 'It is so hard to preserve,' laments Comtesse Guy de Bagneux, the Duchesse's daughter. 'We are only 40 kilometres from Paris. Highways and power lines encroach all the time.' For Comtesse Guy the menace seems all the more threatening – her most nostalgic childhood memories are of intimate afternoon tea in the park with her legendary American grandmother. 'The chef prepared special cakes, but what we all loved best was cinnamon toast.'

Majestic balustrades and exquisite classical lines are softened and broken in the limpid reflections of the lake below the château.

PERDREAUX EN CHARTREUSE

MOULDED PARTRIDGE WITH CABBAGE

This ancient recipe has featured at Le Marais for years. It apparently originated with Catherine de Thouars, who in the 1430s was thrown into a dungeon by her husband, Gilles de Thouars, otherwise known as Bluebeard. While imprisoned, Catherine is said to have amused herself by cooking. This elaborate recipe would certainly have whiled away her time!

6 servings

2 MEDIUM SAVOY CABBAGES (ABOUT 1.6 kg/3½ lb EACH)
500 g/1 lb CARROTS
750 g/1½ lb TURNIPS
1 tbsp VEGETABLE OIL
1×165 g/5½ oz PIECE OF STREAKY BACON, CUT INTO *LARDONS**
3 OVEN-READY PARTRIDGES (ABOUT 500 g/1 lb EACH), GIBLETS REMOVED AND TRUSSED
30 g/1 oz BUTTER, AT ROOM TEMPERATURE
SALT AND PEPPER
375 ml/12 fl oz CHICKEN STOCK (see page 221)

23 cm/9 in SHALLOW ROUND BAKING DISH

Discard any damaged outer leaves from the cabbages. Immerse 8 large green leaves from each cabbage in a large pan of boiling salted water, then remove them as they soften. Refresh the leaves with cold water*. Cut the heart of each cabbage into 8 wedges. Blanch them in the boiling water* until tender, 10 to 15 minutes, then remove with a slotted spoon and refresh them. Shred the cabbage wedges, discarding the core. Keep the water boiling.

Heat the oven to 230°C/450°F/Gas Mark 8. Peel the carrots and turnips and cut them lengthways into 3 mm/⅛ in thick slices. Cook the carrots and turnips separately in the boiling water until just tender, 8 to 10 minutes for the carrots and 5 to 7 minutes for the turnips. Drain them and then refresh with cold water. Using a 3 cm/1¼ in pastry cutter, stamp out rounds from one-third of the carrot and turnip slices. Cut the remaining slices into rectangles, trimming them to the height of the baking dish and to a width of about 1.25 cm/½ in.

Heat the oil in a frying pan. Add the bacon and cook it gently until golden, about 5 minutes. Drain on kitchen paper.

Rub the partridges with the butter and sprinkle them with salt and pepper. Set them in a roasting tin and roast in the heated oven for 20 to 30 minutes until the juice runs pink when a bird is lifted with a two-pronged fork. Baste them often during cooking. When the birds are cooked, remove them to a carving board. Discard the string; cut the legs from the birds and reserve them. Cut off the breast meat and carve each piece into two or three slices on the diagonal. Reserve the carcasses. Reduce the oven temperature to 180°C/350°F/Gas Mark 4.

Pour the stock into the roasting tin and bring it to the boil on top of the stove, stirring to dissolve the roasting juices. Add the reserved carcasses and simmer the stock for 10 to 15 minutes, until reduced by two-thirds, then strain it and taste for seasoning.

To assemble the *chartreuse*, first butter the baking dish and line the bottom and sides with greaseproof paper; butter the paper also. Arrange a ring of alternating carrot and turnip rounds, slightly overlapping, around the bottom of the dish. Arrange a smaller but similar ring of vegetable rounds in the centre. Stand the vegetable rectangles upright round the sides, alternating the carrots and turnips and spacing them slightly apart. Line the dish with the cabbage leaves, saving 2 or 3 leaves for the top. Combine the shredded cabbage and the bacon. Taste the cabbage mixture and adjust the seasoning. Spread one-third of this cabbage mixture in the dish and pour one-third of the reduced stock over it. Arrange half the partridge slices on top. Cover with half the remaining cabbage mixture, pour in half the remaining reduced stock and then add the rest of the partridge slices. Pack the remaining cabbage mixture in the dish, add the

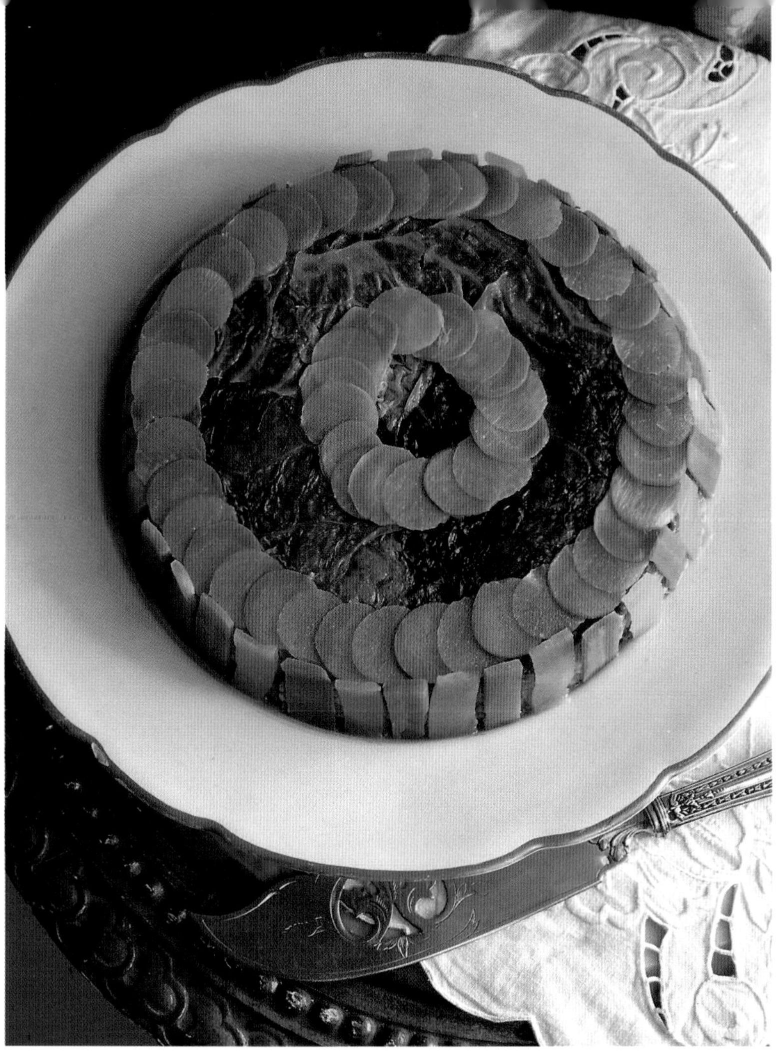

Perdreaux en Chartreuse, moulded partridge with cabbage, is a dish that dates back to the 15th century. It is still made at Le Marais with local partridge and home-grown vegetables.

rest of the stock and set the partridge legs on top. Press the reserved cabbage leaves over the surface, trimming them to fit.

Cover the dish with buttered greaseproof paper or foil and set a heatproof plate, that fits inside the dish, on top to compress the *chartreuse*. Set the dish in a *bain-marie** and bring the water to the boil on top of the stove. Transfer the dish to the heated oven and bake for about 1 hour or until a skewer inserted in the centre for 30 seconds is hot to the touch when withdrawn. Remove from the oven and allow it to stand in the *bain-marie* for at least 2 hours to firm up.

Remove the plate and paper or foil and turn out the *chartreuse* on to a warmed platter. Peel off the lining paper and adjust the decoration if needed. Serve the *chartreuse* cut in wedges.

The *chartreuse* can be kept in the refrigerator overnight; remove it from the *bain-marie* and leave it to come to room temperature first. Before serving, reheat the *chartreuse* in a *bain-marie* in a moderate oven, if necessary.

LIQUEUR A L'ESTRAGON

TARRAGON LIQUEUR

One of the villagers who worked at Le Marais left this recipe with the Bagneux family. French shops sell neutral spirits for conserving fruits in alcohol, but vodka also works well. Other herbs such as rosemary and thyme, or spices such as juniper, can be substituted for the tarragon. Tarragon liqueur adds an unusual flavour to strawberries and to Charentais melon.

Makes 750 ml/1¼ pints liqueur

A LARGE BUNCH OF FRESH TARRAGON (ABOUT 30 g/1 oz)
750 ml/1¼ PINTS NEUTRAL EAU-DE-VIE OR VODKA
300 g/10 oz SUGAR
2 VANILLA PODS, SPLIT

1 LITRE/2 PINT PRESERVING JAR

Reserve 2 tarragon sprigs for decoration. Coarsely chop the remaining tarragon, including the stalks. Combine the chopped tarragon in a saucepan with the eau-de-vie or vodka, sugar and vanilla pods. Heat gently, stirring from time to time, until the sugar dissolves. Take the pan from the heat, cover and leave to cool. Taste the liqueur and add more sugar to taste.

Sterilize the preserving jar*. Pour in the liqueur and seal it. Leave it in a cool place for 2 or 3 days, shaking the jar occasionally.

Strain the liqueur through muslin into a jug. Put the reserved tarragon in the preserving jar and pour in the strained liqueur. Seal the jar and store it in a cool place for at least 1 month before drinking.

A glimpse across the pillared dining room.

BISCUIT GLACÉ CARÊME

STRAWBERRY AND VANILLA ICE CREAM CAKE

At the Congress of Vienna, Marie-Antonin Carême acted as chef to Charles-Maurice de Talleyrand-Périgord, the 'architect of Europe'. No chef could have had a better assignment, for Talleyrand always maintained that the success of political negotiations depended on 'receiving with magnificence and offering the finest cuisine'. The memory of Carême has been preserved in the Talleyrand-Périgord family by this recipe above all others – a typically elegant creation of the greatest of chefs. This cake is also delicious made with raspberry ice cream.

8 to 10 servings

500 ml/$\frac{3}{4}$ PINT VANILLA ICE CREAM
(see page 220)
500 ml/$\frac{3}{4}$ PINT STRAWBERRY ICE CREAM
(see page 220)
1 STRAWBERRY, SLICED

For the sponge
90 g/3 oz PLAIN FLOUR
PINCH OF SALT
3 EGGS, SEPARATED
90 g/3 oz CASTER SUGAR
FEW DROPS VANILLA ESSENCE OR
THE GRATED ZEST OF 1 LEMON
4 tbsp COGNAC OR BRANDY

For the Chantilly cream
125 ml/4 fl oz DOUBLE CREAM
2 tsp ICING SUGAR, SIFTED
FEW DROPS VANILLA ESSENCE

20 cm/8 in SQUARE CAKE TIN; PIPING BAG AND MEDIUM STAR TUBE; ICE CREAM MAKER (OPTIONAL)

For the sponge, butter the cake tin and line the bottom with greaseproof paper. Butter the paper also and coat the tin with flour, discarding the excess. Heat the oven to 180°C/350°F/Gas Mark 4.

Sift the flour with the salt. Whisk the egg yolks with half the sugar and the vanilla essence or lemon zest in a bowl by hand or with an electric mixer until the mixture falls from the whisk in a thick ribbon and holds a slowly dissolving trail, about 5 minutes. In another bowl, whisk the egg whites until stiff. Add the remaining sugar and whisk until glossy to make a light meringue, about 30 seconds longer. Gently fold the meringue into the egg yolk mixture with the flour, adding it in three batches.

Pour the mixture into the prepared tin and bake in the heated oven until the cake shrinks slightly and the top springs back when lightly pressed with a fingertip, 20 to 30 minutes. Run a knife around the cake and turn it out on to a rack to cool. Peel off the lining paper. (The cake can be kept for 1 or 2 days in an airtight container. It freezes well too.)

About 1 to $1\frac{1}{2}$ hours before serving, transfer the ice creams to the refrigerator to soften just until spreadable. Make the Chantilly cream (see page 220) and refrigerate it.

Trim the crusty brown sides from the cake, then cut the cake in half horizontally with a long serrated knife to make two layers. Brush each layer with Cognac or brandy to moisten it.

To assemble the cake, spread one layer with the softened vanilla ice cream using a palette knife. Cover it with the second cake layer and press lightly to flatten it. Spread the top with the softened strawberry ice cream. Freeze the cake until firm, about 20 minutes.

Scoop the Chantilly cream into the piping bag. Pipe a rosette of Chantilly cream in the centre of the cake and top with the sliced strawberry. Pipe rosettes of Chantilly cream in rows around the edge of the cake. (The cake can be kept in the freezer for up to 30 minutes, but is best served as soon as possible after decorating so the Chantilly cream does not freeze.)

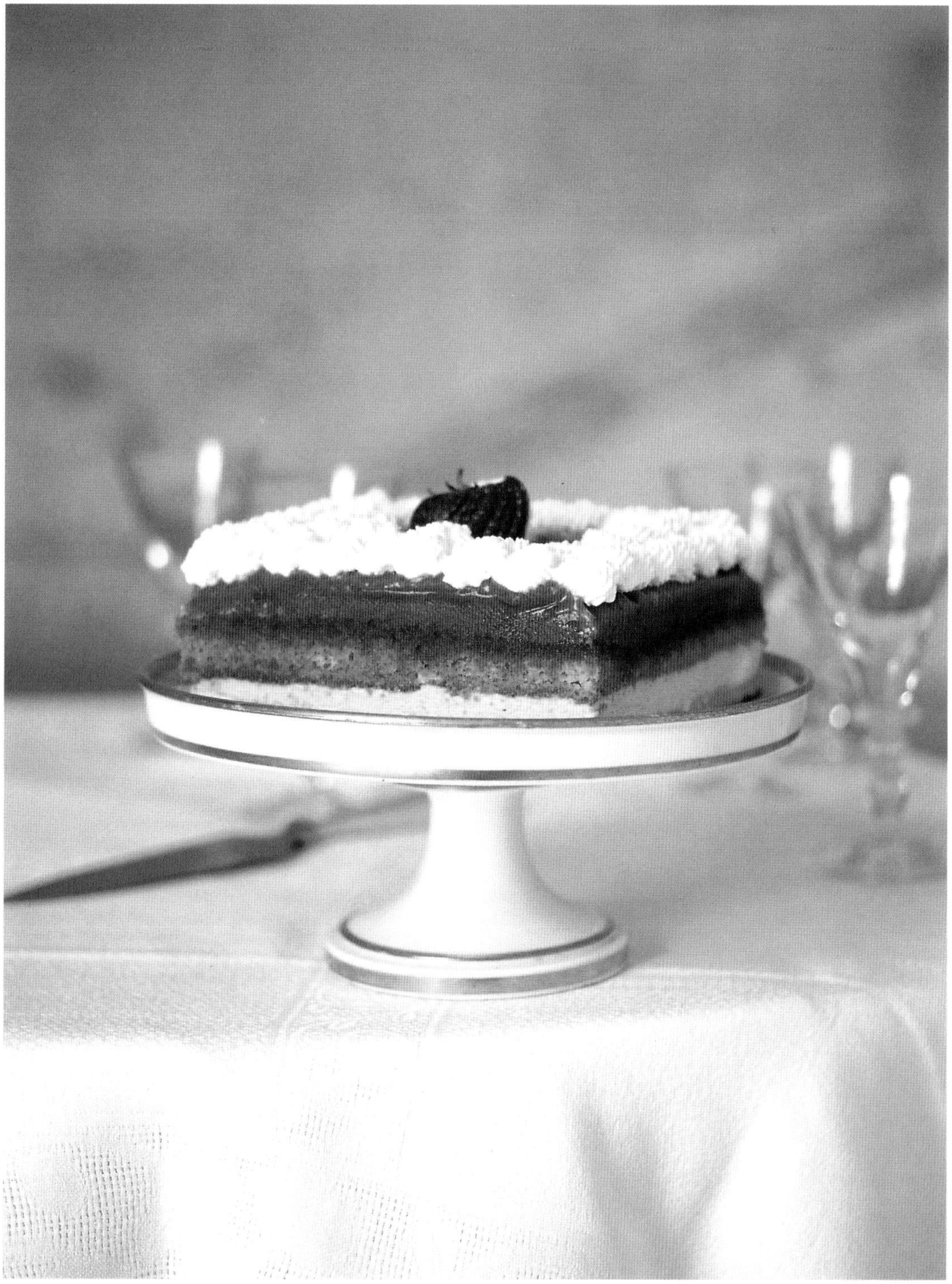

Biscuit Glacé Carême, a sublime dessert created by Marie-Antonin Carême, the famous 19th-century French chef still regarded by many as the greatest of all time.

CHÂTEAU DE COURANCES

Louis XIV much appreciated the fresh water of Courances – 12 springs feed the ornamental gardens. Today the gardens attract visitors from all over the world, who come to see one of the best preserved examples of Le Nôtre landscaping in France.

When I asked the Marquise de Ganay the number of rooms at Courances, she sounded amused. 'Impossible to count!' she replied. 'There are, in any case, six kitchens — one for ourselves, one for the staff, one for parties and one for each of my three daughters who have a home here.' Courances is one of the great châteaux of the Ile-de-France, built in the mid-16th century for Cosme Clausse, Minister of Finance to Henri II. Its name suggests running water — a reference to the many streams that traversed the property before they were tamed in the 17th century by the great landscapist, André Le Nôtre. He endowed Courances with an ornamental lake and a series of cascades and vistas which almost rival those of Versailles.

After 250 years of conspicuous presence, Courances proved too tempting a target for revolutionary France. In 1791 the château was invaded by troops looking for non-existent weapons. Two years later the owner, Marquis 'Le Grand Nicolay' and his son were imprisoned and executed. His widow clung bravely to the family home, but by 1830 the château had been abandoned. In February 1866, artist Jules Coeur noted: 'Renoir, Sisley and I . . . left by carriage for Courances and its beautiful château. Abandoned and surrounded by water, it is crumbling little by little like a piece of sugar in a damp corner.'

Courances is full of ghosts, like that of the young Huguenot Agrippa d'Aubigné, who at the age of 12 danced with such grace that he was spared an imminent death sentence and lived to become a noted 16th-century poet. The diarist Madame de Sévigné spent a rather uncomfortable night here in 1676, complaining of a very damp bed.

In 1870 the Baron de Gaber, great-grandfather of the current Marquis de Ganay, arrived on the scene. He restored what was left of the château and its grounds with the help of another great gardener, Achille Duchène. But the renaissance was short-lived. In World War II Courances became headquarters of the Luftwaffe, which exploded a munitions dump while making a hasty retreat in 1944. Then Courances became an American military prison, and was again badly shaken by an explosion, this time accidental. It was Field Marshal Montgomery who put the property to rights when he chose it as his base during his NATO command after the War.

Today this troubled past is invisible. After ten years of arduous restoration, Marquis and Marquise de Ganay were satisfied with the state of the gardens. Today Marie-Rose de Ganay leaves them in the charge of an Englishman, whose other vocation is music. The château is lively with friends, visitors from abroad, garden openings in spring and hunting in the autumn.

All the daughters have their own living areas, and they bring their families and spend what time they can at Courances. Anne-Marie de Ganay-Meyer runs an international decorating business under the name '*Juste Mauve*'. Valentine is a features writer on literature and gardens, while in the 1970s, Lauraine ran a catering business in Paris. 'My hobby became my *métier*,' she says. 'Everyone thought there must be a chef behind the scenes, but it was actually me peeling the potatoes. I cooked as I would at home. My food was home-made and certainly looked it. There were no lobsters in starched napkins and coatings of aspic, the typical caterer's signature.'

Lauraine was certainly untypical in the world of Parisian cuisine, monopolized as it is by macho chefs. For her parents' anniversary, Lauraine cooked a dinner for 50 of Moroccan-style *bstila* filled with skate, spinach and mushrooms, and a *snob au chocolat*, a moulded speciality of their old Polish cook, with a texture that is half cream, half chocolate truffle. Lauraine had told me 'We are all multilingual at Courances', and I couldn't help thinking that this was equally true of the cooking!

An array of cheeses from the Barthélemy dairy in Fontainebleau, including (clockwise from top right) brie de Meaux, brie de Melun, Coulommiers and fromage de Fontainebleau (right). Guardian geese survey their terrain under a fine canopy of old sycamores (below).

BAVAROIS A LA TOMATE

TOMATO RING FILLED WITH GOAT'S CHEESE AND BASIL

We may think of moulded salads as somewhat old-fashioned, but they have never gone out of style in French households. Lauraine de Ganay updates this fifties classic by filling the ring with a mixture of tangy goat's cheese, olive oil and fresh chopped basil – a wonderful way to enjoy the wealth of local dairy produce. One of the delights of this dish is its convenience. 'Like most of my recipes,' she says, 'it can be prepared well ahead.'

8 servings

1.4 kg/3 lb TOMATOES, SKINNED AND SEEDED*
2 STICKS CELERY, FINELY CHOPPED
SALT AND PEPPER
6 DROPS OF TABASCO SAUCE, MORE IF NEEDED
15 g/½ oz POWDERED GELATINE
90 ml/3 fl oz BROWN STOCK (see page 221)
250 g/8 oz FIRM GOAT'S CHEESE, CUT INTO 1 cm/⅜ in PIECES
4 tbsp OLIVE OIL
2 tbsp CHOPPED FRESH BASIL
FRESH BASIL LEAVES TO DECORATE (OPTIONAL)

1 LITRE/2 PINT RING MOULD

Pureé the tomatoes and celery in a food processor or blender until smooth. Season the purée to taste with salt, pepper and Tabasco sauce.

Sprinkle the gelatine over the stock in a small saucepan and leave until it swells to a spongy consistency, about 5 minutes. Melt the gelatine over low heat, then leave it to cool until tepid, stirring occasionally.

Stir the gelatine smoothly into the tomato purée. Sprinkle the mould with cold water. Then pour the tomato purée into the mould, cover it and refrigerate until set, at least 6 hours. The tomato *bavarois* can be stored for up to a day in the refrigerator, as long as it is not in a metal mould.

To finish, toss the cheese with the oil, chopped basil and pepper to taste. Turn out the *bavarois* on to a platter. Pile the cheese in the centre. Decorate the *bavarois* with basil leaves if you like.

Carré de Porc aux Groseilles

Pork Loin Filled with Redcurrants

Fresh redcurrants from the garden at Courances make an unusual stuffing for pork, as well as flavouring the sauce. At other times of year, tart fruits such as cherries, plums and cranberries can be substituted for the redcurrants. Stone the fruit where necessary and cut it into chunks. A crisp potato cake is an excellent accompaniment.

8 servings

1 PORK LOIN CONSISTING OF 8 CHOPS, RIBS SCRAPED CLEAN
750 g/1½ lb REDCURRANTS
SALT AND PEPPER
2 tbsp VEGETABLE OIL
250 ml/8 fl oz WHITE WINE

Heat the oven to 220°C/425°F/Gas Mark 7.

Set the meat on a carving board, scraped ribs upwards. Cut down between each chop, leaving the base joined, to form pockets for stuffing. Or have the butcher do this for you.

Pull the currants off the stalks with the tines of a fork. Sprinkle the fruit with salt and pepper and push half of it into the pockets between the chops. Tie the joint lengthways tightly with string. Brush the oil over the meat. Put the joint in a roasting tin and roast it in the heated oven for 50 to 60 minutes, basting often, until a skewer inserted in the centre of the meat feels hot to the touch when it is withdrawn after 30 seconds. A meat thermometer should register 75°C/170°F.

Transfer the joint to a carving board with a juice catcher, cover it loosely with foil and leave it to rest while preparing the sauce.

Pour all the fat from the roasting tin, leaving the cooking juices. Add the wine and remaining currants to the tin and bring to the boil, scraping to dissolve the browned roasting juices. Boil until the liquid is reduced by half and the currants are tender, 5 to 7 minutes. Taste the sauce for seasoning.

Remove the string from the joint and carve it, cutting down between each chop. Arrange the chops on a warmed platter. Stir the carving juices into the sauce. Spoon some of the sauce around the chops. Serve the remainder separately in a warm sauceboat.

Carré de Porc aux Groseilles. Home-grown redcurrants marry well with pork in this surprisingly simple dish.

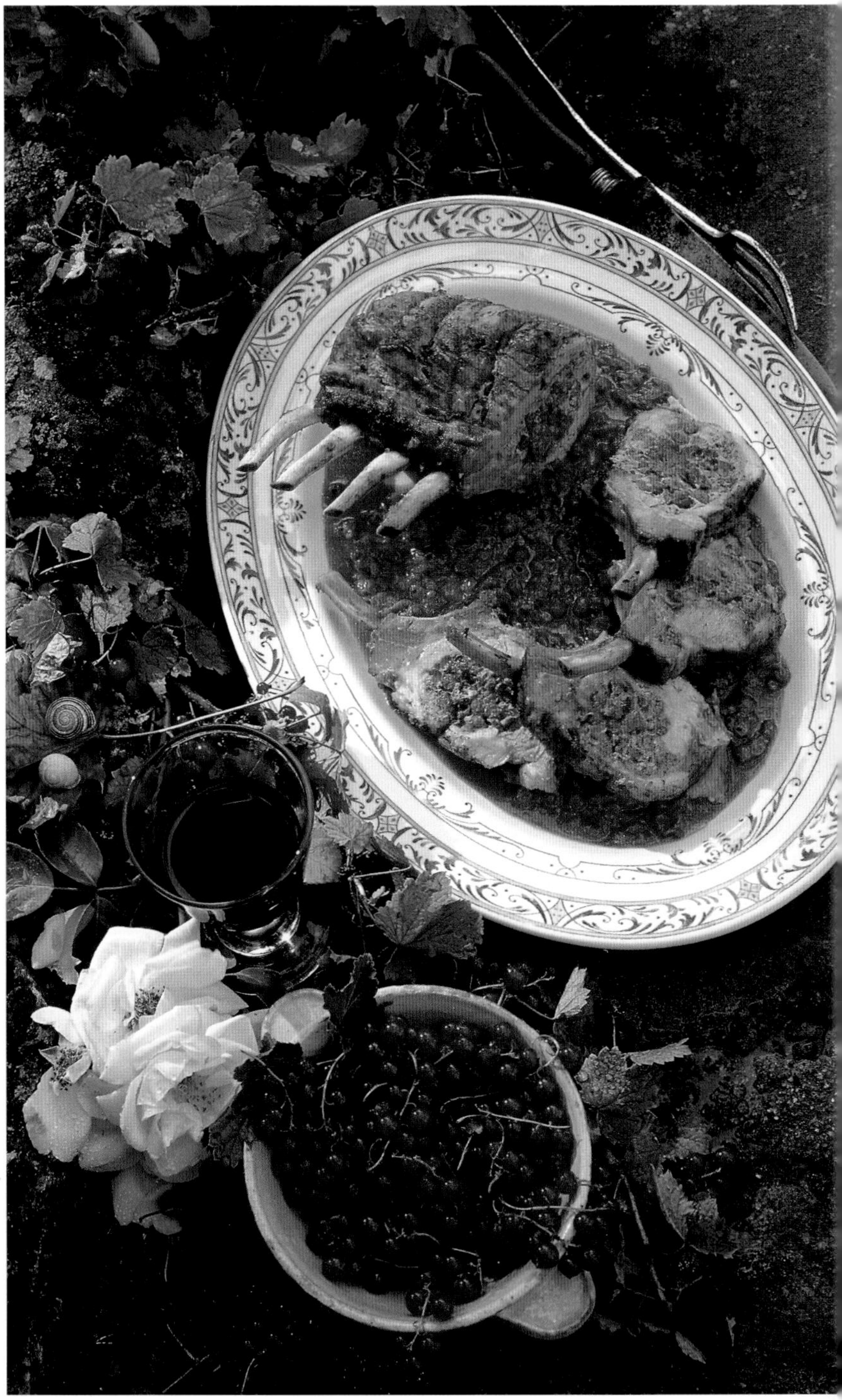

NOUGAT GLACÉ

FROZEN NOUGAT

'This dessert is impressive' says Lauraine de Ganay with authority. 'It can be varied to your liking with different dried and glacé fruits.'

8 to 10 servings

45 g/1½ oz WHOLE UNBLANCHED ALMONDS
3 tbsp ORANGE JUICE
45 g/1½ oz MIXED GLACÉ FRUITS
45 g/1½ oz RAISINS
300 ml/½ PINT DOUBLE CREAM
3 EGG WHITES
30 g/1 oz CASTER SUGAR
3 tbsp HONEY
PRALINE (see page 221)

For the sauce
6 KIWI FRUITS, PEELED
75 g/2½ oz CASTER SUGAR, MORE IF NEEDED

23×12.5×10 cm/9×5×4 in LOAF TIN

Heat the oven to 180°C/350°F/Gas Mark 4. Line the loaf tin with greaseproof paper. Spread the almonds in a single layer in a baking tray. Bake them, shaking the tray occasionally, until they are toasted inside, 5 to 7 minutes. Leave them to cool.

Combine the orange juice with the glacé fruits and raisins and leave them to soak.

Whip the cream until stiff. Beat the egg whites with an electric mixer until stiff. Add half the sugar and continue beating for 30 seconds to make a light meringue. Set aside.

Combine the honey with the remaining sugar in a small heavy saucepan. Heat gently until the honey and sugar melt, stirring occasionally, then boil for 1 minute.

Beating the meringue with the electric mixer, gradually add the hot honey mixture, pouring it directly into the path of the beaters. Continue beating until the meringue is cool and stiff, about 5 minutes.

Nougat Glacé made with dried nuts and raisins and served with fresh kiwi fruit sauce.

Gently fold the whipped cream into the meringue. Then fold in the toasted almonds, praline and drained fruits. Spoon the mixture into the lined tin. Cover and freeze until firm, at least 5 hours. (It will keep for a month in the freezer.)

An hour or so before serving, make the sauce: purée the kiwi fruits with the sugar in a food processor or blender until smooth.

Turn out the *nougat* on to a chilled platter and peel off the lining paper. Cut it into 2 cm/¾ in slices and place on dessert plates. Pour a little sauce around the edge of each slice and serve the rest separately.

Château de Saint-Jean-de-Beauregard

I think of the vegetable garden at Saint-Jean-de-Beauregard as a celebration of the fruits of the earth. Harvest culminates on Armistice Day, 11 November, with a great festival of 'Vegetables Old and New' — a shop window for the amazing variety of apples, pears, grapes, pumpkin and squash, roots and herbs that come to table in autumn from a well-tended garden. Its 16 hectares are the pride and the obsession of Muriel de Curel. In less than a decade, she has brought the garden from a state of neglect to one of joyful abundance.

Since childhood, the Vicomtesse de Curel has always loved gardens. When she and her husband inherited Saint-Jean-de-Beauregard, the handsome Louis XIII château came with one of the earliest *potagers* in France, dating from the mid-1600s and therefore contemporary with the kitchen garden at Versailles. The chance was too good to miss. Soon the borders of the square vegetable beds were replanted with flowers set off by multi-coloured cabbages, oddities like gourds, and such half-forgotten roots as Hamburg parsley, crosnes or Chinese artichokes, and salsify. The fruit trees espaliered along the garden walls to catch the sun were retrimmed with precision. The neglected 17th-century herb garden, once so important for medical remedies but now an essential complement to the table, was brought back to life.

It was in the village of Thoméry, near Fontainebleau, that a system was developed almost 150 years ago for preserving grapes as long as six months. Bunches are picked a week before they are fully ripe, with an extra-long stalk. This is inserted into a glass phial filled with spring water purified with charcoal. The grapes are then left to hang in a dry constant temperature of 5–6°C; any withered fruit is trimmed regularly from the main bunch (far left).

The annual garden festival 'La Fête des Fruits et Légumes', held in November, is renowned for its many unusual varieties. Colourful squashes, pumpkins and yew berries (in the 'Dangerous Fruits' category) are just some of the local fruits on display.

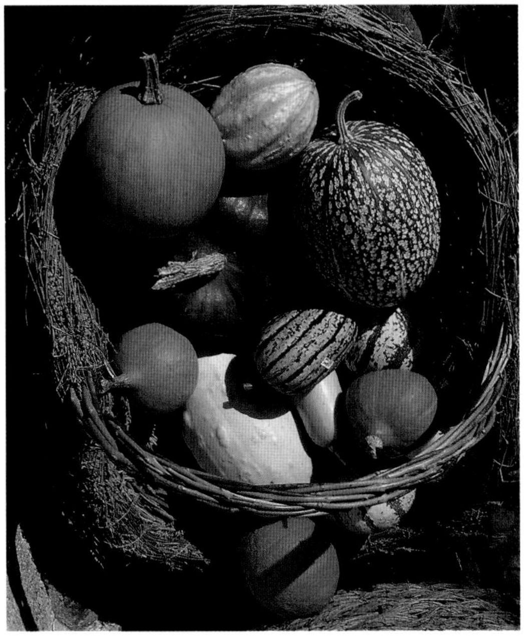

Now all is ordered with logic, a chequerboard of grass paths and beds guarded by bristling cardoons, a member of the thistle family. 'We have neglected so many plants that used to be popular,' laments Muriel de Curel. 'For example, chestnuts, broad beans and chervis (related to cumin) used to flourish here. They were displaced long ago by potatoes, tomatoes and other vegetables brought from the New World.'

November is by no means the end of the season at Saint-Jean-de-Beauregard, for traditional methods of storage are followed to the letter. Apples and pears, picked scarcely ripe so they do not rot, are ranged on wooden slats, each one separated from the next to allow the free circulation of air. Roots are stocked in the old way, layered with dry sand in a 'pie'. In the cool, dim grapery, Chasselas table grapes are preserved for up to six months.

All this is not just for show. 'We supply our own table,' says Muriel de Curel, 'with plenty left over for charity.' She is unusual in liking to cook as well as to cultivate the food she grows. 'Jams and preserves are a speciality of mine,' she declares, 'and sauces too. The copper pots we have at Saint-Jean are put to good use!'

SALADE DU POTAGER

KITCHEN GARDEN SALAD

In late summer and autumn, when the ripening vegetables and ornamental flowers at the Château de Saint-Jean-de-Beauregard are in their prime, salads practically make themselves. For her vinaigrette, Muriel de Curel likes to use one part olive oil to two parts vegetable oil so as to give a hint of the South to this Northern salad. For the perfect accompaniment, serve a bowl of iced red radishes with plenty of fresh baguette and unsalted butter.

6 to 8 servings

125 g/4 oz SMALL TENDER FRENCH BEANS, TRIMMED
125 g/4 oz MANGETOUTS, CUT INTO 3.75 cm/1½ in PIECES ON THE DIAGONAL
90 g/3 oz SMALL BROCCOLI FLORETS
90 g/3 oz SMALL CAULIFLOWER FLORETS
125 g/4 oz BUTTON MUSHROOMS, THINLY SLICED
60 g/2 oz SHREDDED RED CABBAGE
250 g/8 oz MIXED GARDEN LETTUCES, SUCH AS LITTLE GEM, OAKLEAF, ROCKET AND LOLLO ROSSO
1 SMALL RED ONION, THINLY SLICED AND SEPARATED INTO RINGS
½ SMALL CUCUMBER, THINLY SLICED
90 g/3 oz BLACK RADISH OR DAIKON, PEELED AND SHREDDED
1 FRESH YELLOW OR RED CHILLI OR ½ YELLOW PEPPER, SEEDED AND CUT INTO THIN STRIPS

For the vinaigrette
2 tbsp VINEGAR
SALT AND PEPPER
2 tbsp OLIVE OIL
4 tbsp VEGETABLE OIL

Cook the French beans, mangetouts, broccoli and cauliflower separately in boiling salted water until just tender, 5 to 7 minutes. Drain and refresh* each with cold water.

Make the vinaigrette (see page 222). Toss the mushrooms and cabbage separately with a little of the vinaigrette and leave them to marinate for up to 1 hour.

Trim the lettuces, wash them and tear into bite-size pieces. Dry them thoroughly and put in a bowl. (The beans, mangetouts, broccoli, cauliflower, mushrooms, cabbage and lettuces can all be prepared several hours ahead, but add the vinaigrette to the mushrooms and cabbage not more than an hour before serving. Refrigerate the lettuces to keep them crisp.)

To finish, arrange the beans, mangetouts, broccoli, cauliflower, mushrooms, cabbage, onion, cucumber and black radish in small piles on the lettuces. Scatter the chilli or pepper over the top. To serve, add the remaining vinaigrette and toss the salad until the ingredients are evenly coated.

Salade du Potager, with a delicious selection of salad vegetables grown on the estate.

FRICASSÉE DE LAPIN AUX TROIS RACINES

RABBIT STEW WITH ROOT VEGETABLES

The potager or vegetable garden is the pride of St-Jean-de-Beauregard and replete with unusual and old-fashioned vegetables, including Chinese artichokes, black salsify and huge marrows and pumpkins (below). Visitors stroll around the extensive grounds, admiring the espaliered fruit trees and the glorious produce (above right).

Over 2000 varieties of plants grow in the garden of Saint-Jean-de-Beauregard, and Muriel de Curel is constantly adding new ones. In this recipe, created by the young chef Pascal Pineau for the château's autumn fruit and vegetable festival, the hard-to-find roots can be replaced by carrot, turnip and celeriac.

4 to 6 servings

3 tbsp VEGETABLE OIL
1×1.5 kg/3 to 3½ lb RABBIT, JOINTED*
1 CARROT, CHOPPED
1 ONION, CHOPPED
1 STICK CELERY, CHOPPED
2 CLOVES GARLIC, CHOPPED
2 TOMATOES, SKINNED, SEEDED AND CHOPPED*
SALT AND PEPPER
20 g/¾ oz PLAIN FLOUR
125 ml/4 fl oz WHITE WINE
1 LITRE/1¾ PINTS CHICKEN STOCK (see page 221) OR WATER
A BOUQUET GARNI*
1 CLOVE
150 g/5 oz ROOT CHERVIL (CARROT, TURNIP OR CELERIAC WILL DO), CUT INTO 2.5 cm/1 in CHUNKS
150 g/5 oz HAMBURG (ROOT) PARSLEY, CUT INTO 2.5 cm/1 in CHUNKS
150 g/5 oz PARSNIP, CUT INTO 2.5 cm/1 in CHUNKS
45 g/1½ oz BUTTER
FRESH CHERVIL SPRIGS TO DECORATE

Heat the oil in a sauté pan or flameproof casserole. Brown the rabbit joints a few at a time over moderate heat. Add the carrot, onion, celery, garlic, tomatoes and a little salt and pepper to the pan. Sprinkle the flour over the rabbit and vegetables and cook until foaming, 2 or 3 minutes. Stir in the wine and stock and add the bouquet garni and clove, then bring to the boil. Reduce the heat to low and simmer, covered, until the rabbit is tender, about 40 minutes. (The rabbit can be cooked up to 2 days ahead and refrigerated in the cooking liquid.)

Remove the rabbit joints from the pan. Discard the bouquet garni and clove. Purée the vegetables with the cooking liquid in a food processor or blender until smooth. Return this purée to the pan and bring it to the boil. Add the vegetable chunks and simmer them until tender, 15 to 20 minutes. Using a slotted spoon, transfer them to a warmed serving dish and keep warm.

The sauce should be thick enough to coat a spoon lightly, so if necessary boil it to the desired consistency. Reheat the rabbit pieces in the sauce, then transfer them to the serving dish and keep warm.

Turn the heat under the sauce to very low and gradually whisk in the butter in small pieces. Taste for seasoning. Spoon the sauce over the rabbit and vegetables, decorate with chervil sprigs and serve.

FONDANT AUX POMMES

OLD-FASHIONED APPLE CAKE

'Just an old family recipe,' insists the Vicomtesse de Curel. 'But it's the best!' This is a very good way to use the aged, slightly dry apples that have been stored in clayettes, *or wooden drying racks.*

8 servings

2 EGGS
100 g/3½ oz CASTER SUGAR
125 g/4 oz PLAIN FLOUR
1 tbsp BAKING POWDER
1 VANILLA POD, SPLIT
100 g/3½ oz UNSALTED BUTTER, AT ROOM TEMPERATURE
3 DESSERT APPLES (ABOUT 625 g/1¼ lb TOTAL WEIGHT), PEELED, CORED AND CUT INTO SMALL CUBES
ICING SUGAR FOR SPRINKLING (OPTIONAL)

23 cm/9 in ROUND CAKE TIN OR SPRINGFORM TIN

Butter the tin and line the bottom with greaseproof paper. Butter the paper. Coat the tin with flour and caster sugar, discarding the excess. Heat the oven to 190°C/375°F/Gas Mark 5.

Whisk the eggs with the sugar until thick and light. Sift the flour and baking powder into the bowl, then stir them in. Scrape the seeds from the vanilla pod into the mixture. Cream the butter and stir it in, then stir in the apples. Spoon the mixture into the prepared tin.

Bake the cake in the heated oven for 40 to 45 minutes or until it shrinks from the sides of the tin and a wooden cocktail stick inserted into the centre comes out clean. Allow the cake to cool slightly in the tin, about 5 minutes, then turn it out on to a rack to cool completely, discarding the lining paper. (The cake keeps for up to 3 days in an airtight container.)

Sprinkle the cake with sifted icing sugar just before serving, if you like.

Apples, quince and pears are stored in the capacious cellars, ranged on wooden slats to prevent rotting. Darkness is essential for storage otherwise the fruit will spoil.

Château d'Anet

Hunting was the passion of Diane de Poitiers, mistress of Henri II (King of France from 1547 to 1559) and builder of the Château d'Anet. Diana, goddess of the hunt, is featured in the statuary, while over the main gateway of Anet stands a stag at bay, flanked by hounds. Only an hour from Paris, the forest of Anet is still prime hunting ground, and the sport remains a love of the current châtelaine, Laurette de Yturbe. 'I used to ride in a "pillbox",' she says, 'a horsedrawn carriage with high wheels and extra springs for the bumps, but most people follow the hunt on horseback or even bicycle. On foot is too slow.'

Rules for the traditional *chasse à courre* date back hundreds of years, as do the huge circular horns and costumes of the huntsmen. 'The struggle between stag and hounds is dramatic and carefully staged,' Madame de Yturbe told me. 'Early in the day, the master of the hunt selects the quarry. Only that particular animal is pursued. When the chase begins, selected huntsmen use a complex system of calls on the horn as signals for the hounds and hunters patrolling the forest alleys in search of the stag. If the animal escapes, then the hunt is abandoned for the day. This happens often. Once in my father's time we recognised a stag we had already hunted three times. Its courage could be acknowledged only by letting it go free.'

Most châteaux have character, but Anet's sense of identity, stemming from a gay and sophisticated past, is stronger than most. 'A charming valley, haven of peace, of greening trees and murmuring streams,' wrote an enamoured 18th-century visitor. 'Your pride, Anet, rests on thee. You alone possess the gifts of this world: love, glory, spirit and virtue.'

The inscription on the entrance portal reads 'This ample dwelling was consecrated by Phoebus to the good Diana who in return is grateful for everything she has received.' Diana was, of course, Diane de Poitiers, and Phoebus, Henri II (right).

The eastern façade of Anet, the only surviving wing of the original château.

Such chivalry harks back to another age when Anet was very much on centre stage. The original château, built in the 1540s, was recognised even then as a landmark of French Renaissance architecture, the ultimate hunting lodge and *château de plaisance*, on a par with the grandest of the Loire. Famous artists, including the Florentine silversmith and sculptor Benvenuto Cellini, decorated the Italianate buildings of architect Philibert de l'Orme. The beautiful Diane reigned supreme in France – she was 20 years older than her lover the King, who had grown tired of his wife, Catherine de Medicis. When the King was killed in a joust, Diane retired to Anet and passed her time in its embellishment until her death in 1566.

The 17th and 18th centuries brought the social and literary world to the château, including celebrities like La Fontaine and Saint-Simon. Voltaire took advantage of a stay at Anet not only to write a play, but also to act in it with other guests. When the Duc de Vendôme, owner of the day, received the Grand Dauphin (the King's putative heir), Jean-Baptiste Lully presented a new opera, and the Duc organised a grand banquet. The menu included 30 soups, 132 hors d'oeuvres, and a huge spread of game birds including pheasant, pigeon, woodcock, grey and red partridge, and plover, not to mention 334 roast game joints and four whole wild boar. In the style of the times this would have been served in two or three 'removes' or courses, in which hundreds of dishes were arranged in careful geometric patterns on huge tables for maximum show. Ostentatious display was the name of the game.

As so often, the French Revolution brought a sad change in fortune. Anet was sold piece by piece as public property; panelling was torn out, tiles stripped off, and the walls of dressed stone demolished for use elsewhere. Of the main château, only a wing has survived, along with the chapel, entrance gate and flanking pavilions. Happily, after nearly two centuries of work by devoted owners, all these structures have been fully restored, though what was lost in the Revolution has gone forever. In 1929 Madame de Yturbe's father was one of the first to open a privately owned château to the public. 'He felt that history should be shared,' she explains. 'We open Anet only in the afternoons, so that for at least half the day we can lead a normal life with our children and grandchildren. The château is self-supporting, and we cannot ask for more.'

The blessing of the hounds on the feast of St Hubert takes place in a village chapel near Anet. Huntsmen, hunters and spectators gather at the shrine, not to mention the eager hounds, who were originally allowed inside the chapel as well.

CUISSOT DE CHEVREUIL, SAUCE POIVRADE

MARINATED ROAST LEG OF VENISON WITH A PEPPERY SAUCE

Cuissot de Chevreuil is now reserved for special occasions at Anet, and is served with tart red berries called airelles.

The hunting season at Anet lasts from October until 'you can smell the violets', says Madame de Yturbe, but venison is less common on the château table than you might think. 'We never eat the mature stags hunted on the property; they would be far too tough,' she says. 'And we leave the females and young males to keep up the breeding stock.' However, she much enjoys this marinated leg of venison, served with the classic piquant sauce poivrade, *braised chestnuts and a purée of celeriac. As a condiment, the tart French berries called* airelles *are suggested. Cranberry sauce is a good alternative.*

8 servings

1×2.7 kg/6 lb LEG OF VENISON
30 g/1 oz BUTTER, AT ROOM TEMPERATURE
SALT AND PEPPER

For the marinade
3 PARSLEY STALKS
A BRANCH OF FRESH THYME
1 BAY LEAF
1 tsp PEPPERCORNS
2 CLOVES
2 BOTTLES (750 ml/1¼ PINTS EACH) FULL-BODIED WHITE WINE
300 ml/½ PINT WHITE WINE VINEGAR
125 ml/4 fl oz VEGETABLE OIL
2 CARROTS, THINLY SLICED
2 ONIONS, THINLY SLICED
2 SHALLOTS, THINLY SLICED
1 STICK CELERY, THINLY SLICED
2 CLOVES GARLIC

For the sauce

125 ml/4 fl oz WHITE WINE VINEGAR
175 ml/6 fl oz FULL-BODIED WHITE WINE
2 LITRES/3¼ PINTS BROWN VEAL OR
BEEF STOCK (see page 221)
4 PEPPERCORNS, CRUSHED
75 g/2½ oz BUTTER, CUT INTO SMALL PIECES

For the marinade, combine the herbs, peppercorns, cloves, wine and vinegar in a large saucepan and bring just to the boil. Reduce the heat and simmer for 30 minutes. Heat 2 tablespoons of the oil in a frying pan. Add the carrots, onions, shallots, celery and garlic and sauté, stirring often, until they begin to colour, 7 to 10 minutes. Add the sautéed vegetables and remaining oil to the marinade and leave to cool.

Put the venison in a deep bowl (not aluminium) and pour over the cooled marinade. Cover and refrigerate for 2 or 3 days, turning the meat occasionally.

Lift the meat out of the marinade and reserve it. For the sauce, boil the marinade in a saucepan until reduced to 1.25 litres/2 pints, then strain it and return to the pan. Add the vinegar, wine and stock. Simmer for about 2 hours or until reduced to 750 ml/1¼ pints. Add the peppercorns 10 minutes before the end of cooking. Strain again and season to taste. (The sauce and venison can be prepared to this point 12 hours ahead and refrigerated.)

Heat the oven to 200°C/400°F/Gas Mark 6. Pat the joint of venison dry with kitchen paper. Lay it in a large roasting tin, rub the surface with the butter and season. Roast for ¾ to 1 hour, basting often, until the meat is rare: the juices should run slightly pink when the meat is pierced, or a meat thermometer should register 51°C/125°F. For well-done meat, the juices should run clear, or the temperature on a meat thermometer should be 60°C/140°F. Transfer the meat to a carving board, cover it with foil and leave to rest for 15 minutes.

Reheat the sauce, if necessary. Whisk in the butter over low heat, but do not boil.

Carve the venison and arrange it on a warmed platter. Pour a little of the sauce around the venison and serve the rest separately.

LA POMME CHÂTEAU D'ANET

BAKED APPLE SLICES WITH CINNAMON AND RAISINS

In case weekend visitors from Paris are delayed, Madame de Yturbe likes to serve country dishes that reheat well, such as blanquette de veau *(see page 129) and* boeuf bourguignon. *Desserts are equally simple – in summer strawberries with fresh cheese or a tart of figs from the garden, and in winter this baked apple dish. Since Anet borders on Normandy, the land of apples and Calvados, it's not surprising that Madame de Yturbe adds a generous glass of apple brandy to her baked apples just before serving. Serve the baked apple slices very hot, with chilled vanilla custard (see page 222) or crème fraîche* as an accompaniment.*

4 servings

3 tbsp RAISINS
4 tbsp CALVADOS,
MORE IF LIKED
4 COOKING APPLES (ABOUT 750 g/1½ lb
TOTAL WEIGHT), PEELED, CORED AND
CUT INTO 3 mm/⅛ in SLICES
50 g/1¾ oz SUGAR
1 tsp GROUND CINNAMON
45 g/1½ oz UNSALTED BUTTER

1 LITRE/2 PINT BAKING DISH

Heat the oven to 180°C/350°F/Gas Mark 4 and butter the baking dish. Soak the raisins in the Calvados to plump them.

Arrange the apple slices, overlapping, in layers in a neat pattern in the baking dish. Sprinkle them with the sugar, cinnamon and drained raisins (reserve the Calvados). Dot the top with the butter and bake in the heated oven until the apples are tender, about 35 minutes. Sprinkle with the reserved Calvados and serve very hot.

Château de Dampierre

Even before the present château was built, Dampierre — a property associated for centuries with the ducal titles of Luynes and Chevreuse — was a haven for celebrated guests. Anne of Austria spent several days there in 1661 with her daughter-in-law, Henrietta of England. Only a few years later the property was described as 'big, very old and by now completely run down'. But not for long, for the new Duc de Chevreuse had made a strategic marriage with the daughter of France's Minister of Finance, Jean-Baptiste Colbert.

This gave the young Duc the means to rebuild and redesign his domain, using the services of the great architects of the time — Mansart for the château and Le Nôtre for the garden. Both the château itself — in graceful pink brick and golden stone — and the huge lakes and lawns that surround it have changed little since these two master craftsmen laid out Dampierre. Inside, the royal apartments where Louis XIV, Louis XV and Louis XVI all stayed at one time or another remain untouched, echoing the grandeur of Versailles.

The elegant Château de Dampierre was built between 1675 and 1683 by one of the greatest of French architects – Jules Hardouin Mansart. Today visitors are attracted not only by the classical architecture but by the impressive restaurant Les Écuries du Château, housed in the old stables and set up by the present Duc de Chevreuse.

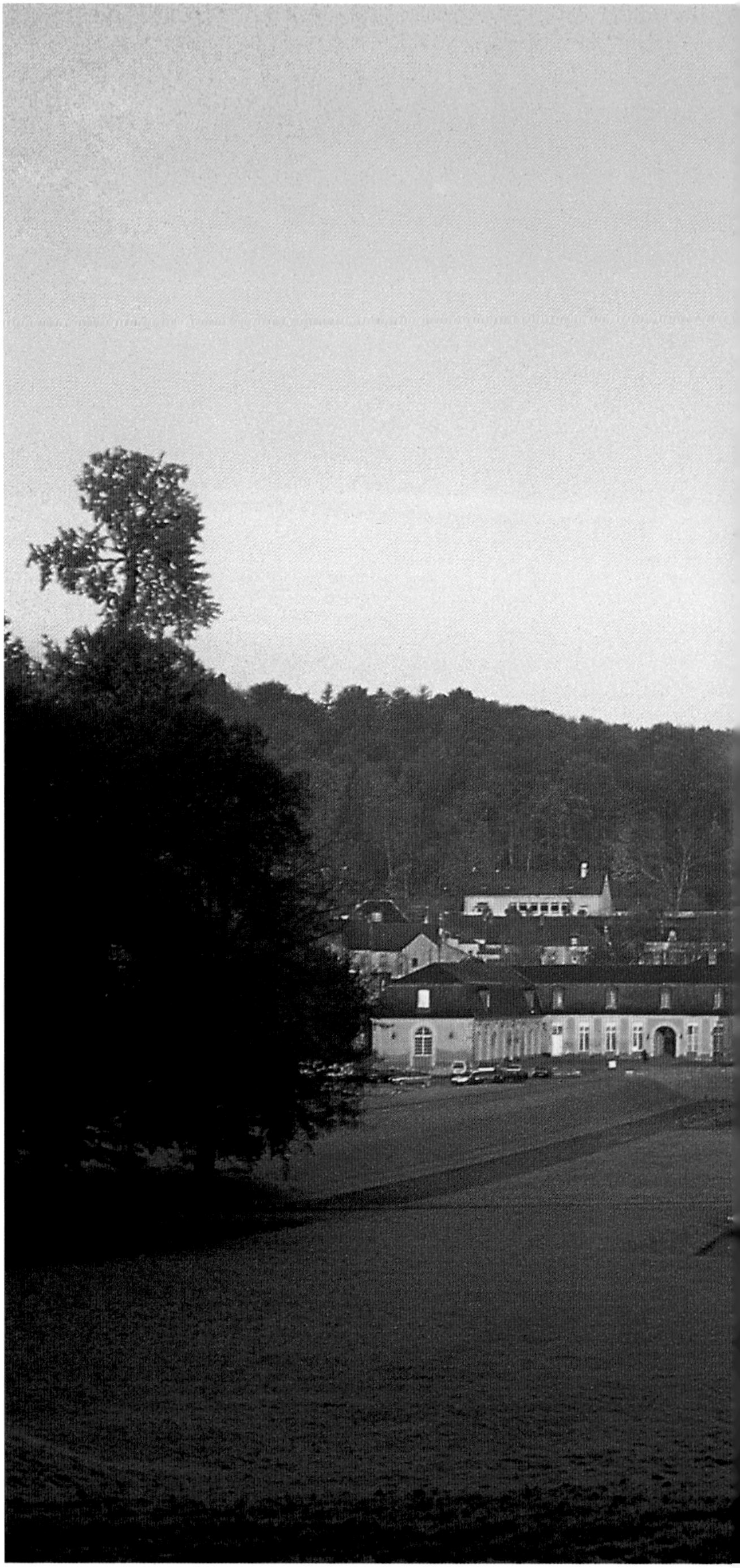

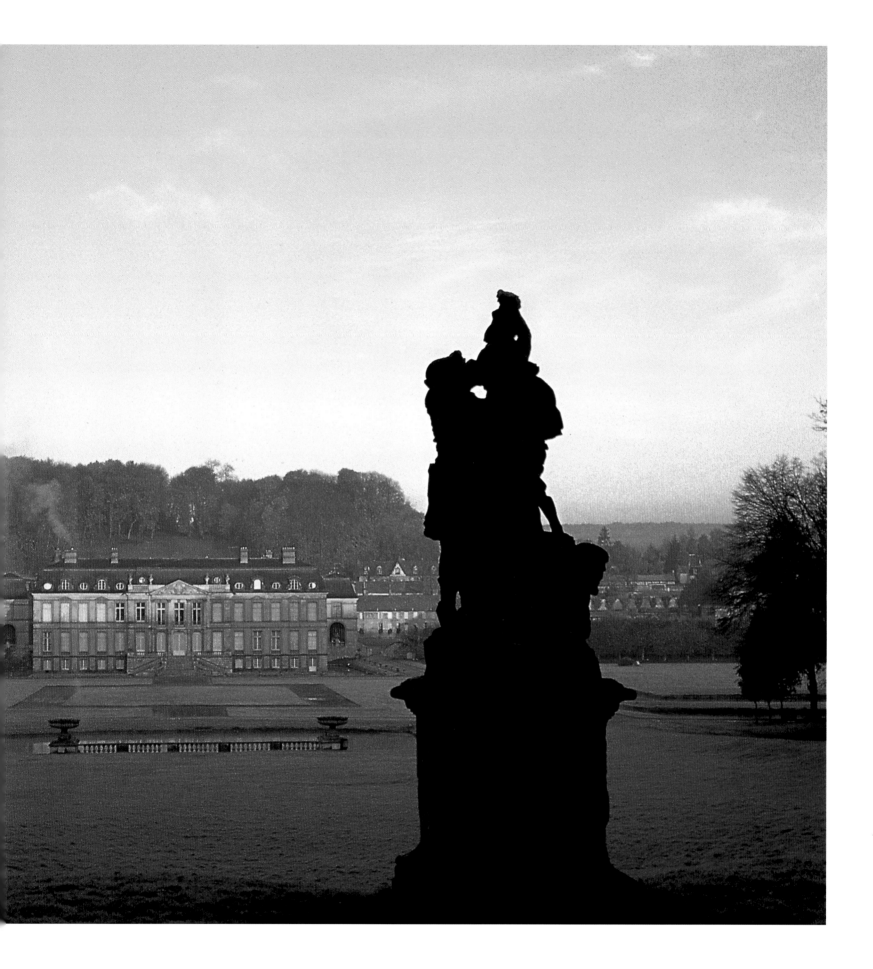

One of the more notorious occupants of Dampierre, Marie de Rohan-Montbazon, pretended to spend hot summer nights in the summerhouse by the lake, when really it was a cover for her illicit liaisons in Paris.

The link between Dampierre and the Ducs de Luynes and Chevreuse remains extraordinarily close (the two titles are separate, being held by father and son in alternating succession). The family survived the Revolution thanks to the affection in which they were held by the local community. When the Duc and Duchesse were arrested with their daughter in 1794, villagers hid the heir to the dukedom, young Honoré. What is more, each day they sent a carriage-load of meat and vegetables to the prison, for the Duc was a gourmand of renown. It is said that the provisions were equally appreciated by the prison governor, who eventually arranged for the release of his noble detainees.

A love of good food runs in the family and can be traced back to the Duc de Chevreuse who built Dampierre. For all his distinction as tutor to the King's grandson (and would-be heir), he was a true eccentric: 'He once poisoned his stomach with chicory water throughout the entire course of the meal, just for the sake of drinking a bumper of wine with sugar and nutmeg at the end,' the diarist Saint-Simon reported. 'He never appeared at meals until the second course was served; then he would hastily devour a shoulder of rabbit or a grill, whatever was least acid, and for dessert, a few sweetmeats, which he thought were good for the digestion, with a weighed portion of bread from which the crust had been removed . . . towards midnight he would eat some kind of an egg dish or fish cooked in water and oil.'

The present family's favourites are a bit different. 'Philippe is so lucky,' sighs the Duchesse de Chevreuse of her teenage son. 'He is tall and thin and loves to try everything – another Gargantua. He'll take a double helping just to test the difference between the common grey partridge and the Savoy red partridge, found mainly in the Midi.'

His father is an equal enthusiast, not hesitating to wander into famous kitchens for a chat with the chef. He insists that the fruit and vegetables on the family table be grown at Dampierre and 'would never go out and buy a chicken from a shop,' says the Duchesse – 'it must be raised at home.'

Both the Duc and Duchesse like to cook, 'I act as *marmiton* (the lowest rung in French kitchen hierarchy),' she laughs. 'I'm more fussy about food than Jean, though I'm crazy about chocolate. He is a true gourmand, he enjoys everything.' 'Nothing beats a *rable de lièvre à la royale*,' interjects the Duc, more tempted than some by marinated saddle of hare served in a dark red wine sauce thickened with the blood of the animal.

In spending a good deal of time at Dampierre and working hard to give it life, the Duc is inspired by his father, the Duc de Luynes, who has been a moving force behind Demeure Historique, the action group for châteaux proprietors. The Duc de Chevreuse surprised some of his clan by installing a charming restaurant, Les Écuries du Château, in the stables. Few if any historic monuments offer notable food, but the cuisine of chef Christian Deluchey, based on modern classics such as *ragoût de boeuf aux morilles et pâtes fraîches* and *gratin de mandarines*, has already achieved recognition in the gastronomic guides. For her part, the Duchesse oversees the flower garden and coordinates visiting groups. She is president of the local tourist office. 'A big property like this is demanding,' she admits. 'But we would never think of giving it up. That is unimaginable.'

Bécasses en Salmis

Pan-Roasted Woodcock on Croûtes

Diminutive woodcock, with distinctive, straight beaks, are prized as much for their earthy insides as their tasty flesh, for they are the only birds traditionally cooked with the innards left intact. Since their sale has been outlawed in France, you would have to befriend a generous hunter to taste one – quail is not quite the same thing, although delicious prepared en cocotte *as here. If cooking quail, substitute 2 or 3 chicken livers (about 60 g/2 oz) for the woodcock innards.*

4 servings as a first course

4 OVEN-READY WOODCOCK OR QUAIL (ABOUT 125 g/4 oz EACH), WITH THE INNARDS
SALT AND PEPPER
60 g/2 oz CLARIFIED BUTTER (see page 220)
150 ml/¼ PINT COGNAC
2 SHALLOTS, FINELY CHOPPED
1 CLOVE GARLIC
1 SMALL CARROT, VERY THINLY SLICED

1 BAY LEAF
A SPRIG OF FRESH THYME
75 ml/2½ fl oz PORT
500 ml/16 fl oz CHICKEN STOCK (see page 221)
125 g/4 oz *PÂTÉ DE FOIE GRAS*

4 SQUARE *CROÛTES*, FRIED IN OIL AND BUTTER (see page 220)

Sprinkle the birds inside and out with salt and pepper. Tie them into shape with string. Heat three-quarters of the clarified butter in a sauté pan or flameproof casserole and brown the birds over moderate heat, 6 to 7 minutes.

Add half the Cognac, bring it to the boil and set it alight. (Stand back from the flame.) Simmer the Cognac for about 30 seconds, basting the birds until the flame dies. Add the shallots, garlic, carrot, bay leaf and thyme. Cover the pan and continue cooking the birds for 10 to 15 minutes or until they are barely done: the juice from the cavity should run pink when a bird is lifted with a two-pronged fork.

Transfer the birds to a carving board, cover loosely with foil and leave them to rest.

Pour all the fat from the pan, leaving the cooking juices. Stir in the port, remaining Cognac and the stock and bring to the boil, scraping to dissolve the browned pan juices. Season. Reduce the heat and simmer the sauce until it lightly coats a spoon, 10 to 15 minutes.

Strain the sauce into a saucepan, set it over very low heat and gradually whisk in half the *pâté de foie gras*. Move the pan on and off the heat, so the pâté softens creamily to form a smooth sauce. Do not heat it too much or it will melt to oil. Taste the sauce for seasoning.

Cut the birds into quarters – 2 legs and 2 breasts; discard the back. Scoop out the innards. Heat the remaining clarified butter in a small frying pan. Add the innards (or chicken livers if using quail) and sauté them, stirring often, until brown on the outside but still pink in the centre, about 1 minute. Mash together the remaining *pâté de foie gras* and the innards or livers.

Spread this mixture on the *croûtes*. Set a piece of bird on top of each *croûte*, arrange on warmed plates, spoon over the sauce and serve.

Pheasant hunting in the forest begins in the autumn, and feathered game features regularly in family meals (above).

Bécasses en Salmis – woodcock was traditionally used for this dish, but quails make a perfectly suitable alternative, as used here (left).

The grand stone staircase dominates the front of the château and affords a marvellous vantage point over the Le Nôtre parterres below.

SOLE COLBERT

GOLDEN SOLE WITH HERB BUTTER

This old family recipe must be served at once so the cold herb butter is firm inside the crisp hot fish. If you like, garnish it with deep-fried parsley.

4 servings

4 DOVER SOLE (ABOUT 300 g/10 oz EACH), CLEANED AND TRIMMED
125 g/4 oz CLARIFIED BUTTER (see page 220)

For the parsley butter
125 g/4 oz BUTTER, AT ROOM TEMPERATURE
2 tbsp FINELY CHOPPED PARSLEY
1 tbsp LEMON JUICE
SALT AND PEPPER

For the coating
60 g/2 oz SEASONED FLOUR
2 EGGS, BEATEN TO MIX WITH 1 tbsp DIJON-STYLE MUSTARD AND 1 tbsp VEGETABLE OIL
100 g/3½ oz DRY WHITE BREADCRUMBS

PIPING BAG AND MEDIUM STAR TUBE (OPTIONAL)

For the parsley butter, cream the butter, then beat in the parsley and lemon juice. Season. (This can be prepared 2 or 3 days ahead and refrigerated, but allow the butter to soften again by the time the fish are done.)

Prepare the fish or have it done by the fishmonger as follows: Remove top and bottom skin. Set a fish flat on a work surface. Using a flexible knife, cut along the edge of the right fillet. Holding the knife almost parallel to the bones, slice between the fillet and the bones. Continue cutting over and beyond the backbone until the whole fillet is loosened in one piece. Cut to the edge of the traverse bones but do not remove the fillet completely. Turn the fish over and again loosen the fillet from the bones, taking care to work from the same cut side. With scissors, snip the backbone at head and tail. Cut all around the traverse bones so they are easy to remove after cooking. Fold the fillet back in place. Repeat for all the fish.

Coat the fish first with the seasoned flour, then the eggs and finally with breadcrumbs.

Heat the clarified butter in a large frying pan. Add 2 fish and brown them over moderate heat, 2 to 3 minutes on each side. Continue cooking over fairly low heat until the fillets are opaque next to the bone, 5 to 7 minutes. Transfer the fish to kitchen paper to drain, then keep warm on a platter while you cook the remaining fish.

Pull out the backbone from the open side of each fish so the fillets remain intact, attached at the head and tail. Spoon or pipe the parsley butter into the backbone cavity. Serve at once.

TERRINE DE CANARD

WILD DUCK TERRINE WITH PISTACHIOS

The Duc de Chevreuse enjoys organizing hunting parties for his friends in the walled forest of Dampierre. Of course you can use domestic duck in this recipe too.

16 to 18 servings

3 OVEN-READY MALLARD DUCKS (ABOUT 750 g/1½ lb EACH)
30 g/1 oz BUTTER
60 g/2 oz SHELLED PISTACHIOS, BLANCHED AND SKINNED*
625 g/1¼ lb MINCED PORK
2 tbsp SALT, MORE IF NEEDED
1 tbsp PEPPER, MORE IF NEEDED
3 SHALLOTS, FINELY CHOPPED
75 ml/2½ fl oz WHITE WINE
4 tbsp COGNAC
125 g/4 oz BARDING FAT*
A SPRIG OF FRESH THYME
2 BAY LEAVES

1.5 LITRE/2½ PINT TERRINE WITH LID

Ask the butcher to bone the duck breasts, or do it yourself: place a duck, breast up, on a board and cut out the wishbone. Cut the breast meat away from the bone on one side until you reach the ridge of the breastbone, where the skin and bones meet. Turn the bird around and repeat on the other side. Pull to separate the breastbone and carcass from the meat. Discard the skin from the meat. Repeat the process with the remaining ducks.

Cut 3 of the duck breasts lengthways into 4 or 5 strips each. Heat the butter in a frying pan, add the strips of duck breast and sauté them on all sides, stirring constantly, until they are lightly browned but still pink in the centre, 1 to 2 minutes. Remove them. Cut the remaining breasts into pieces.

Scrape the meat off the legs, discarding the skin and any tendons and sinews. Work the leg and breast meat with the giblets through a mincer fitted with a medium disc. Or, purée them a little at a time in a food processor.

Mix together the pistachios, 625 g/1¼ lb of the minced duck, the pork, salt, pepper, shallots, wine and Cognac. Beat with a wooden spoon until this forcemeat holds together. Sauté a small piece in a frying pan and taste it, then adjust the seasoning of the remaining forcemeat.

Heat the oven to 180°C/350°F/Gas Mark 4. Line the terrine with the barding fat, reserving some for the top. Spread half the forcemeat in the lined terrine. Top with the strips of duck breast, laying them lengthways. Spread the remaining forcemeat on top and cover with the reserved barding fat. Add the thyme and bay leaves and put the lid on the terrine.

Set the terrine in a *bain-marie** and bring the water to the boil on top of the stove. Transfer to the heated oven and cook for about 1½ hours or until a skewer inserted in the centre of the terrine for 30 seconds is hot to the touch when withdrawn. Leave the terrine to cool until tepid. Remove the lid and set a 500 g/1 lb weight on top so the mixture will compress (this ensures it will slice well). Keep the terrine in the refrigerator for at least 3 days or up to a week before serving to allow the flavour to mellow. Serve the terrine directly from the dish.

Terrine de Canard. The forest of Dampierre is enclosed by 14 kilometres of wall and is well-stocked with a wide variety of game birds including wild duck.

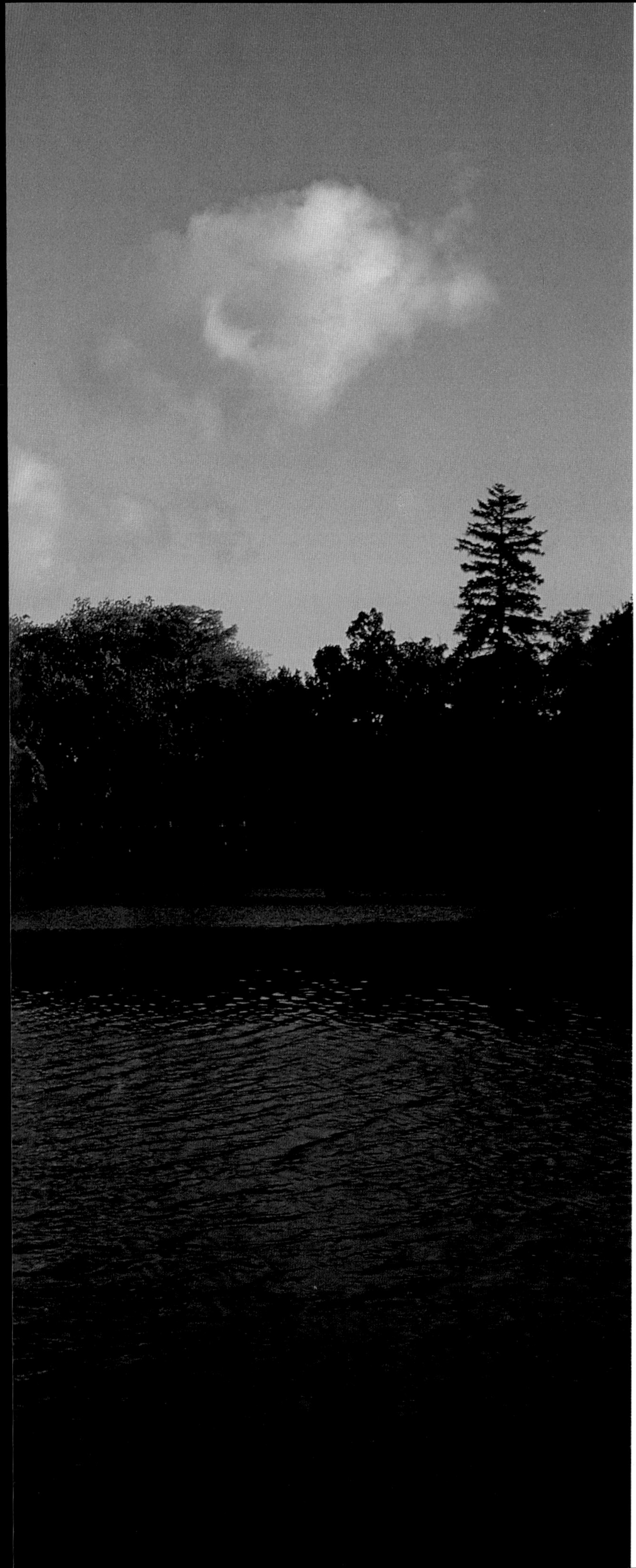

Château de La Ferté-Saint-Aubin

Jacques Guyot bought La Ferté-Saint-Aubin in 1987 as a calculated business risk. He first heard about the property by the classic country method, word of mouth, and was attracted at once. La Ferté is in Sologne, a flat but distinctive region of pine forest and heather, dotted with lakes and well stocked with game, which Jacques Guyot knew from childhood. To all appearances, however, La Ferté was unsaleable, having crumbled over the years in the hands of an elderly owner. But Monsieur Guyot knew better as he had already been partner with his brother in the restoration of the now-famous Château de Saint-Fargeau. 'Old places must live again,' he insists. The bankers were less enthusiastic. 'I had to work like the devil to convince them,' he laughs.

Since then he has invested an additional six million francs, almost all of it earned by the château itself, with a minimum of government help. A master of public relations, Jacques Guyot tells visitors that each 35-franc entrance fee buys three new slates for the roof, which covers about a hectare. The first area to be restored at La Ferté was the stables — two sets of them — for Jacques Guyot was once a riding instructor. 'The château belonged to two marshals of France, so of course horses were important,' he explains. Riding and carriage displays are held each weekend, with regular dressage competitions.

The imposing Château de La Ferté-Saint-Aubin is surrounded by over 7 hectares of water. After years of neglect, it is now being restored by its energetic owner, Jacques Guyot.

La Ferté is covered with over 8000 square metres of roofing – a considerable area when so many of the slates need repairing or replacing. In fact, the châtelain, Monsieur Guyot delights in telling visitors how each entrance fee pays for 3 new slates precisely.

From horses, the transition to other animals was easy. The park now houses deer, mountain sheep and goats, as well as a model farm with poultry, ponies and miniature goats. An *Île Enchantée* for children has been created, where they can visit Snow White and other fairytale characters. The orangery has recently been restored for receptions and banquets, while within the château, visitors may tour 25 rooms from attic to cellar, including a magnificent period kitchen with old work tables, cast-iron pans and an open fireplace with a working spit. It was to this kitchen that a 19th-century owner, a retired chef and hotelkeeper, would descend in the morning to sniff the air for clues to the day's fare. 'Leopold,' he would cry, 'your ragoût is not *à point*.' It lacks this, or there is too much of that, he would say – with which the nervous chef always concurred, mindful that a gourmet's nose must not be contradicted.

In the midst of all his activity, Jacques Guyot still finds time to cook. He holds clear views about this, too, dividing responsibility with his wife. He likes to roast game birds with a whole onion inside to keep them moist, and he sautés *trompettes de la mort*, or 'trumpets of death', (a species of wild mushroom that he gathers in the park) in butter with salt, pepper and a whole garlic clove, which is discarded before serving. Crushed garlic, he believes, is too strong. A few spoons of cream are added at the end of cooking: 'I like to cook with cream, though I'm not Norman,' he remarks.

Meanwhile, business goes from strength to strength. 'We try to offer a whole day of country entertainment,' explains Jacques Guyot, 'tempting people to come back again and again, particularly with children.' His success can be measured in attendance figures, which have grown from 25,000 in 1987 to over 60,000 in 1990. 'We were so pleased to jump the 40,000 mark, the average for châteaux open to the public,' he says. His crowning achievement came in 1990 with the award for the restoration of the orangery – listed as a *chef d'oeuvre en péril* – which had been ruined by fire in 1944. For Jacques Guyot, it was a public recognition of his personal belief that 'like nature, stones can talk'.

DAIM LOWENDAL

VENISON SIMMERED IN LOIRE VALLEY WINE

La Ferté is known as 'Château des Maréchaux' as it was built by Henri de Saint-Nectaire, Duc de La Ferté and a marshal of France, then later bought by one of Napoleon's marshals, the famous André Masséna. Jacques Guyot recommends a fruity red Loire wine such as a Bourgueil for this recipe, in which venison is marinated and then simmered very slowly.

4 servings

750 g/1½ lb BONELESS STEWING VENISON, CUT INTO 2.5 cm/1 in CUBES
250 g/8 oz BUTTER
1 ONION, SLICED
45 g/1½ oz PLAIN FLOUR
SALT AND PEPPER

For the marinade
1 ONION, HALVED
2 BAY LEAVES
1 tsp PEPPERCORNS
1 BOTTLE (750 ml/1¼ PINTS) RED WINE, PREFERABLY FROM THE LOIRE VALLEY

Combine the meat with the marinade ingredients in a large bowl (not aluminium). Cover and refrigerate for 2 days.

Lift the meat out of the marinade and drain it in a sieve, then pat dry with kitchen paper. Clarify one-quarter of the butter (see page 220). Heat the clarified butter in a flameproof casserole. Add the onion and sauté it, stirring often, until it browns, about 5 minutes. Remove it. Coat the pieces of meat with half the flour, tossing to discard the excess. Brown the pieces of meat, a few at a time, in the casserole over very high heat, stirring constantly. Return them all to the casserole with the onion.

Heat the oven to 160°C/325°F/Gas Mark 3. Strain the marinade into a saucepan and bring it to a simmer. Cream the remaining butter and, with a whisk, work in the remaining flour to make a smooth paste. Drop pieces of this *beurre manié* into the simmering marinade, whisking rapidly until smooth and thickened. Stir into the casserole containing the meat and season with salt and pepper. Cover and bring just to the boil, then transfer to the heated oven and cook until the meat is very tender, about 4 hours. Stir occasionally and add a little water if the meat gets too dry.

Taste the stew for seasoning before serving. (It can be cooked up to 3 days ahead and the flavour will improve.)

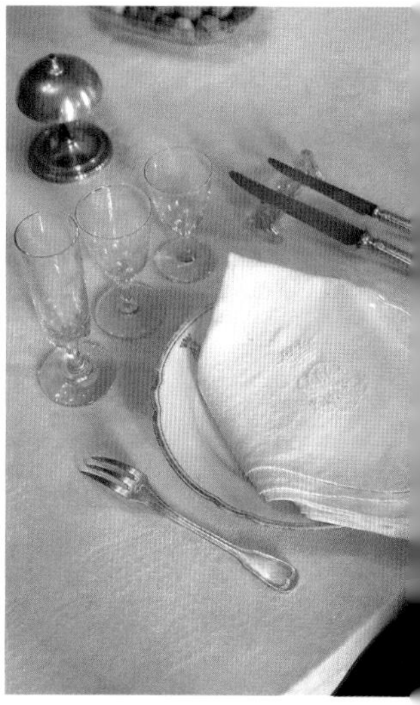

In restoring La Ferté, Jacques Guyot was keen to preserve as much of the elegance and character of the property as he could. He and his wife try to use all the rooms at different times of the year in order to keep the château looking and feeling like a real home.

Faisan a la Masséna

Roast Pheasant Stuffed with Wild Mushrooms

Out of game season, this recipe can be made with chicken or guinea fowl and cultivated button mushrooms. If you would like a more generous serving of mushrooms than fits comfortably inside the birds, sauté more separately.

4 servings

75 g/2½ oz BUTTER, MORE IF NEEDED
1 CLOVE GARLIC, PEELED
500 g/1 lb FRESH WILD MUSHROOMS, SUCH AS IVORY AND BLACK VARIETIES OF CHANTERELLES AND OYSTER MUSHROOMS, CLEANED* AND CUT INTO 1 cm/⅜ in SLICES IF LARGE
SALT AND PEPPER
3 to 4 tbsp CHOPPED PARSLEY
2 tbsp CRÈME FRAÎCHE* OR DOUBLE CREAM
2 YOUNG OVEN-READY PHEASANTS (ABOUT 1 kg/2 lb EACH)
2 STRIPS OF BARDING FAT* (OPTIONAL)
250 ml/8 fl oz CHICKEN STOCK (see page 221)
4 SMALL FIRM APPLES, SUCH AS GOLDEN DELICIOUS, PEELED, CORED, THICKLY SLICED INTO RINGS AND HALVED
1 tbsp SUGAR
4 tbsp ARMAGNAC OR BRANDY

TRUSSING NEEDLE AND STRING

Heat the oven to 190°C/375°F/Gas Mark 5. Melt half the butter in a frying pan. Add the garlic clove and cook, stirring, until fragrant, then add the mushrooms with salt and pepper. Toss the mushrooms over moderately high heat until they lose most of their moisture, about 5 minutes, then pour off any liquid. Add the parsley, cover and cook over low heat until the mushrooms are tender, about 10 minutes. Stir in the crème fraîche or cream and adjust the seasoning. Discard the garlic clove.

Season the cavities of the birds. Stuff them with the mushrooms and truss the birds*. If using barding fat, drape it over the breasts and tie it in place with string. Otherwise, spread about 15 g/½ oz of softened butter over each breast. Set the birds in a roasting tin and roast them in the oven until just done, about 30 minutes. The juice from the breast should run slightly pink when pierced with a fork, if you like meat pink at the bone. For well done birds, continue roasting for 5 to 10 minutes longer.

Transfer the birds to a carving board, cover them with foil and leave to rest while finishing the dish. Pour off the fat from the roasting tin, leaving the cooking juices. Add the stock to the tin and boil, stirring to dissolve the juices. Simmer until it reduces by half, 10 to 15 minutes. Strain, and taste for seasoning.

Wipe out the frying pan used to cook the mushrooms and in it melt the remaining butter. Add the apples, sugar, salt and pepper and sauté, turning the apples often so they cook evenly, until tender, 10 to 12 minutes. Add the Armagnac or brandy to the pan, heat it and set it alight. (Stand back from the flame.) Continue cooking for about 30 seconds shaking the pan until the flame subsides. The apples should taste peppery.

Remove the string and barding fat, if used, from the birds and carve them. Arrange the meat on a platter or plates with the mushrooms and apples. Pour a little of the cooking juices over the meat and serve the rest separately.

Faisan à la Masséna (left). Named after André Masséna (a previous owner of La Ferté) who was one of Napoleon's marshals, this dish is prepared in the autumn when pheasant, apples and wild mushrooms are all in season.

TARTE TATIN

CARAMELIZED UPSIDE-DOWN APPLE TART

Tarte Tatin – succulent baked apples with a caramel topping. The tart is baked in the oven with a pastry lid, then turned out upside down just before serving.

Tarte Tatin originated in Lamotte-Beuvron, a small town only a few kilometres from Château de La Ferté. The story goes that the Tatin sisters, left penniless when their father died, started selling a rustic apple tart topped with caramel that their father had much enjoyed. With the railway age, Lamotte became an important junction and the sisters' baking flourished. There is still a Hotel Tatin near the station.

The secret of Tarte Tatin is to cook the apple halves so the butter-flavoured caramel penetrates deep inside them.

8 to 10 servings

175 g/6 oz UNSALTED BUTTER
300 g/10 oz CASTER SUGAR
2.5 kg/5 to 6 lb FIRM DESSERT APPLES, SUCH AS GOLDEN DELICIOUS

For the pâte sucrée
175 g/6 oz PLAIN FLOUR
90 g/3 oz UNSALTED BUTTER
½ tsp SALT
90 g/3 oz CASTER SUGAR
3 EGG YOLKS

30 cm/12 in ROUND HEAVY TIN

Make the *pâte sucrée* (see page 221) and chill it.

Melt the butter in the tin and sprinkle with the sugar. Cook over moderate heat, stirring occasionally, until the sugar caramelizes to a deep golden brown. Allow the tin to cool.

Peel the apples, cut them in half and core them. Arrange them upright in concentric rings to fill the tin, packing them tightly. Cook the apples in the caramel until they are a dark brown and the juice they have rendered has evaporated, 15 to 20 minutes. Leave to cool.

Heat the oven to 190°C/375°F/Gas Mark 5. Roll out the *pâte sucrée* on a floured surface to a 30 cm/12 in round. Lay the round over the apples so they are completely covered. Chill until the dough is firm, 10 to 15 minutes.

Bake the tart in the heated oven until the pastry is golden, about 15 minutes. Allow the tart to cool to tepid in the tin, then turn it out on to a large platter. (Do this carefully because the caramel juice from the bottom of the apples may splash.) Serve the tart warm, with crème fraîche* or vanilla ice cream (see page 220).

(Tarte Tatin may be cooked up to 8 hours ahead and left in the tin, provided it is not made of uncoated cast iron or aluminium. Warm it over low heat before turning out.)

Château de Beauregard

The great royal châteaux of the Loire are without equal, but for all their grandeur and beauty, they seem to lack a soul, standing empty and living out their years in the care of the State. I get so much more pleasure out of visiting a château like Beauregard. 'The building is not large,' the architect Androuët du Cerceau noted in his inventory of 1576, 'but it is charming and fitted out in impeccable style.' The ambiance has survived almost untouched, from the painted ceilings to the 17th-century floor of hand-painted tiles from Holland, no one alike. The greatest treasures are the 327 portraits of the kings and notables of France spanning 300 years, from the 14th-century Philippe VI de Valois to Louis XIII of France.

The château was built in the 1550s by Jean du Thier, Controller General of Finance for Henri II, and a man of immense wealth, known for his love of art, music, hunting and outdoor games. Paintings celebrating these diversions adorn Beauregard's magnificent *cabinet des grelots*, so named because its carved panelling features sleigh-bells. Du Thier was also a lover of gardens; the ground plans for Beauregard show that he adopted Italian principles there, with the knots of box hedge so arranged that a gardener could reach out to any plant without treading on the surrounding soil. Down river from Beauregard, at Villandry, a similar vegetable garden has been replanted and undoubtedly is one of the great sights of the Loire.

Elegant Château de Beauregard, dating from the 16th century, is a superb and rare example of a prominent Loire château that is still a family home.

(Top) The old kitchen equipped with an impressive range of copper pans was used by the family until a decade ago, when the antiquated cast iron range was removed and the two immense open chimneys were restored to their original state (right).

When today's owners of Beauregard, Comte and Comtesse Alain du Pavillon, inherited the château in 1968, they were determined that it should not just be a '*monument historique*' but a family home as well. In practice this meant dividing the château into two parts. The public rooms are open to visitors most of the year, with exhibitions and concerts held in the summer.

On the family side, Comtesse du Pavillon talked to me animatedly about the gatherings in her dining room: 'We may be two, we may be twenty-five,' she says. Many classic recipes have been handed down in the family – the Comtesse was born Anne-Marie Suchet d'Albuféra and can claim title to *sole à la Suchet*, with carrots in a wine sauce, and *poularde Albuféra*, a poached chicken stuffed with rice, truffles and *foie gras*. But such outmoded fare is not for the Pavillon family. 'My cooking is simple, with plenty of fish and vegetables, salads and fruit tarts,' says Anne-Marie du Pavillon.

I was especially pleased to hear this comment because to my mind this is what the cooking of

the Loire is all about. There are almost as many fruit tarts as there are fruit trees in the region – open-faced tarts of sweet pastry brushed with jam and filled with fresh berries; rhubarb or plum tarts with the fruit cooked first with sugar as a compote and then baked in a double crust, or packed under a single crust as in an English-style pie. In winter Anne-Marie du Pavillon makes a spectacular *tarte demi-deuil* (half-mourning) filled with whipped Chantilly cream which camouflages prunes soaked in tea.

For a first course, the Pavillons often serve the delicious asparagus of the Loire with a walnut vinaigrette dressing and chopped hard-boiled egg for colour. An alternative starter (or sometimes a light main dish) is a *feuilleté* of goat's cheese wrapped in puff pastry – hot and golden brown – served with a green salad. Dozens of goat's cheeses are found along the Loire: from the Beauregard area come Selles-sur-Cher, a disc rolled in powdered charcoal, as well as the taller, narrower Cornilly, and little cheese rounds sold specifically for baking.

The portrait gallery at Beauregard testifies to the history of France, with 327 portraits from Philippe VI of Valois up to Louis XIII. Family portraits rub shoulders with royal figures and the colourful mosaic-like composition complements the regularity of the tiled Delft floor (above). The famous 'Cabinet des Grelots' is a lavish oak-panelled room decorated with paintings depicting various human pleasures and pastimes. The 'grelots' or bells are embossed decorations carved out of the panelling.

TOMATES CAMBACÉRÈS

TOMATOES STUFFED WITH ARTICHOKES

Jean-Jacques Régis de Cambacérès, a famous forbear of the Comtesse du Pavillon, was consul and then High Chancellor of France under Napoleon. He also made his mark as a gourmet, leaving this family recipe of tomatoes stuffed with artichokes and mayonnaise. Serve with rye toasts topped with hard-boiled egg, tomato and anchovy.

4 servings

4 LARGE RIPE TOMATOES
SALT AND PEPPER
4 ARTICHOKE BOTTOMS, COOKED AND COOLED (see page 220)
125 ml/4 fl oz MAYONNAISE (see page 221)
4 LETTUCE LEAVES

For the toasts
2 HARD-BOILED EGGS
1 tbsp SMALL CAPERS
4 tbsp MAYONNAISE
8 THIN SLICES OF RYE BREAD, OR 4 LARGE SLICES CUT IN HALF
2 SMALL RIPE TOMATOES, THINLY SLICED
8 ANCHOVY FILLETS IN OIL, DRAINED AND HALVED

Cut off the top of each tomato about one-quarter of the way down and discard. Cut out the core and seeds, and cut a thin slice from the base of each tomato so it will sit flat. Sprinkle the inside of the shells with salt and pepper, turn them upside down and leave to drain.

Dice the artichoke bottoms and stir them into the mayonnaise. Taste for seasoning.

For the toasts, slice the hard-boiled eggs. Chop the capers, reserving 8 whole ones to decorate. Stir the chopped capers into the mayonnaise. (The stuffed tomatoes and toasts may be prepared to this point up to 2 hours ahead. Cover and refrigerate the mayonnaise.)

To finish, toast the rye bread. Spread each slice of toast with caper mayonnaise. On each, arrange one slice of tomato sprinkled with salt and pepper, one slice of egg and two anchovy halves crossed on top. Top with a whole caper.

Carefully spoon the artichoke and mayonnaise mixture into the tomato shells. Arrange a lettuce leaf, a stuffed tomato and 2 decorated toasts on each plate.

Tomates Cambacérès. Fresh, perfectly ripe tomatoes are essential for this simple but eye-catching dish.

Saumon au Beurre Blanc

Roasted Salmon with White Butter Sauce

'No one tolerates fish bones nowadays,' remarks the Comtesse du Pavillon. So she opts for salmon or sea trout rather than the bonier pike, which is also native to the Loire. White butter sauce originated in the western reaches of the Loire where Poitou-Charentes, home of fine butter, meets the Pays Nantais, land of Muscadet wine.

8 servings

1×2.5 kg/5½ lb WHOLE SALMON, FILLETED WITH SKIN AND CUT INTO 8 PIECES
1 tbsp VEGETABLE OIL
SEA SALT AND PEPPER

For the white butter sauce
4 tbsp WHITE WINE VINEGAR
4 tbsp DRY WHITE WINE
2 SHALLOTS, FINELY CHOPPED
1 tsp CRUSHED WHITE PEPPERCORNS
SALT
250 g/8 oz CHILLED UNSALTED BUTTER, CUT INTO SMALL PIECES
½ LEMON

Heat the oven to 230°C/450°F/Gas Mark 8. Brush the skin side of the fish with the oil, and sprinkle with salt and pepper. Brush a large baking sheet with oil and place the pieces of fish on it, skin side up. Roast the fish for 8 to 12 minutes until the skin is crisp and slightly blackened and the flesh just flakes easily. When ready, transfer the fish to a warmed platter and keep warm.

While the fish is roasting, make the white butter sauce: boil the vinegar and wine with the shallots, peppercorns and a little salt in a heavy saucepan for 5 to 10 minutes until the liquid is reduced to 1 tablespoon. Reduce the heat to very low and gradually add the butter, whisking vigorously so the sauce foams. Move the pan on and off the heat so the butter softens creamily to form a smooth sauce. Do not heat it too much or it will melt to oil. Strain the sauce. Squeeze a teaspoon of juice from the lemon and stir it in. Taste for seasoning. Serve as soon as possible.

Roasted Saumon au Beurre Blanc, with its distinctive blackened and crispy skin.

CHÂTEAUX OF

Mist and Sea

Château de Creullet

From Bayeux, seat of the Dukes of Normandy, lush meadows stretch without interruption to the sea. This fertile region caught the eye of the Vikings just as it did that of Louis XIV, but his intent was rather different. The King wanted to create a jewel, in the style of the Petit Trianon at Versailles, as a retreat for a young mistress. Reputedly she did not enjoy the favours of the king long enough to earn her reward. Since then, the charming Château de Creullet, with its balustraded gardens and ornamental lake inspired by Le Nôtre, has been passed from hand to hand, down to its current owners, the Marquis and Marquise de Canchy.

Château de Creullet was a key command post for the allied liberating forces in 1944 and the headquarters for Field Marshal Montgomery.

Maintaining Creullet from a base in Paris is a struggle for a growing family — the Canchys have five young children — but Norman traditions are maintained at weekends and during holidays. What a fine domain this is for everyone, young and old — a hectare of walled vegetable garden, a greenhouse sheltering special pink Muscat grapes with a flavour of raspberry, a thriving herb garden, and an apple orchard with 100-year-old trees espaliered to catch the sun. A dozen or more varieties can be counted, some ripening early, some late, some for cooking, others for the table and still other small bitter cider apples, destined for preserves and for juice. 'In summer we live off the garden,' says Hélène de Canchy. 'We have our own chickens and salt-marsh lamb — we are only five kilometres from the sea — and the sole and scallops from the little villages on the coast are outstanding.'

The Château de Creullet lies in Calvados, the Normandy region famous for apple brandy. Once a year the cider press arrives at the farmhouse, a venerable truck fitted out with clanking machinery.

The vintages stored in the scarred oak barrels in the cellars at Creullet are identified with chalk.

A famous stretch of ground! On 5 June, 1944 the first invasion beachhead was established here, and Field Marshal Montgomery made Creullet his headquarters during the Normandy landings. Distinguished visitors included Général de Gaulle, General Eisenhower and King George VI, who held an impromptu inspection of troops in the garden. After the War, Montgomery returned several times: 'My Normandy home,' he called the château.

Apples naturally find their way into the cooking at Creullet. Roast chicken is basted with cider, and crêpes are filled with sautéed apples and flamed with Calvados. This is Creullet's very own Calvados, for Jean-François de Canchy holds the right to distil his own cider under a personal licence, which is now quite rare in France. At one time all of this happened furtively. In the château cellars you will still find an old fireplace which was used as an escape route for the tell-tale apple-scented vapours produced during distillation. It was then bricked up from season to season in case an excise inspector passed by!

FONDS D'ARTICHAUTS FARCIS MORNAY

STUFFED ARTICHOKE BOTTOMS WITH CHEESE SAUCE

Artichokes flourish in the garden at Creullet and are at their classic best served hot with this mushroom stuffing topped with cheese sauce.

6 servings

125 g/4 oz *PÂTÉ DE FOIE GRAS* OR CHICKEN LIVER PÂTÉ
100 g/3½ oz FRESH BREADCRUMBS
60 g/2 oz MUSHROOMS, FINELY CHOPPED
2 tbsp MADEIRA, MORE IF NEEDED
SALT AND PEPPER
6 ARTICHOKE BOTTOMS, COOKED AND DRAINED (see page 220)

For the sauce

250 ml/8 fl oz MILK
A SLICE OF ONION
1 BAY LEAF
30 g/1 oz BUTTER
2 tbsp FLOUR
GRATED NUTMEG
SALT AND WHITE PEPPER
20 g/¾ oz GRUYÈRE CHEESE, GRATED

Heat the oven to 190°C/375°F/Gas Mark 5.

Mash together the pâté, breadcrumbs and mushrooms with a fork until fairly smooth. Add enough of the Madeira to make a spreadable mixture. Adjust the seasoning if necessary.

Mound the mixture on the artichoke bottoms, spreading it to the edges. Dot the top with the butter. Arrange in a buttered baking dish, cover with buttered foil and bake in the heated oven until the stuffing is very hot, about 15 minutes.

Meanwhile, prepare the white sauce (see page 222); it will be thick enough to spread. Off the heat, beat in the cheese. Taste the sauce and adjust the seasoning if necessary.

Heat the grill to high. Cover the artichoke stuffing with the sauce using a palette knife. (The artichokes can be prepared to this point a day ahead and refrigerated; reheat them in a low oven before finishing.) Grill for several seconds until the top is golden, watching carefully so they do not burn. Serve immediately.

Haricots blancs, white kidney beans, are hung up to dry in an airy attic to catch the breeze.

As for all such preserves, the way to keep rose petal and apple jelly clear is not to press on the fruit in the jelly bag.

Confiture de Rose

Rose Petal Jelly

Creullet is famous for its roses. In September, the second flowering of the rose garden comes hand in hand with the appearance of apples. Hélène de Canchy's rose petal jelly is the happy result of this accidental convergence.

Makes about 1.15 kg/2½ lb jelly

400 g/13 oz JUST-PICKED, UNBLEMISHED ROSE PETALS
400 ml/13 fl oz BOILING WATER
APPLE JELLY (see below)
250 g/8 oz SUGAR
JUICE OF 2 SMALL LEMONS

4 PRESERVING JARS (250 ml/8 fl oz EACH)

In a covered heatproof bowl steep the petals in the boiling water for 3 or 4 hours.

Melt the jelly in a preserving pan over low heat. Stir in the petals with their steeping water, the sugar and lemon juice and boil as fast as possible to setting point, 105°C/220°F on a sugar thermometer (see below).

Allow the jelly to cool slightly, then pour it into sterilized jars*. Seal the jars. Store them in a cool place.

Gelée de Pommes

Apple Jelly

This pure apple jelly is delicious on its own but is perfect for the addition of other flavours.

Makes about 600 g/1¼ lb

1 kg/2 lb CRAB APPLES
ABOUT 300 g/10 oz SUGAR

2 PRESERVING JARS (250 ml/8 fl oz EACH)

Scrub the apples, especially at the blossom ends, and discard the stalks. Cut the fruit into quarters (skins and cores are left on to add flavour and pectin). Put the fruit in a pan with water barely to cover. Simmer, stirring occasionally, until they are very soft, about 20 minutes.

Remove the pan from the heat and allow to cool slightly, then spoon the fruit and juice into a jelly bag, or a colander lined with several layers of muslin, set over a bowl. Leave the bag or colander in place overnight to allow the juice to drip slowly into the bowl.

Measure the juice. Bring the juice to the boil and stir in 150 g/5 oz sugar for each 250 ml/8 fl oz juice. Boil as fast as possible to setting point, 105°C/220°F on a sugar thermometer. At this temperature, the jelly falls from a spoon in a characteristic 'sheet' of drips. Alternatively, remove the pan from the heat, pour a few drops of jelly on to a cold saucer and wait for a moment to see if the drops begin to set. Push them with your finger – if setting point has been reached, the surface of the jelly will wrinkle.

Allow the jelly to cool slightly, then pour it into sterilized jars*. Seal the jars. Store them in a cool place.

As well as the elegant Le Nôtre gardens, Creullet boasts a walled vegetable garden, a greenhouse sheltering pink muscat grapes, and an apple orchard with 100-year-old trees espaliered to catch the sun. The young de Canchys help out with the annual ritual of apple picking.

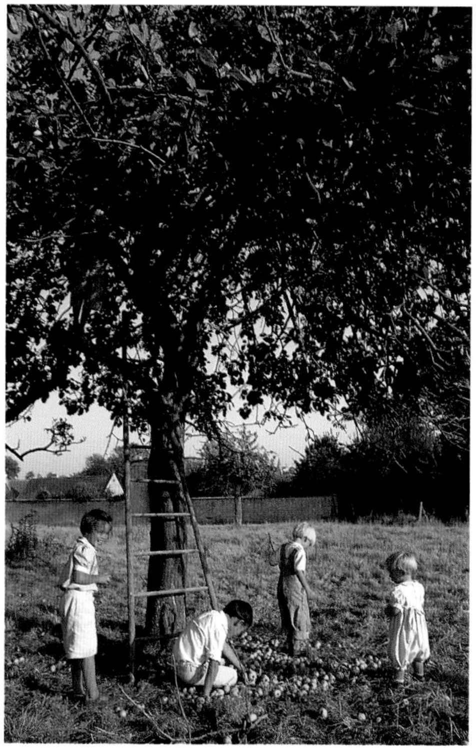

Le Pain Farci, a savoury ham and olive loaf taken on beach picnics by the family.

LE PAIN FARCI

HAM AND OLIVE LOAF FOR A PICNIC

A regular event at Château de Creullet are seaside picnics, held on the nearby beaches, site of the Normandy invasion. This unusual savoury bread raised with baking powder is a popular part of the feast.

Makes 1 loaf

375 g/12 oz PLAIN FLOUR
1 tbsp BAKING POWDER
½ tsp SALT
165 g/5½ oz BACK BACON, RINDED AND CHOPPED
250 g/8 oz BUTTER, AT ROOM TEMPERATURE
5 EGGS
165 g/5½ oz COOKED HAM, CHOPPED
60 g/2 oz OIL-CURED BLACK OLIVES, STONED AND CHOPPED

23×12.5×10 cm/9×5×4 in LOAF TIN

Heat the oven to 180°C/350°F/Gas Mark 4. Butter the loaf tin. Combine the flour, baking powder and salt. Fry the bacon gently in a frying pan so the fat runs, then cook it until golden, about 5 minutes. Drain on kitchen paper.

In a large bowl, cream the butter. Beat in the eggs, one by one, adding a little of the flour mixture with the first egg. Sift the remaining flour mixture over the butter mixture in three batches, stirring until smooth after each addition. Stir in the ham, bacon and olives.

Transfer the dough to the prepared loaf tin and smooth the top. Bake in the heated oven for 1¼ to 1½ hours or until the bread is golden brown and shrinks slightly from the sides of the tin. It should sound hollow when tapped on the base. Transfer the loaf to a rack to cool.

The bread is best eaten the day of baking, although it freezes well. It's also good toasted the following day.

DOUILLONS NORMANDS

APPLES BAKED IN PASTRY

Firm dessert apples such as Golden Delicious, which hold their shape during cooking, are essential to a good apple dumpling. Serve the douillons *with apricot sauce (see page 174) or vanilla custard (see page 222) if you like.*

6 servings

500 g/1 lb PUFF PASTRY DOUGH (see page 221)
90 g/3 oz UNSALTED BUTTER, AT ROOM TEMPERATURE
100 g/3¼ oz CASTER SUGAR
6 SMALL DESSERT APPLES (ABOUT 1 kg/2 lb TOTAL WEIGHT), PEELED AND CORED
1 EGG, BEATEN TO MIX WITH ¼ tsp WATER TO GLAZE

Sprinkle a baking sheet with water. Roll out the dough to a 51.5×35 cm/21×14 in rectangle. Cut out six 17.5 cm/7 in rounds. Transfer them to the baking sheet and chill until firm, about 15 minutes. Save the trimmings for decoration.

Cream the butter and beat in the sugar. Set an apple on each dough round. Spoon some of the butter mixture into the core cavity of each apple. Brush the dough with egg glaze*, then bring up the dough around the apples, pleating it at the top to seal tightly. Brush the dumplings with egg glaze and chill them until firm, about 30 minutes.

Heat the oven to 220°C/425°F/Gas Mark 7.

Roll out the reserved dough and cut out six 5 cm/2 in rounds. Press a round over the seam on each dumpling and brush it with a little egg glaze. Bake the dumplings in the heated oven until the pastry begins to brown, about 15 minutes. Reduce the oven temperature to 180°C/350°F/Gas Mark 4 and continue baking for ¾ to 1 hour or until the pastry is brown and crisp and the apples are very tender when pierced with a knife. Allow the dumplings to cool for 10 minutes before serving.

Canon-les-Bonnes-Gens – a dream of 18th-century Arcadia (top).

An ancient apple press stands in an out building (middle).

Bulbs and branches are dried out in the abandoned orangery (below).

Old gardening tools suspended in time and space (right).

Château de Canon-les-Bonnes-Gens

'We live in the 18th century,' exclaims François de Mézerac. 'How lucky we are!' He is referring not only to the property itself, with its extensive gardens, lakes, avenues and carefully landscaped views, but also to his ancestor who created the ensemble. This was Jean-Baptiste Elie de Beaumont, famous as a Paris advocate who campaigned with Voltaire for human rights and justice under the *Ancien Régime*. The archives at Canon record how Elie de Beaumont travelled to England before planning the transformation of the property in the 1770s so that it would express, through nature, libertarian ideals of beauty and harmony.

Were he to return today, Elie de Beaumont would approve: parts of Canon are wilderness, other parts are manicured paths leading one to another and offering here a vista of grazing sheep, there a folly lacquered in brilliant Chinese red. Most entertaining of all are the *chartreuses* — a corridor of 13 walled gardens, like a series of square houses without roofs, the walls angled to trap maximum sun. Protected from winter frost, not to mention Norman mists and breezes, espaliered pears, plums, apples, peaches and even kiwi fruits bask in the warmth retained by the stone walls even after sunset. Apricots ripen in May and June, figs in August, a good month ahead of the local average. Apples may be typical of Normandy, but at Canon-les-Bonnes-Gens they take a back seat.

When in Paris, Elie de Beaumont supplied his table from Canon. 'Be sure', he instructed his bailiff 'to include a hare, several game birds, two ducks so we have an old one to braise with turnips and the other to roast on the spit, two fat chickens . . . and if you can add a couple of pigeons, all the better.' The delivery, by express coach in a wicker hamper, was expensive but 'my health is more important than my pocket,' wrote Canon's proud owner.

Today, François de Mézerac runs the farm attached to the property, while his brother and sister live in the château itself, overseeing and often personally guiding summer visitors. His wife, Marie-Josèphe, laughs when told her cooking is 'the admiration of everyone'. 'No, no,' she says, 'it is simply that we have big dishes for big appetites.' (The Mézeracs have six children, as well as a dozen nieces and nephews for whom Canon is home.)

Evening meals usually begin with *le potage du potager* – a soup supplied from the vegetable garden – followed perhaps by a roast leg of home-raised lamb basted with local cider and served with haricot beans, or a whole fish baked in cider, or simply an open tart filled with cheese in a cream sauce. Dessert is mandatory, and equally simple: sponge cake, a vanilla cream or Madame de Mézerac's favourite *tarte Alsacienne* – sweet pastry topped with rhubarb, baked so the juice combines with the crisp pastry. 'I like to cook everything slowly, so it simmers but never burns,' she says. 'In winter we have a big wood-fired stove and that's ideal.'

Canon has seen some troubled times. German soldiers were billeted there for four years during the War. 'At least we did not have to feed them,' says Monsieur de Mézerac, alluding to 1815 and the aftermath of Waterloo, when 24 Prussians and their horses arrived at the château. 'I rounded up chickens and hens,' the bailiff of the day recorded distractedly. 'I had two rabbits killed but it worries me that the meat smells. The women were put to work with the men setting the tables . . . but all went well. They departed at five in the morning, after a breakfast of three bottles of eau-de-vie, coffee, *soupe au lait*, meat and butter, taking with them all the eau-de-vie that was left.'

The Château de Canon survives scarcely touched by time. 'This is a happy place, always sunny, always gay,' declares François de Mézerac. Its 18th-century park and gardens, full of *fabriques* (statues and ornamental fantasies) and bold perspectives, are an unusual marriage of the English and French styles. A sign, perhaps, that these two battling nations could find common ground in landscaping long before they edged towards an *entente cordiale* in more worldly realms.

The first apple blossom of early summer (top).

A fully-stocked cider cellar (below).

The name Canon-les-Bonnes-Gens dates from 1776 when owner Elie de Beaumont launched an annual fête to choose the best villager of the year. First it was for the Best Young Girl. Next year it was the turn of the Best Old Man, followed by the Best Mother. The custom was eventually dropped, however, the name stuck.

Hay drying in the summer sun (below left).

Stone arches lead into the 13 chartreuses, a series of walled gardens angled to trap the sun and protect tender plants from winter blasts (middle).

One of several follies in the park, designed to delight 18th-century strollers (right).

LE BON JEUNE HOMME

RICH CHOCOLATE CREAMS

The curious name in French for this recipe, 'the nice young man', recalls a bit of parental mischief. Whenever a suitor came to dinner in Madame de Mézerac's family, her mother always served this dessert. At the appropriate moment, everyone turned to look at the mystified guest as she announced, 'And now let's eat up le bon jeune homme!' *Madame de Mézerac serves it in the traditional 'pots' used for* petits pots de crème; *ramekins or espresso cups are quite suitable though.*

4 to 6 servings

165 g/5½ oz BITTERSWEET CHOCOLATE, CHOPPED
125 g/4 oz CASTER SUGAR
560 ml/18 fl oz MILK

4 OR 6 POT-DE-CRÈME CONTAINERS OR RAMEKINS

Combine the chocolate, sugar and milk in a heavy saucepan over low heat. Stir often until the chocolate melts and the sugar dissolves. Raise the heat and simmer the mixture for about 45 minutes, stirring occasionally, until it coats a spoon thickly.

Pour the mixture into the chosen containers and allow to cool completely, at least 2 hours. (The creams can be prepared up to 2 days ahead and refrigerated.)

TEURGOULE

CREAMY BAKED RICE PUDDING

Genuine rice pudding, baked with milk for hours until creamy, never falls from favour. 'When we were children at Canon,' says Monsieur de

Le Bon Jeune Homme, rich chocolate creams (right).

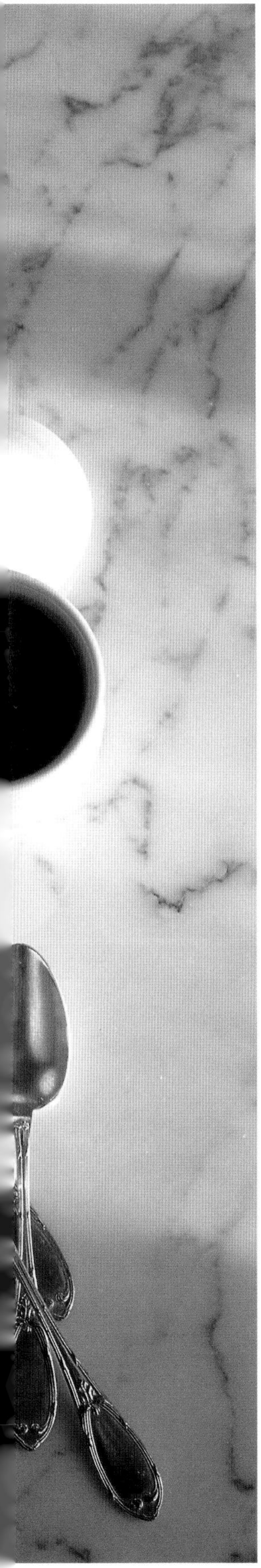

Mézerac, 'we were served this pudding on Saturday nights.' The family was especially fond of this homely dish during the War when they best appreciated its nourishing qualities. Serve it straight from the oven in its glazed earthenware dish or allow it to cool to room temperature first.

6 to 8 servings

2 LITRES/3½ PINTS MILK, MORE IF NEEDED
125 g/4 oz SUGAR
125 g/4 oz SHORT-GRAIN (PUDDING) RICE
PINCH OF SALT
PINCH OF GROUND CINNAMON

2.5 LITRE/4 PINT DEEP EARTHENWARE BAKING DISH

Heat the oven to 150°C/300°F/Gas Mark 2.

Mix all the ingredients together in the baking dish and bake in the heated oven for 1 hour. If all the milk has been absorbed after this time, stir in more to make the mixture soupy. Continue baking until the rice is very soft, 1 to 2 hours longer. At the end of cooking, a golden crust will have formed and the pudding will be lightly set when the baking dish is shaken.

GÂTEAU NINITE

COFFEE GÂTEAU WITH CHOCOLATE GLAZE

According to family tradition, this recipe was invented by Ninite, trusted old cook to François de Mézerac's great-aunt. It was and still remains the traditional dessert at Christmas dinner, which unites this large, far-flung family. Many French families seem to have a version of this gâteau in their repertoire. It's one of the first recipes mothers allow their children to make on their own; grown-ups love it too.

8 to 10 servings

250 g/8 oz BUTTER, AT ROOM TEMPERATURE
100 g/3½ oz CASTER SUGAR
4 EGGS, SEPARATED
60 PETIT BEURRE BISCUITS
250 ml/8 fl oz STRONG BLACK COFFEE, CHILLED, MORE IF NEEDED
250 g/8 oz BITTERSWEET CHOCOLATE, CHOPPED

23×12.5×7 cm/9×5×2¾ in LOAF TIN

Set aside 30 g/1 oz of the butter, and cream the remainder with half the sugar. Beat in the egg yolks. Whisk the egg whites with the remaining sugar until the mixture stiffens and forms a long peak when the whisk is lifted, about 5 minutes. Mix this meringue into the butter mixture. (If the butter separates, whisk the mixture over a pan of hot water until it is smooth.)

Butter the loaf tin. Moisten about 7 of the biscuits in the coffee. Arrange them in a layer on the bottom of the tin, trimming them to fit as needed. Cover with a layer of the butter mixture. Moisten more biscuits in the coffee as you use them, layering them with the butter mixture until all the ingredients are used, finishing with a layer of biscuits. Cover and refrigerate until firm, at least 4 hours and up to 2 days.

To finish, turn out the gâteau on to a platter. Melt the chocolate on a heatproof plate set over a pan of hot water. Stir in the reserved butter until the mixture is smooth. Allow it to cool slightly, then spread it evenly over the top and sides of the gâteau, using a palette knife. Refrigerate the gâteau until the chocolate is set.

Norman cows, the wealth of this ancient province.

Château de Miromesnil

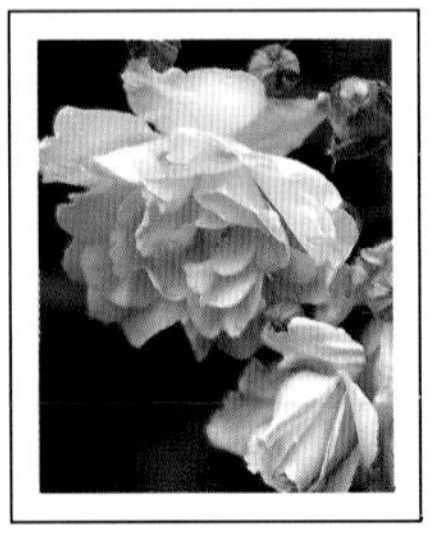

'Good cooking starts in the garden,' was Comtesse Bertrand de Vogüé's reply to my question about her cuisine. So when she and her late husband bought the Château de Miromesnil in 1938, her first thought was to restore the vegetable garden. They had to wait ten years until the property recovered from the aftermath of the occupation by German and Allied troops. And it was many years, tons of compost and innumerable packets of seeds later that the garden began to approach its current glory.

Now cabbages burgeon beneath Miromesnil's windows and the walled *potager* is abloom with flowers as well as vegetables. The Comtesse is also an avid collector of new varieties, bringing plants from England, and even from North America where her son lives. 'Flowers are so much better in England,' she says. 'They are selected and bred more carefully. But, except for a few exotica, France is best for vegetables.' However, her choice is limited by the climate. 'Here in Normandy we are too far north for tomatoes, for instance. After 15 August it's autumnal here around Dieppe. Pears are a lot of work — they need individual protective bags — and even apples do less well than 50 kilometres south along the Seine valley.'

The walled kitchen garden at Miromesnil burgeons with cottage flowers, vegetables and soft fruit.

Tall stems of eremurus from the kitchen garden decorate the cool stone staircase of the hallway.

Built in 1589 after an earlier house had been ruined by the English at the battle of Arques, the château presents two faces to the world. To the south, the pink brick is unadorned, a friendly grand country house open to the sun. The north façade is severely classical in the style of Louis XIII, though its sobriety is relieved with carved stone dormer windows and whimsical tall chimneys. Miromesnil's beech trees, like those of the forest of Eawy nearby, are famous – and afford much-needed protection from the coastal winds.

Set just behind Dieppe near the old highway to Paris, Miromesnil used to be within earshot of the *chasse marée* or tidal express – an infernal clatter of horse carts racing the 115 kilometres to Paris, day and night, to deliver the fish catch to the markets on the northern side of the city. (The faubourg Poissonière remains as a reminder.) Today, Dieppe still has a bustling Saturday market but, for the rest, it's a town of memories: the commercial port is moribund, the colony of famous artists and fashionable sea-bathers has disappeared, and the Channel tunnel further north will put the town even further off the map. For the Comtesse de Vogüé, who remembers the halcyon pre-War days, this decline occasions sadness.

The old map of the original château is carefully protected with a sheet of glass.

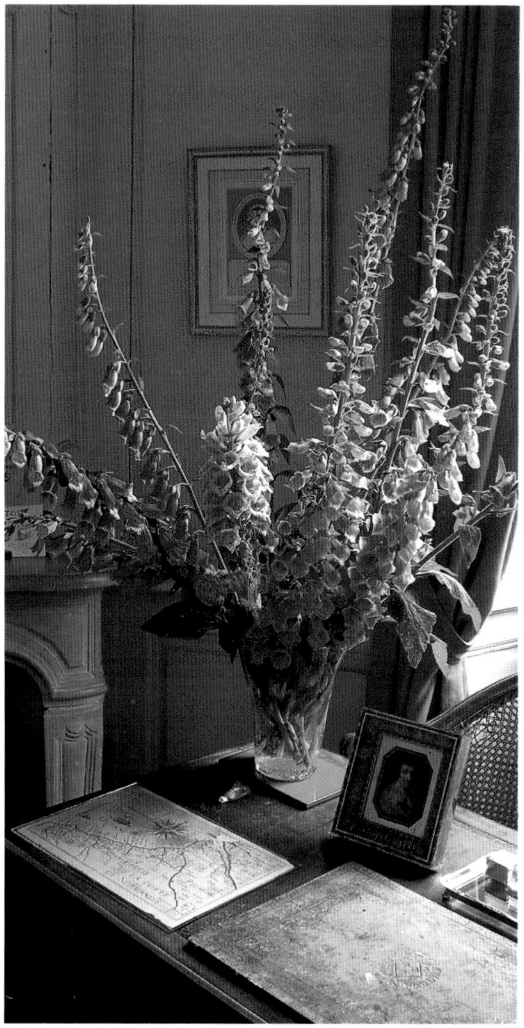

The 17th-century house still contains several items belonging to the writer Guy de Maupassant, who was born at Miromesnil and lived there from 1849 to 1853.

The Comtesse de Vogüé has tended Miromesnil's gardens for over 50 years and she takes great pride in showing visitors round the vegetable plots, lined with daffodils, delphiniums, clematis and roses, and encircled by ancient brick walls.

Miromesnil was the birthplace of the writer Guy de Maupassant, who was brought up just along the coast at Fécamp. Many of his short stories portray the tough life in the Pays de Caux (land of chalk) – the jealousies and cunning of the peasantry and the rough justice meted out by the local dignitaries. Appropriately for a Norman, Maupassant was succinct when it came to eating: 'Only an imbecile could fail to be a gourmand,' he wrote.

A lighthouse off the Norman coast near Dieppe (above).

Sole a la Rosalie

Baked Sole with Sorrel Sauce

Rosalie was the first wife of Chancellor Hue de Miromesnil, the builder of the château, and she is remembered by the de Vogüé family in this namesake recipe. It's an easy and elegant dish. Serve it with steamed rice for a main course. Fish fillets cooked by this simple method are excellent with other sauces too. Try them with hollandaise, white butter sauce (see page 222) or even a vinaigrette (see page 222).

6 servings as a main course, 8 to 10 as a first course

750 g/1½ lb DOVER SOLE FILLETS
SALT AND PEPPER
2 tbsp DRY WHITE WINE
30 g/1 oz BUTTER
375 g/12 oz SORREL, RINSED AND STALKS REMOVED
250 ml/8 fl oz CRÈME FRAÎCHE* OR DOUBLE CREAM, MORE IF NEEDED

Heat the oven to 180°C/350°F/Gas Mark 4. Butter two large baking dishes.

Put the fish in the prepared dishes and sprinkle with salt, pepper and the wine. Bake in the heated oven until the fish is firm and opaque, 10 to 12 minutes. Take the dishes from the oven and keep the fish warm.

Meanwhile, melt the butter in a large saucepan. Add the sorrel and cook over moderate heat for 3 to 5 minutes, stirring often, until the leaves wilt and have given up most of their liquid. Add the crème fraîche or cream and boil, stirring often, until the sauce thickens, 3 to 5 minutes, then briskly whisk until smooth. If the sorrel is very acid, add more cream and continue cooking for 2 or 3 minutes. Season.

Spread the sorrel sauce on warmed dinner plates. Lay the fish on top of the sauce using a fish slice and serve.

A local fishing boat heads out to sea (right).

CHAPEAU DU MARQUIS A LA FRAISE

FROZEN STRAWBERRY SOUFFLÉ

Named for the Marquis Thomas-Hue de Miromesnil, keeper of the Seals for Louis XIV, this cool and airy 'top hat' dessert should rise above the rim of its dish like a traditional hot soufflé. The strawberries for this recipe are picked in Miromesnil's thriving kitchen garden, but it can also be made with raspberries. The large proportion of fruit purée gives the soufflé an incomparable flavour and a texture similar to that of a granité.

10 servings

1 kg/2 lb STRAWBERRIES, HULLED
6 EGGS, SEPARATED
JUICE OF 1 LEMON
JUICE OF 2 ORANGES
150 g/5 oz CASTER SUGAR
PINCH OF SALT

For the Chantilly cream
250 ml/8 fl oz DOUBLE CREAM
1 tbsp ICING SUGAR
FEW DROPS VANILLA ESSENCE

For the decoration (optional)
ICING SUGAR FOR SPRINKLING
10 SMALL STRAWBERRIES WITH HULLS

1 LITRE/2 PINT SOUFFLÉ DISH

To prepare the soufflé dish, cut out a piece of greaseproof paper about 5 cm/2 in longer than the circumference of the soufflé dish. Fold the paper in half lengthways to make it sturdier and wrap it around the dish; it should extend about 5 cm/2 in above the rim. Secure the paper tightly with adhesive tape.

Purée the strawberries in a food processor or blender until smooth. There should be 750 ml/$1\frac{1}{4}$ pints of purée. Make the Chantilly cream (see page 220).

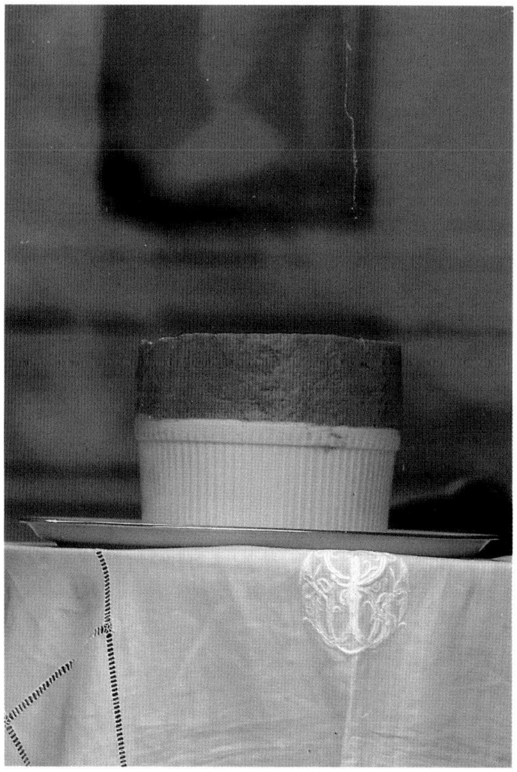

This glorious dessert is delightfully named after the top hat of the Marquis de Miromesnil.

Whisk together the egg yolks, juices and two-thirds of the sugar by hand in a heatproof bowl until mixed. Set the bowl over a pan of hot, not boiling, water and continue whisking, by hand or with an electric mixer, until the mixture falls from the whisk in a thick ribbon and holds a slowly dissolving trail, about 5 minutes. Take the bowl from the hot water and continue whisking until cool.

In another bowl, whisk 4 of the egg whites with the salt until stiff. Add the remaining sugar and continue whisking until glossy to make a light meringue, about 30 seconds. Gently fold the meringue into the egg yolk mixture. Then fold in the Chantilly cream and fruit purée.

Pour the soufflé mixture into the prepared dish; it should extend at least 4 cm/$1\frac{1}{2}$ in above the rim of the dish. Freeze it until firm, at least 6 hours. (The soufflé can be stored for up to 2 weeks in the freezer.)

About $\frac{1}{2}$ to 1 hour before serving, transfer the soufflé to the refrigerator to soften slightly. Just before serving, if you like, sprinkle the soufflé very generously with sifted icing sugar. Remove the greaseproof paper and decorate the soufflé with strawberries if you like.

Malouinière du Bos

The Picard family acquired the Malouinière du Bos in 1976 with the express intention of restoring an historic house for their six children. 'If we were to take the road to ruin, we decided to do it with panache!' says René Picard. The Malouinière du Bos is an outstanding example of the type of grand country houses built by Malouin corsairs — licensed pirates if you will — who made their fortune in the busy port of Saint-Malo both by ordinary trade and by attacking enemy ships from the Channel down to the Mediterranean, then selling the booty. The 50 or so examples of these houses that cluster around the town are unique. Built in the 17th and 18th centuries on the proceeds of this privateer trade. But what trade!

Ships from Saint-Malo plied the route from Brittany's northern coast to South America, the Indies and the Far East, culminating in ten golden years at the turn of the 17th century when Louis XIV gave the Malouin corsairs exclusive trading rights with the French East India Company. In return, the crown took a fifth of the profits. By 1712 the Malouins had taken control of the Compagnie des Indes. For a short while Saint-Malo was renowned as one of the richest towns in France. However, it was far from salubrious. Built in a coastal hollow and surrounded by massive fortifications. Soon the corsairs decided to live more comfortably outside the city walls and built country houses known as *malouinières*.

At Le Bos the panelling is remarkable, deeply carved in solid wood by Breton carpenters released from their usual occupation of building ships. The doors, on the left, were given an asymmetrical design to ease the passage of trays to and from the kitchen.

This stone crucifix is part of the simple decoration of the chapel at Le Bos.

Saint-Malo's most famous son, the writer François-René de Chateaubriand, was born there in 1768. In his memoirs, he described the *malouinières* as 'extremely luxurious. Bonnaban, the château of Monsieur and Madame de la Saudre, is partly built of marble brought from Genoa, and has a magnificence of which we have no idea in Paris. La Briantais, Le Bos, Le Montmarin, La Balue and Le Colombier are or were adorned with orangeries, fountains and statues. Some of the gardens slope down to the water through arcades of lime trees, and through colonnades of pines. Seen across beds of tulips, the sea displays its ships, its calms and its storms.'

So wealthy were the Magon de la Lande family, who built Le Bos in 1717, that a saying ran 'Paris for the Bourbons, Saint-Malo for the Magons'. The handsome house, with its decorative features picked out in local granite, is an archetypal *malouinière*, positioned so that the windows could overlook traffic on the River Rance. Only a cluster of tall chimneys is visible over the high wall sheltering the property – the Magons were discreet about their wealth and preferred a small estate of little more than eight hectares. 'A *malouinière* was in essence a town house in the country,' explains René Picard.

Le Bos attracted the Picards not only because it lived up to their expectations of beauty – the name is pronounced '*beau*' – but also because the property had changed little since 1763, when a younger Magon took over his inheritance. The process was reported to have taken 12 hours, for the new owner ceremoniously opened and closed every window, and lit a fire in each chimney. The doors of the chapel and sacristy were also opened and closed, and the altar panels unfolded. In the garden the young Magon planted a tree, then promptly uprooted it, presumably to remind the gazing crowd that the Magons always called the shots.

Such vignettes of times past provide much pleasure for René Picard as he combs the archives at Le Bos for insights into its history and the people who lived there. 'Notice how the curve of the façade is repeated in the lawn,' he points out. As for the marble statues, 'they represent the four seasons, brought back from Italy in the hold of Malouin ships which had taken salt cod to Genoa'.

The garden is another of René Picard's pleasures – he was called in from picking French beans to talk to me. 'When the children come, I often do the cooking,' he says. 'Lots of simple food – baked ham, chocolate mousse and our own potatoes to feed a multitude.' His wife, Jacqueline, inclines towards fish, perhaps monkfish in a cream sauce, or salmon *en papillote*. Both are lovers of artichokes, a symbol of Breton agriculture. 'We grow them to eat and for their splendid blue flowers,' says Madame Picard warmly.

The Picard children and grandchildren surely enjoy a happier table than Chateaubriand remembered: 'I had an intense dislike for certain dishes, but I was forced to eat them. I used to look imploringly at my nurse so that she could nimbly remove my plate when my father was looking the other way.'

Old wooden beehives.

LA MORUE JACQUES CARTIER

SALT COD WITH POTATOES, ARTICHOKES AND RED PEPPER

'When we eat salt cod,' says Madame Picard, 'we always think of past centuries and the grande pêche *off the coast of the New World.' The Bishop of Rennes would bless the fleet when it sailed from Saint-Malo, then the boats (or 'galleons of the fog', as they were called) disappeared for months at a time, some never to return. The fishermen swore that they would never go back to sea, yet when the time came, they could never resist another adventure.*

It is a good idea to start preparing the cod well ahead as it may need soaking as long as 2 days if it is very salty. Salt cod is particularly good in broth soups and stews with vegetables that need salt, such as potatoes or turnips.

6 servings

750 g/1½ lb SALT COD
BLACK PEPPER
175 ml/6 fl oz MILK
100 g/3¼ oz PLAIN FLOUR
125 ml/4 fl oz VEGETABLE OIL
60 g/2 oz BUTTER
JUICE OF ½ LEMON

For the garnish

3 tbsp VEGETABLE OIL
1 ONION, FINELY CHOPPED
4 CLOVES GARLIC, FINELY CHOPPED
3 RED PEPPERS, CORED, SEEDED AND SLICED
SALT AND BLACK PEPPER
CAYENNE PEPPER
3 ARTICHOKE BOTTOMS, COOKED AND DRAINED (see page 220)
60 g/2 oz BUTTER
500 g/1 lb SMALL NEW POTATOES, WASHED AND PEELED
2 tbsp CHOPPED PARSLEY

Put the cod in a large basin of cold water, cover it and leave it in the refrigerator to soak for at least 12 hours and up to 2 days, depending on the saltiness. Change the water three or four times during this time to remove excess salt. Drain and rinse the fish, then pat it dry with kitchen paper.

To prepare the garnish, heat the oil in a frying pan. Add the onion and cook over moderate heat, stirring often, until soft, 3 to 5 minutes. Stir in the garlic and cook for 1 minute. Reduce the heat to low and add the red peppers, salt, black pepper and cayenne pepper. Cover and cook for 20 to 30 minutes until tender, stirring occasionally. Taste for seasoning and add more salt and pepper if necessary.

Meanwhile, quarter the artichoke bottoms and set them aside. Melt the butter in a sauté pan or frying pan and add the potatoes – each one should touch the bottom of the pan. Cover tightly and cook over moderate heat for 15 to 20 minutes, shaking the pan occasionally, until the potatoes are tender and golden. Sprinkle with salt and pepper. (The garnish can be prepared 3 or 4 hours ahead and reheated.)

Sprinkle the fish with pepper, dip it in the milk and coat it with flour, patting to discard the excess. Heat the oil and half the butter in a frying pan. Brown the fish in batches over moderate heat, 2 to 3 minutes on each side, adding more oil if necessary so the fish is half covered.

Reduce the heat to low and return all the fish to the pan. Cook for 12 to 20 minutes, basting it often, until it flakes (cooking time depends on the age of the fish).

Transfer the cod to kitchen paper to drain and keep the fish warm.

Reheat the garnish if necessary. Arrange the red pepper mixture in a layer on a warmed platter. Set the fish on top and sprinkle it with the lemon juice. Surround the fish with the potatoes and artichokes and sprinkle them with the chopped parsley.

Melt the remaining butter in a small saucepan and cook until it is a hazelnut colour, about 2 minutes, then pour it over the fish and serve immediately.

Artichokes and potatoes are staple vegetables of the region. They are cooked with salt cod in the typically Breton dish 'Morue Jacques Cartier', named after the famous French explorer who discovered Canada.

POULET EN GELÉE DE CIDRE

CHICKEN IN CIDER JELLY

'The Bretons have long been great drinkers of cider in cups called bolées,*' recounts René Picard. 'After several* bolées *downed in Saint-Malo's rue de la Soif (Street of Thirst), the corsairs would heat piastre coins and throw them from the windows to the crowd, who would burn their fingers as they fought to catch them.'*

Most Breton cider is cidre bouché, *or corked cider, the dry, fermented drink popular for cooking as well as sipping. Here, a chicken poaches in stock made with cider and vegetables, then the meat is layered with the strained cooking liquid in a terrine. The calf's feet add natural gelatine to the stock, ensuring that it sets.*

12 servings

2 CALF'S FEET, SPLIT IN HALF
2 LITRES/3¼ PINTS DRY CIDER
2 LITRES/3¼ PINTS WATER
2 CARROTS, THINLY SLICED
2 ONIONS, THINLY SLICED
2 LEEKS (WHITE PART ONLY), THINLY SLICED
1 STICK CELERY, THINLY SLICED
A BOUQUET GARNI*
3 CLOVES GARLIC
1×2.25 kg/5 lb CHICKEN, TRUSSED*
SALT AND PEPPER
A BUNCH OF PARSLEY
CORNICHONS OR GHERKINS
PICKLED ONIONS

TRUSSING NEEDLE AND STRING; 2 LITRE/3½ PINT TERRINE

Blanch the calf's feet* by putting them in a pan of cold water, bringing to the boil and boiling for 5 minutes; drain and rinse them. Put the calf's feet, cider, water, carrots, onions, leeks, celery, bouquet garni and garlic in a flameproof casserole and bring slowly to the boil, skimming often. Simmer over low heat for 1½ hours, skimming occasionally.

Add the chicken to the casserole with a little salt and pepper and enough water to cover the chicken. Cover and continue simmering for about 1½ hours until the juices from the chicken run clear when the thigh is pierced with a fork. Be sure there is always enough liquid to cover the chicken.

Lift the chicken out of the casserole, letting the juice drain, and allow it to cool. Remove the string and skin and cut the meat off the bones, reserving the carcass. Cut the meat into strips.

Meanwhile, simmer the cooking liquid with the chicken carcass until it reduces by three-quarters. Strain it and taste it for seasoning. Allow it to cool, then skim off any surface fat. Pour enough cooking liquid into the terrine to make a 2 cm/¾ in layer and refrigerate it until set.

Strip the parsley sprigs, discarding the stalks. Pour boiling water over the parsley leaves, leave 1 minute and then drain them. (This makes them a bright green.) Arrange a few leaves of parsley on the jellied liquid in the terrine and

This terrine of chicken in cider jelly is made with traditional Breton cider. A cool glass of the same dry cider is the perfect accompaniment.

cover with the nicest chicken strips. Add more cooking liquid and chill until it is set. Continue layering the cooking liquid, parsley and chicken strips until all the ingredients are used. Finish with a layer of cooking liquid. (The terrine can be made up to 3 days ahead and kept in the refrigerator.)

To serve, run a knife around the sides of the terrine. Serve directly from the dish, with the *cornichons* and pickled onions.

One of several statues representing the Four Seasons in the garden at Le Bos. The statues are Italian, dating from the 18th century, and were brought back by the corsairs from their trading trips to Genoa. Like many malouinières, the garden at Le Bos overlooks the Rance river.

MOKA AUX NOIX

COFFEE AND WALNUT GÂTEAU

One of the districts of Saint-Malo still bears the name Moka, a reminder that it was the town from which sailors voyaged to Arabia, to return with coffee and other riches of the East.

8 servings

For the génoise

125 g/4 oz PLAIN FLOUR
PINCH OF SALT
3 EGGS
100 g/3¼ oz CASTER SUGAR
1 tbsp INSTANT COFFEE DISSOLVED IN 2 tbsp WATER
45 g/1½ oz UNSALTED BUTTER, MELTED AND COOLED

For the icing

375 g/12 oz UNSALTED BUTTER, AT ROOM TEMPERATURE
200 g/6½ oz ICING SUGAR, SIFTED
15 g/½ oz INSTANT COFFEE DISSOLVED IN 4 tbsp WATER
125 g/4 oz WALNUT HALVES

20 cm/8 in ROUND CAKE TIN; PIPING BAG AND MEDIUM STAR TUBE (OPTIONAL)

Butter the cake tin and line the bottom with greaseproof paper. Butter the paper also and coat the tin with flour, discarding the excess. Heat the oven to 180°C/350°F/Gas Mark 4.

For the *génoise*, sift the flour with the salt. In a heatproof bowl set over a pan of hot, not boiling, water whisk the eggs with the sugar until the mixture falls from the whisk in a thick ribbon and holds a slowly dissolving trail, about 5 minutes. (An electric mixer can also be used, in which case the pan of hot water is not needed.) Sift the flour over the mixture in three batches and fold together lightly. Add the coffee and melted butter with the last batch.

Pour the mixture into the prepared tin and bake in the heated oven for 30 to 40 minutes or until the cake shrinks slightly and the top springs back when lightly pressed with a fingertip. Run a knife around the cake and turn it out on to a rack to cool. Peel off the lining paper. (The cake can be kept 1 or 2 days in an airtight container. It freezes well too.)

To make the icing, cream the butter and gradually beat in the sugar and coffee. Reserve 125 ml/4 fl oz of the icing. Finely chop the walnuts, reserving 8 halves for decoration. Beat the chopped nuts into the larger portion of icing.

Cut the cake in half horizontally using a long serrated knife, to make two layers. Spread one cake layer with one-third of the walnut icing. Set the second cake layer on top and press lightly to flatten it. Spread the top and sides of the gâteau with the remaining walnut icing. Scoop the reserved coffee icing into the piping bag and decorate the gâteau with 8 rosettes. Set a reserved walnut half on each rosette. (The gâteau can be made ahead and refrigerated.)

Manoir du Vau-de-Quip

Vicomte Maurice de Kervenoaël is Breton born and bred and has always been determined to maintain roots in this isolated western region of France. So in 1976 he bought the Manoir du Vau-de-Quip near Redon, in the heart of Brittany. Not only was the manoir in a sad state of disrepair, but the property had been dismembered into house, farm and woodland, victim of the French inheritance laws. Little by little the Kervenoaëls have pieced Vau-de-Quip together again. Now the manoir is again owner of the surrounding valley, and of woods of wild chestnut, oak and maritime pine. 'You could say we have recreated the old estate,' says Catherine de Kervenoaël. 'All we are still missing is part of the woodlands.'

Restoration of the manoir has been a painstaking affair. First priority was a kitchen and bathroom so the house would be at least habitable. Next was to apply for an historic monument listing — eventually this enabled the de Kervenoaëls to get a government subsidy to dry out the north wall of Vau-de-Quip and seal it from pervasive damp. In summer, students came along to help them paint and hang wallpaper in the seven bedrooms.

Terraces of huge trees surround Vau-de-Quip, with the nearest towering taller than the three-storied main building. Close by cluster the classic Breton adjuncts to the property – farmhouse, chapel, stables and outbuildings (right). The stone gateway proudly displays a time-worn family crest (right above). A turret protrudes from the woodland of wild chestnut, oak and maritime pine (right centre).

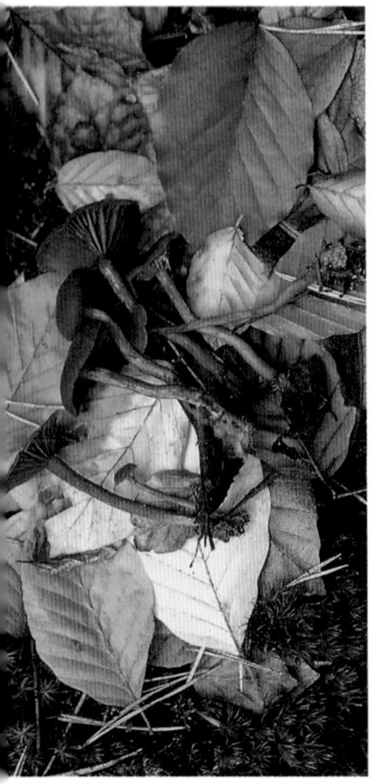

Edible mushrooms picked after a light shower from the woods around Vau-de-Quip (top left). The great kitchen-dining room with its dark beams and terracotta tiled floor (top right). Dating from the 15th century, the stone fireplace is decorated with animal motifs.

Now, after 15 years, the dozen ugly reinforced steel joists used by the previous owners to prop up the sagging main beams of the ground floor have gone. Finance is on the way for work on the great open fireplaces with their Renaissance carving. Surprisingly, the roof, usually the first source of trouble in an old house like this, has come last. 'The most recent roof repairs were 100 years ago so it certainly needs attention,' says the Vicomtesse, 'especially the dormer windows, whose stone carvings have been badly eroded by the weather.'

Central heating is still something of a luxury at Vau-de-Quip and in winter the family gathers in the great kitchen-dining room with its terracotta tiles and overhead beams. At the side of the fireplace is a curious niche – a 'petit four' for baking small cakes and side dishes. (Most baking would have been done in a bread oven sited away from the main building because of the heat and danger of fire.) The Vicomtesse looks after the cooking and at Christmas turns to simple dishes like a moulded dessert made with wild chestnuts from the property. 'I notice how much friends appreciate regional dishes, so different from the cooking in restaurants,' she says.

The Kervenoaëls told me how lucky they had been to find Vau-de-Quip since Bretons hold on closely to their land; the property had passed to a new family only three times since the title deeds began in 1488. One owner was the beautiful Louise du Bot du Grég, notorious for her two-faced conduct during the Napoleonic Wars. Married to one of the Royalist Breton leaders fighting against the new Republic, she joined the revolutionaries by engaging in an affair with General Hoche, who had been sent from Paris to suppress the Royalists. Vau-de-Quip was confiscated, but Louise managed to recover her property thanks to her liaison with Hoche. Bold as brass, she hung on to it by marrying a Napoleonic general once Hoche and her husband were out of the way.

Vau-de-Quip lies on the edge of Breton-speaking territory. The land is generously watered by streams – '*vau*' means valley while '*quip*' probably denotes a water spring. It could hardly be more appropriate to its current owners, for Vicomte de Kervenoaël is known teasingly by his friends as 'Mr Mineral Water' because he presides over the company which bottles Evian and Source Badoit.

TARTE AU THON

WARM TUNA FLAN

Since the Middle Ages, tuna has been one of the mainstays of Breton fishermen, and boats range hundreds of miles, as far as Senegal, in search of the giant fish.

8 servings

30 g/1 oz BUTTER
3 SHALLOTS, CHOPPED
4 HARD-BOILED EGGS
1 × 195 g/6½ oz CAN OF TUNA IN WATER OR BRINE, DRAINED
50 g/1¾ oz FRESH BREADCRUMBS SOAKED IN 125 ml/4 fl oz MILK AND SQUEEZED DRY
3 tbsp OLIVE OIL
4 tbsp CHOPPED PARSLEY
1 EGG, BEATEN TO MIX WITH ½ tsp SALT TO GLAZE

For the pâte brisée

300 g/10 oz PLAIN FLOUR
150 g/5 oz UNSALTED BUTTER
1 EGG YOLK
½ tsp SALT
4 tbsp WATER

For the sauce

2 tbsp LEMON JUICE, MORE TO TASTE
2 tbsp MIXED CHOPPED FRESH HERBS
SALT AND PEPPER
250 ml/8 fl oz CRÈME FRAÎCHE* OR DOUBLE CREAM

20 cm/8 in FLAN TIN WITH REMOVABLE BOTTOM

Make the *pâte brisée* (see page 221) and chill it for at least 30 minutes.

Melt the butter and cook the shallots until soft, 3 to 5 minutes. Chop the hard-boiled eggs. Flake the tuna with a fork. Mix together the eggs, tuna, soaked breadcrumbs, olive oil, shallots and parsley.

A leaping stone fish adorns the fireplace – a territorial symbol declaring that the châtelain held the right to fish the local seas.

Butter the flan tin. Divide the *pâte brisée* in half. Line the tin with half the dough, overlapping the edges of the tin*. Brush the dough edges with egg glaze*. Spoon the tuna mixture into the pastry case.

Roll out the remaining dough to a round 5 cm/2 in larger than the flan tin and cover the flan with it. Trim the edges and seal the pastry lid to the case with a fork or scallop with the back of a knife. Brush the lid with egg glaze. Using a sharp knife, slash the lid every 2.5 cm/1 in so steam can escape. Chill until the pastry dough is firm, about 30 minutes.

Heat the oven to 220°C/425°F/Gas Mark 7 and put in a baking sheet to heat.

Bake the flan on the hot baking sheet until the pastry starts to brown, 10 to 15 minutes. Reduce the oven temperature to 180°C/350°F/Gas Mark 4 and continue baking until the pastry is browned, 15 to 20 minutes longer. (The flan can be baked up to 2 days ahead and refrigerated. Reheat and serve it warm or at room temperature.)

Meanwhile, to make the sauce, mix the lemon juice, herbs, salt and pepper in a bowl. Gradually whisk in the crème fraîche or cream – the lemon juice will thicken it lightly. Taste and add more salt, pepper and lemon juice if needed.

Serve the flan hot, with the sauce.

SAUMON EN CROÛTE DE SEL

SALMON BAKED IN A SALT CRUST

This method of preparing salmon in a salt crust is good with other thick fish fillets – especially cod. The crust is removed before eating.

8 servings

1 × 1.4 kg/3 lb PIECE OF SALMON FILLET, WITH THE SKIN, CUT INTO 8 PIECES
8 SPRIGS OF FRESH THYME
1 EGG, BEATEN TO MIX
750 g/1½ lb UNPEELED BOILING POTATOES
375 g/12 oz SPINACH, WASHED AND STALKS REMOVED
30 g/1 oz BUTTER
SALT AND PEPPER

For the salt crust

375 g/12 oz SEA SALT
300 g/10 oz PLAIN WHOLEMEAL FLOUR
5 EGG WHITES, MORE IF NEEDED

For the white butter sauce

4 tbsp WHITE WINE VINEGAR
4 tbsp WHITE WINE
2 SHALLOTS, CHOPPED
250 g/8 oz UNSALTED BUTTER
2 tbsp MIXED CHOPPED FRESH HERBS

For the salt crust, beat together the salt, flour and egg whites, adding more egg white if necessary to form a dough that holds together. Cover the dough and leave it to rest for at least 15 minutes, and up to 4 hours.

Divide the salt crust dough into 8 equal pieces. Roll out a piece to a 20 cm/8 in square. Put a piece of fish, skin side down, in the centre of the dough square. Top with a sprig of thyme. Brush the surrounding dough with beaten egg, then bring up the dough over the fish and seal into a parcel with the salmon flat inside. Keep it

Saumon en Croûte de Sel – a gutsy taste of the sea. The salt crust is discarded at the table before eating.

in the refrigerator while preparing the remaining parcels. Chill all the fish parcels for at least 15 minutes, and up to 2 hours.

Heat the oven to 200°C/400°F/Gas Mark 6 and put in a baking sheet to heat. Put the fish parcels on the hot baking sheet and bake in the heated oven for 12 minutes. Remove the parcels and leave at room temperature for 10 minutes.

While the fish is baking and resting, cook the potatoes in a large pan of boiling salted water until just tender, 15 to 20 minutes. Cook the spinach in a large pan of boiling salted water until tender, 1 to 2 minutes. Drain the spinach and refresh it*. When cool enough to handle, squeeze the spinach by handfuls to remove excess moisture. Make the white butter sauce (see page 55) and stir in the herbs.

Drain the potatoes, peel them and cut into thick slices. Keep warm. Melt the butter in a frying pan. Add the spinach with a little salt and pepper and cook over moderate heat, stirring often, until heated through. Taste for seasoning.

To serve, put the fish, still in the salt crust, on warmed plates. Arrange the potatoes and spinach around the fish and serve. Hand the sauce separately. Leave guests to remove the salt crust at the table.

LE REDONNAIS

CHESTNUT LOAF WITH WHIPPED CREAM

The wild chestnut trees around Redon are famous – the locals say they have a special savoury taste and will not survive if planted elsewhere. 'When I make the cake in Paris with chestnuts bought there,' says the Vicomtesse de Kervenoaël, 'it simply isn't the same.' Though nothing can replace the taste of fresh chestnuts, the results are very good with canned ones.

8 servings

875 g/1¾ lb FRESH CHESTNUTS OR 500 g/1 lb CANNED UNSWEETENED CHESTNUTS
600 ml/1 PINT MILK, MORE IF NEEDED
250 g/8 oz UNSALTED BUTTER, AT ROOM TEMPERATURE
135 g/4½ oz CASTER SUGAR
2 to 3 tsp RUM
125 g/4 oz BITTERSWEET CHOCOLATE, CHOPPED
½ tsp VEGETABLE OIL

For the Chantilly cream
125 ml/4 fl oz DOUBLE CREAM
1½ tsp ICING SUGAR
FEW DROPS VANILLA ESSENCE

23×12.5×10 cm/9×5×4 in LOAF TIN; PIPING BAG AND MEDIUM STAR TUBE (OPTIONAL)

Lightly butter the loaf tin. Line the bottom with greaseproof paper, and butter the paper also.

If using fresh chestnuts, make a slit at the end of each nut with a small knife. Put them in a pan of cold water and bring just to the boil. Use a slotted spoon to lift out a few nuts at a time and peel them while still hot, removing both the thick outer skin and the thin inner skin. If the chestnuts cool and become difficult to peel, quickly reheat them. Do not allow them to heat too long, or they will become soft and fall apart. Put the peeled fresh nuts in a saucepan with the milk, cover the pan and simmer gently over low heat until the nuts are tender, 25 to 30 minutes.

If using canned chestnuts, just drain them. Purée fresh or canned chestnuts in a food processor or work them through a food mill.

Beat the butter and sugar together until soft. Beat this mixture together with the rum into the nut purée until smooth. Pack the mixture into the prepared tin and smooth the top. Cover and refrigerate overnight, or up to a week.

To finish, turn out the chestnut loaf on to a platter and peel off the lining paper. Melt the chocolate on a heatproof plate set over a pan of hot water. Stir in the oil until the mixture is smooth. Allow it to cool slightly, then spread the chocolate evenly over the top and sides of the chestnut loaf using a palette knife. Put it in the refrigerator to set.

Make the Chantilly cream (see page 220) and scoop it into the piping bag if using. Cut the loaf in thin slices using a knife dipped in hot water and set the slices on individual plates. Decorate with rosettes of Chantilly cream, if using a piping bag, or spoon the cream on to the slices by hand.

The caretakers of the château cradling two young ducks (left).

Château du Vert-Bois

Thanks to the loving care of Anne Prouvost and her late husband, the 18th-century Château du Vert-Bois is an oasis of beauty in the chill plains of northern France. They inherited the château with all its original decoration, fine furniture and collection of Delft faïence, to which Madame Prouvost's father had added 19th- and 20th-century paintings by such masters as Renoir, Bonnard, Dufy and Chagall. The Prouvosts themselves expanded the collection with modern artists and added a remarkable group of rare minerals collected on their travels. In 1975, the Fondation Septentrion (Foundation of the North) was opened at Le Vert-Bois to help local artists exhibit their work. Regular classes are held in drawing, painting, decorating furniture and bookbinding, while the appraisal of antiques is particularly popular.

The classical, moated Château du Vert-Bois is pure Louis XV, but in miniature. 'The building is only one room deep,' explains owner Madame Prouvost, 'so with floor to ceiling windows on both sides we have wonderful light, but few bedrooms.' The bridge across the moat – survivor of an earlier fortified farm – is scarcely carriage-width. The gatehouse at Le Vert-Bois (inset above) is almost a century older than the château, and was originally a hunting lodge. It is built in a Flemish style, a striking contrast to the classical lines of the château itself.

Between the two World Wars, when the French textile business was still prosperous, wool merchants like the Prouvosts had close connections with their counterparts in the United States, even opening up mills there. Much of the business was centred in Rhode Island around Woonsocket – as Anne Prouvost told me, 'there were plenty of French-speaking Catholics'. Very soon the family was at ease in Boston and New York social circles. It was in this company that Madame Prouvost first encountered 'the obligatory after-dinner hour of powder room and *crème de menthe* for the ladies while our husbands savoured a splendid Cognac'. New York memories include filling in as a volunteer waitress at the charity restaurant that is run by the Alliance Française.

Later, in Hollywood, the Prouvosts were entertained by movie mogul Jack Warner – 'electronic gates, uniformed guards, fierce dogs . . . and a private road peppered with reproduction Greek statues and fountains,' recalls Anne Prouvost. Next, the Prouvosts opened a textile mill in South Carolina near Charleston, returning to France with a taste for jambalaya but 'not for that horrible fried chicken'.

The Prouvosts were great yachtsmen, regularly taking their children to the Mediterranean. Anne Prouvost was always in charge of the food. 'I'm the queen of fish soup and ratatouille,' she confesses. 'You could always find chicken, however tough, so stewed chicken in sauce is my speciality too.' Back home she has made her cook an expert at *waterzoï*, a Flemish version of *pot-au-feu* which is finished with crème fraîche and huge quantities of chopped parsley. Madame Prouvost also enjoys *flamiche*, a Flemish leek tart baked in *pâte brisée* with a topping of creamy custard. 'But when I'm alone I simply cook an egg.'

The elegant grand salon is presided over by a glittering chandelier and fine impressionist paintings.

FAISANS EN ESCABÈCHE

OIL AND VINEGAR BRAISED PHEASANTS IN ASPIC

Though only a few kilometres from the industrial city of Lille, the Château du Vert-Bois is in rustic and idyllic surroundings and aptly lives up to its name of 'green woods'. Game birds and hare are plentiful here. In this unusual recipe, the musky flavour of wild pheasant is enhanced with vinegar, while oil is used to keep the bird moist. For serving, the halved birds are brushed with a light coating of aspic.

4 servings

2 OVEN-READY PHEASANTS
(ABOUT 1 kg/2 lb EACH)
SALT AND PEPPER
1 ONION, CHOPPED
2 BAY LEAVES
175 ml/6 fl oz WHITE WINE VINEGAR
4 tbsp OLIVE OIL
1 LITRE/1¾ PINTS CLEAR CHICKEN STOCK
(see page 221), AT ROOM TEMPERATURE
15 g/½ oz POWDERED GELATINE
1 SMALL LEAFY LETTUCE OR
1 BUNCH OF WATERCRESS

TRUSSING NEEDLE AND STRING

Heat the oven to 180°C/350°F/Gas Mark 4. Season the cavities of the birds with salt and pepper and truss them*. Put them in a large flameproof casserole with the onion, bay leaves, vinegar, oil, salt and pepper. Cover the casserole and bring the liquid just to the boil on top of the stove.

Transfer the casserole to the heated oven and cook the birds until they are tender, about 1½ hours. Baste the birds often and turn them from time to time during cooking.

Drain the birds and allow to cool to room temperature, then cover them and refrigerate until they are well chilled, about 2 hours. Discard the cooking liquid.

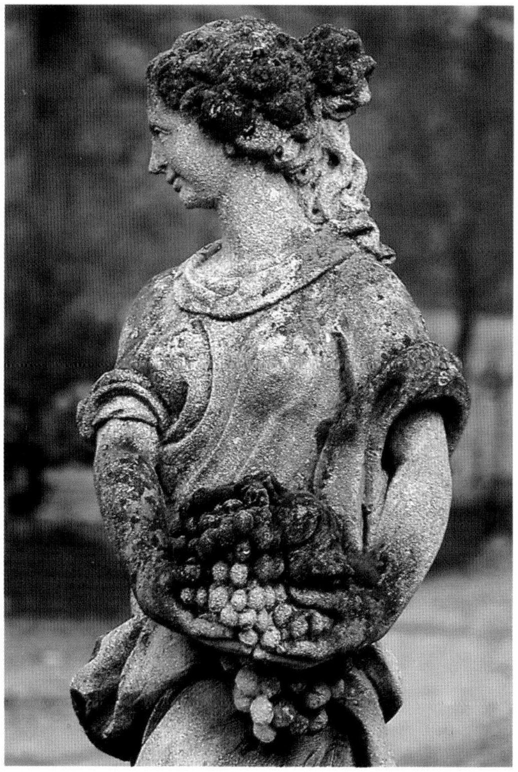

The garden at Le Vert-Bois dates from the mid-18th century and includes a formal French park, an orchard and the English-style 'jardin du curé', designed by Russell Page, the influential English landscape architect.

Remove the string from the birds and pat them dry with kitchen paper. Halve each bird, cutting along the breastbone and backbone. Set the halves on a rack, skin side up, over a tray to catch the drips and refrigerate them.

Put 3 or 4 tablespoons of the stock in a small saucepan. Sprinkle over the gelatine and leave until it swells to a spongy consistency, about 5 minutes. Melt it over low heat, gently shaking the pan. (Do not stir or strings will form.) Add the gelatine mixture to the remaining stock to make aspic. Taste it for seasoning. Leave it to cool until tepid, stirring occasionally.

Pour about one-quarter of the aspic into a metal bowl set over ice and stir gently until it is very cold, turns syrupy and starts to set. Working quickly, brush or spoon a thin coating of this aspic over the birds. Chill them until the aspic sets.

Chill more aspic until it is on the point of setting and coat the birds again. Repeat the process twice.

Set the birds on a platter lined with lettuce or decorate the birds with watercress. Cover the birds and refrigerate them for up to 24 hours, until ready to serve.

Exquisite Persian bowls from the prestigious collection of porcelain, sculpture and fine china displayed at Le Vert-Bois.

Pudding de Cabinet

Brioche Pudding with Glacé Fruit and Jam

This extravagant version of bread and butter pudding was the speciality of a great-grandmother who left 'lasting memories. It was she who preserved the house in its pristine state,' says Madame Prouvost. The recipe calls for kramik *– a local brioche – instead of the more usual sponge fingers or boudoir biscuits. If you don't have time to bake the* kramik *(see next recipe), this dessert is quickly made with a shop-bought loaf of brioche, weighing about 500 g/1 lb, sliced and trimmed to fit the dish.*

10 to 12 servings

30 g/1 oz SULTANAS
60 g/2 oz MIXED GLACÉ FRUITS, CHOPPED
KRAMIK (see opposite), CUT CROSSWAYS INTO 3 LAYERS
300 g/10 oz APRICOT JAM
6 EGGS
200 g/6½ oz CASTER SUGAR
1 LITRE/1⅔ PINTS MILK

For the vanilla custard
500 ml/16 fl oz MILK
1 VANILLA POD, SPLIT,
OR FEW DROPS VANILLA ESSENCE
6 EGG YOLKS
60 g/2 oz CASTER SUGAR

2 LITRE/3½ PINT SOUFFLÉ OR OTHER ROUND BAKING DISH

Generously butter the baking dish. Put it in the freezer until the butter is firm, and then butter it once again.

Heat the oven to 180°C/350°F/Gas Mark 4.

Sprinkle sultanas and glacé fruits over the bottom of the baking dish. Top with a layer of brioche. Spread with a thin layer of jam and sprinkle with more sultanas and glacé fruits.

Whisk the eggs and sugar together until light. Gradually whisk in the milk. Pour a little of this custard slowly over the bread so it is absorbed.

Put the dish in a *bain-marie** and bring the water to the boil on top of the stove. Transfer it to the heated oven and bake until the custard sets, about 30 minutes. Remove the dish from the oven and layer the remaining bread, jam, sultanas and glacé fruits in the dish until all the ingredients are used, finishing with a layer of bread. Pour in the remaining custard. If the bread floats, gently press it into the custard. Bring the *bain-marie* back to the boil on top of the stove, then return the dish to the oven and bake until the custard sets, 1½ to 2 hours.

Meanwhile, make the vanilla custard (see page 222). Allow the pudding to cool for at least 15 minutes before serving it, or serve it at room temperature. Run a knife around the dish and turn out the pudding on to a platter. Pour a little of the vanilla custard around it and pass the remaining sauce separately.

Pudding de Cabinet, the ultimate bread and butter pudding.

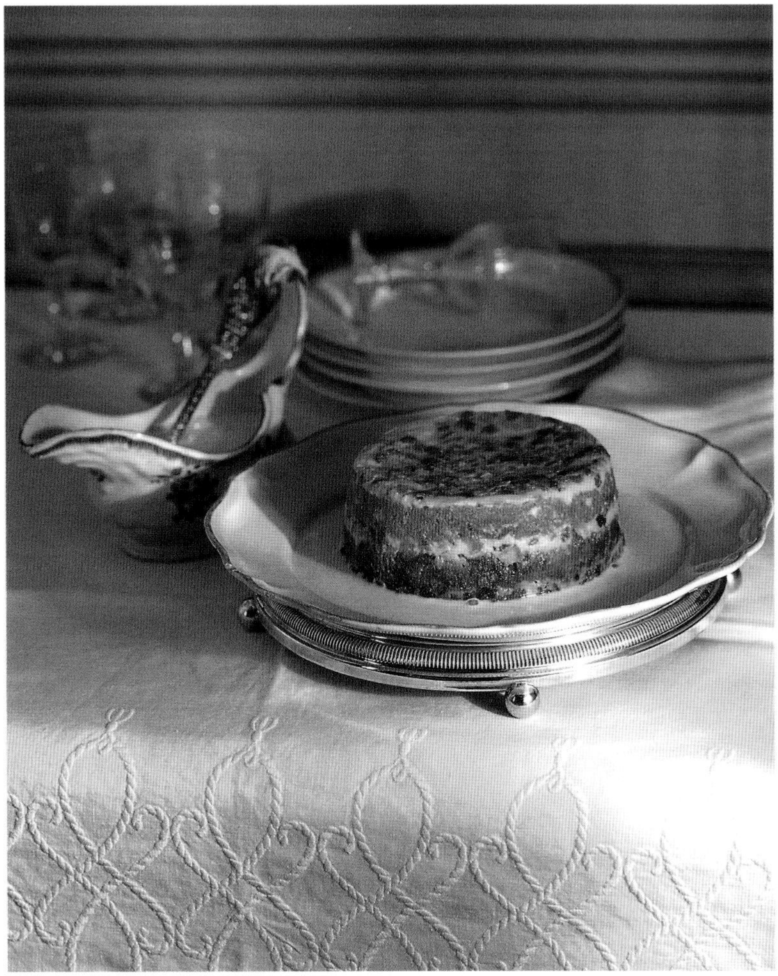

KRAMIK

BROWN SUGAR BRIOCHE

Some of France's great 19th-century fortunes were made in the northern fields of sugar beet, so not surprisingly, the local rich yeast bread is sprinkled with brown sugar. Other versions appear throughout Flanders and in neighbouring Belgium. It's a treat toasted for breakfast.

75 ml/2½ fl oz MILK
1½ tsp DRY YEAST OR 10 g/⅓ oz FRESH YEAST*
200 g/6½ oz PLAIN FLOUR, MORE IF NEEDED
PINCH OF SALT
1 tbsp GRANULATED SUGAR
2 EGGS, BEATEN TO MIX
100 g/3¼ oz UNSALTED BUTTER

For the topping
45 g/1½ oz BUTTER, AT ROOM TEMPERATURE
75 g/2½ oz LIGHT OR DARK SOFT BROWN SUGAR

20 cm/8 in ROUND CAKE TIN

Heat the milk in a small saucepan until bubbles form round the edge, then allow it to cool to lukewarm. Sprinkle or crumble over the yeast and leave to dissolve, about 5 minutes.

Sift the flour with the salt into a bowl and make a well in the centre. Add the yeast mixture, granulated sugar and eggs to the well. With your fingertips, stir the ingredients in the well, gradually drawing in the flour to make a smooth dough. It should be very soft. Using your cupped hand, knead the dough by slapping it against the side of the bowl. Continue kneading until the dough is shiny and very smooth, about 10 minutes.

Pound the butter with your fist to soften it first, then work it into the dough until thoroughly incorporated. (Alternatively, you can mix and knead the dough in an electric mixer fitted with a dough hook.)

Transfer the dough to an oiled bowl, flipping it so the top is oiled. Cover it with a damp cloth and leave to rise in a warm place until doubled in bulk, 1 to 1½ hours.

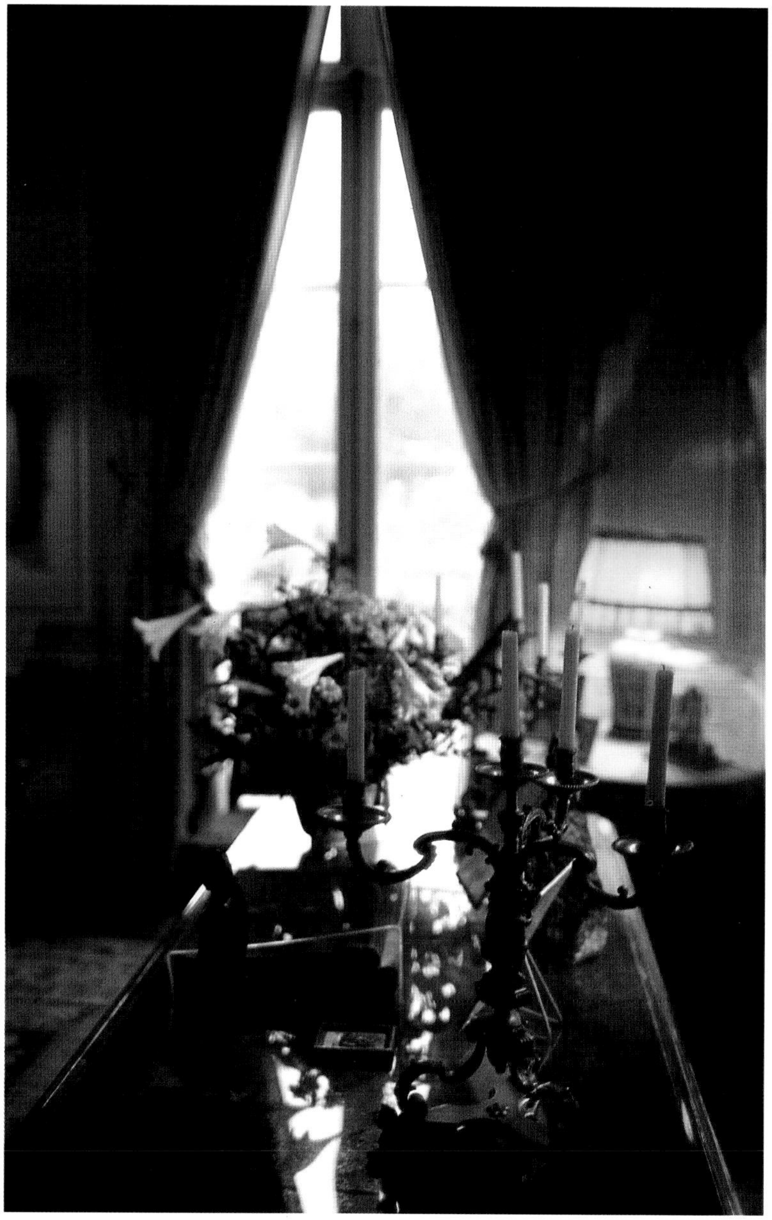

The elegant rooms at Le Vert-Bois are sumptuously furnished and still retain much of their original decoration.

Meanwhile, butter the cake tin.

Transfer the dough to a floured work surface and knead it lightly to knock out the air. Shape it into a ball and transfer it to the tin. Flour your hands and flatten the dough into the bottom (not the sides) of the tin. Spread it with the butter for the topping and sprinkle with the brown sugar. Leave it to rise in a warm place until almost doubled in bulk, 15 to 30 minutes. Heat the oven to 200°C/400°F/Gas Mark 6.

Bake the *kramik* in the oven until it is brown and firm, 25 to 30 minutes. Turn it out on to a rack to cool. It is best eaten warm on the day of baking, but can be stored for up to a day.

Château d'Ittenwiller

Each year in October François-Joseph d'Andlau-Hombourg takes two weeks' holiday to pick his own grapes. The *vendange* at the Château d'Ittenwiller in Alsace has become something of a festival, with the Comte, his two brothers and their children joined by a bevy of friends. Picking is done by hand in the old way. 'This means we can cut the vines right back for lower yield and higher quality. We are one of only two châteaux in Alsace that press and bottle wine on the property itself,' he recounts with pride. 'So many friends want to help, we have to turn away volunteers!'

His wife, Christine d'Andlau-Hombourg, is in charge of the cooking. 'We're expecting about 50 people for the harvest weekend this year,' she told me. 'We take a picnic to the vines in late morning — hot rolls, ham and pâté sandwiches with *cornichons*, plenty of wine and beer. Everyone must be well fed to be strong and happy!' After this second breakfast, lunch back home does not start until late afternoon and it, too, is generous. An enormous *choucroute* is followed by the local Munster cheese (milder types are available for the faint-hearted) and a dessert of chocolate cake or perhaps floating island.

17th-century Château d'Ittenwiller, a reconstruction of an ancient fortified manor, is busiest in the autumn when grape-picking dominates château life. The building is typically Alsatian with ivy-covered turrets, and the presence of antlers around the house and the grounds is explained by the well-stocked deer-park in the grounds.

A stone archway above the entrance to the wine cellar is shaded by a magnificent maple tree (above).

Lunch the following day is similarly matched to the exigencies of outdoor life. Main course is the Alsatian meat and potato dish called *back-eöfe*, which precedes salad, cheese and assorted fruit tarts of apples, pears or plums topped in Alsatian fashion with a creamy custard. As for the evenings, a *quiche lorraine* is always available. The Comtesse's recipe is again a local classic, flavoured with ham in a custard of whole eggs and cream, and sprinkled with a little Gruyère cheese for a crisp brown crust.

Good food is but a background for the matter in hand – the harvest itself. The enduring concern is the weather as some sun is vital during the ten days before picking. Heavy rain during picking dilutes the grape juice and encourages rot (but not the 'noble rot' so necessary to the luscious sweet wines made from late-picked grapes). Once in cask, a wine can develop unpredictably, particularly in the first few weeks. 'We all mess up a barrel from time to time, though no one likes to admit it,' the Comte acknowledges with a laugh. He speaks with the authority of experience – Alsace has been home to the Andlau-Hombourg family for more than a millenium.

He is particularly proud of the Château d'Ittenwiller Comte d'Andlau-Hombourg white wine, a blend originally made by the Benedictine monks who planted vineyards at Ittenwiller after displacing a nunnery dating back to 1115. The Benedictine 'recipe' is based on four grape varieties: Sylvaner (a typically Alsatian grape valued for its acidity), Pinot Blanc for volume, a small amount of Tokay (known in the rest of France as Pinot Gris), and finally Muscat for fragrance and finesse. 'It's a wine to drink throughout the meal, good with all but the richest red meats,' says the Comte. Two other white wines are also produced on the property: a Riesling, dry and ideally suited to fish dishes, and a fruity Gewürztraminer, at its best as an aperitif, with dessert or with a slice of the best Alsatian *foie gras*.

The vines at Château d'Ittenwiller extend over three hectares – just sufficient, says the Comte, 'for us to maintain the property and enjoy ourselves at the same time'. There is certainly much to take pleasure in, for Ittenwiller is a quintessentially Alsatian cluster of buildings, complete with decorative painted shutters, geranium window boxes, an encircling moat and the slightly surreal touch of stags' antlers here, there and everywhere. There is no problem renewing the stock as the Château d'Ittenwiller also has its own deer park!

The Château d'Ittenwiller vineyard on a mellow autumn afternoon. It extends over 3 hectares.

Wine aged well in oak casks acquires an unmistakable character. The Gewürztraminer in this cask is a favourite aperitif wine.

Bottles of Château d'Ittenwiller white, Riesling and Gewürztraminer (above).

Backeöfe

Pork, Lamb and Beef Baked with Potatoes

This traditional Alsatian stew is commonly prepared and served in oval terrines of the local earthenware pottery. These are still hand-crafted by artisans and painted with country designs. In the old days, housewives carried their terrines filled with backeöfe *to the village communal oven, which was hot from bread-baking. Even today Comte d'Andlau-Hombourg gives old-fashioned instructions. 'Cook your* backeöfe *in the baker's oven for 2 to 2½ hours,' he writes, 'or bake it in your oven at home for 3½ hours.'*

8 servings

500 g/1 lb STEWING PORK, CUT INTO 5 cm/2 in CUBES
500 g/1 lb BONED LAMB SHOULDER, CUT INTO 5 cm/2 in CUBES
500 g/1 lb STEWING BEEF, CUT INTO 5 cm/2 in CUBES
500 ml/16 fl oz DRY WHITE WINE, PREFERABLY ALSATIAN
250 g/8 oz ONIONS, SLICED
2 CLOVES GARLIC, CHOPPED
A BOUQUET GARNI*
1 tsp CRUSHED PEPPERCORNS
1 kg/2 lb POTATOES, PEELED AND SLICED
SALT

Combine the pork, lamb, beef, wine, onions, garlic, bouquet garni and peppercorns in a large bowl (not aluminium). Stir well, cover and refrigerate overnight.

Heat the oven to 160°C/325°F/Gas Mark 3. Line a flameproof casserole with half the potatoes and sprinkle them lightly with salt. Cover the potatoes with all the meats and half the onions and season them. Layer the remaining potatoes and onions in the casserole and add a little more salt. Strain in the wine.

Cover the casserole and bring to a simmer on top of the stove. Transfer to the heated oven and bake until the meats are very tender, 3 to 4 hours. If you like, uncover the casserole during the last 30 minutes of cooking, to allow the top to brown.

Taste the cooking liquid for seasoning before serving, in the casserole. (The stew can be refrigerated for 1 or 2 days. The flavour mellows with time.)

The local Backeöfe, a dish that requires good dry white wine and slow gentle cooking.

KUGELHOPF

ALSATIAN YEAST CAKE

'Kugelhopf,' says Christine d'Andlau-Hombourg, 'is a sweet yeast cake flavoured with raisins and almonds that we eat for breakfast, for tea, and even at wine tastings.' For a crisp brown crust it is best baked in the traditional deep, fluted ring mould made of earthenware.

Makes 2 loaves

175 ml/6 fl oz MILK
1 tbsp DRY YEAST OR
20 g/¾ oz FRESH YEAST*
175 g/6 oz UNSALTED BUTTER
500 g/1 lb PLAIN FLOUR
PINCH OF SALT
75 g/2½ oz CASTER SUGAR
2 EGGS, BEATEN TO MIX
75 g/2½ oz RAISINS, SOAKED IN WARM WATER UNTIL PLUMP AND DRAINED
45 g/1½ oz WHOLE UNBLANCHED ALMONDS

2×1.5 LITRE/2½ PINT KUGELHOPF MOULDS

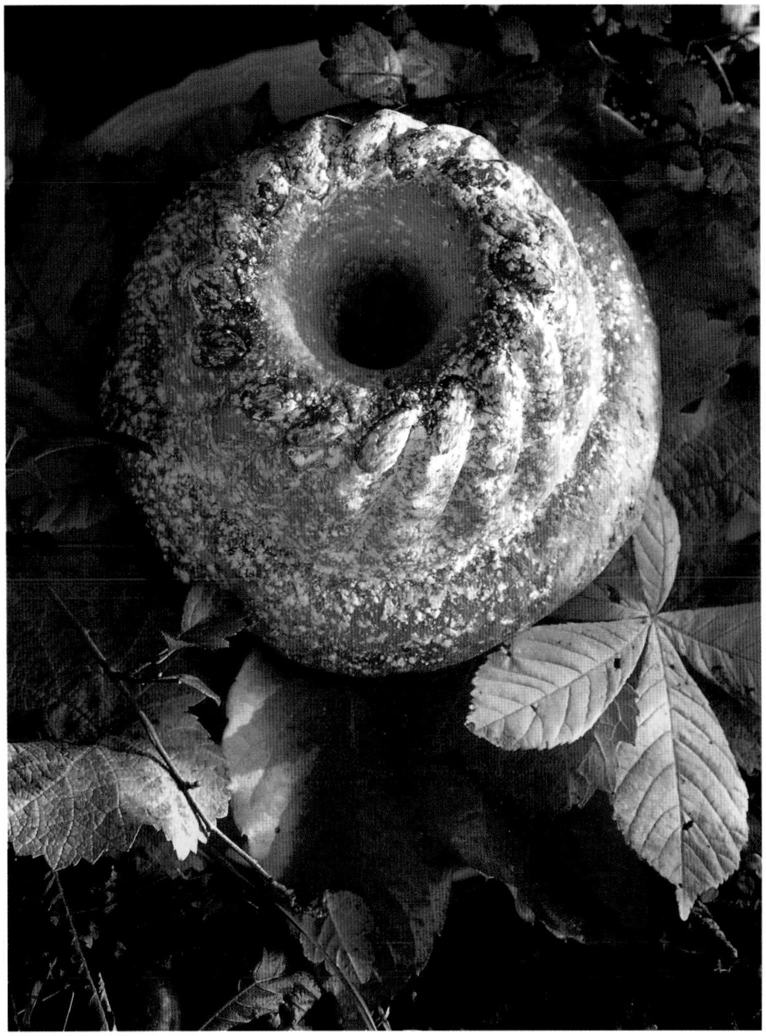

Kugelhopf, sweet yeast cake, is a staple of Alsace and a favourite at breakfast.

Heat the milk in a small saucepan until bubbles form round the edge. Pour about half of it into a small bowl and allow it to cool to lukewarm, then sprinkle or crumble over the yeast and leave to dissolve, about 5 minutes. Meanwhile, add the butter to the remaining milk in the saucepan and continue heating, stirring, until the butter melts, 2 to 3 minutes. Leave it to cool to tepid.

Sift the flour with the salt into a large bowl and make a well in the centre. Add the butter and yeast mixtures, the sugar and eggs to the well. With your fingertips, stir the ingredients in the well, gradually drawing in the flour to make a smooth dough. It should be very soft. Using your cupped hand, knead the dough by slapping it against the side of the bowl. Continue kneading until the dough is shiny and very smooth, about 10 minutes. Gently work in the raisins. (Alternatively, you can mix and knead the dough in an electric mixer fitted with a dough hook.)

Oil a large bowl and transfer the dough into it. Cover the bowl with a damp cloth and leave the dough to rise in a warm place until doubled in bulk, 1 to 1½ hours. Butter the kugelhopf moulds. Press the whole almonds evenly around the sides and bottom.

When risen, knead the dough lightly to knock out the air. Divide the dough in half and put it in the moulds; it should fill them by one-third. Cover with a damp cloth and leave to rise in a warm place until the dough has almost reached the top of the moulds, ¾ to 1 hour. Heat the oven to 190°C/375°F/Gas Mark 5.

Bake the kugelhopfs in the heated oven until puffed and brown, 40 to 50 minutes. Turn them out on to a rack to cool.

The kugelhopfs are best eaten on the day of baking, but can be stored in an airtight container for up to 3 days.

Parc de Schoppenwihr

'Alsace is a garden,' remarks Baron Christian de Watteville-Berckheim. His home at Schoppenwihr is a small part of this garden, with a park which is a microcosm of the province itself, a reflection too of Nature's struggle to survive 20th-century progress. The property includes eight hectares of forest, farmland for growing maize and wheat, and a network of lakes and streams inhabited by carp, pike, perch and the other freshwater fish. 'Recently they've been doing poorly,' laments the Baron, 'what with pollution from the paper mill and two years of drought.'

Schoppenwihr is an ancient property which has been in the Watteville-Berckheim family since the 15th century. The park is landscaped *à l'anglaise*, with splendid trees, including American and Asian species, and rolling vistas dotted with sheep which are kept 'to look pretty'. Sadly, this beautiful landscape is under double threat — from incursion by electrical pylons, and the intrusion of yet another autoroute. Not that the Watteville-Berckheims are unaccustomed to adversities — German, American and British soldiers fought over the ground in January 1945, leaving the château in ruins and age-old trees badly damaged by shrapnel.

The landscaped gardens of Schoppenwihr were laid out in a romantic English style in the 19th century and planted with rare and exotic trees.

Intricately carved chair backs add to the grandeur of the great dining room (above).

Now the family live in a picturesque domain that once housed a vast wine press. It is typically Alsatian, dating largely from the early 1800s, with overhanging eaves, precipitous tiled roofs and gabled windows.

The Schoppenwihr domain is supplied with game, though as with fish, stocks are fragile. 'With the sweeping expanse of modern fields, birds have nowhere to shelter,' explains Christian Watteville-Berckheim, who has memories of a landscape intersected with hedgerows and copses. 'Crop-spraying in early June is also to blame since it kills the insects on which game birds feed. This is why so much game is raised on artificial foodstuffs, and can taste unpleasantly of fish when it comes to table,' the Baron added. As a result, the legendary Auberge de l'Ill, one of the finest restaurants in Alsace, has banned pheasant from its menus for the present.

Fortunately game birds, venison and even the occasional hare still find their way to the Schoppenwihr table. Young birds are wrapped in vine leaves and barded with fat to roast in classic style, then set on a buttered *croûte* of bread spread with a pâté of the liver and heart made piquant with herbs and a thread of Cognac. Older birds may be simmered in wine *en cocotte*, then served in a cream sauce sharpened with horseradish – the Alsatian mustard. 'Old birds can be so bland,' warns the Baron. He prefers to bake them with sauerkraut until the meat is tender and falls from the bones, soft enough to chop and mix back into the cabbage.

CANARD AU SANG BERCKHEIM

ROAST DUCK WITH MUSTARD SAUCE

This recipe is equally good for other game birds, or for young pigeon. 'Serve the bird', says Christian de Watteville-Berckheim, 'with a glass of good Alsatian Tokay.'

4 servings

2 OVEN-READY WILD MALLARD DUCKS (ABOUT 750 g/1½ lb EACH)
60 g/2 oz BUTTER, AT ROOM TEMPERATURE
SALT AND PEPPER

For the sauce
2 tbsp DIJON MUSTARD FLAVOURED WITH TARRAGON
2 tsp CORNFLOUR
4 tsp OLIVE OIL
125 g/4 oz COLD BUTTER, CUT INTO PIECES

TRUSSING NEEDLE AND STRING

Heat the oven to 260°C/500°F/Gas Mark 10. Truss the birds*. Spread them with the butter and sprinkle with salt and pepper. Set them on one leg in a roasting tin and roast in the heated oven for 8 minutes. Turn them on to the other leg, baste well and roast for 5 minutes longer. Turn the birds on to their backs, baste and continue roasting for 5 to 8 minutes until the juice from the centre runs pink when the bird is lifted on a two-pronged fork. At this point the meat will be rare. If you prefer it well done, continue roasting for another 5 to 8 minutes.

Transfer the birds to a carving board with a well to catch the juices. Cut the birds in half, discarding the backbone. Cover the ducks loosely with foil and leave to rest. Pour off all the fat from the roasting tin, leaving the cooking juices. Add the juice from the carving board to the roasting tin and heat, stirring to dissolve the browned juices in the tin. Boil to reduce them to about 2 tablespoons.

For the sauce, whisk together the mustard and cornflour in a saucepan until smooth. Whisk in the oil a few drops at a time at first, then in a thin stream as for mayonnaise. Warm gently for 30 seconds. Whisk in the reduced roasting juices, then whisk in the butter a few pieces at a time, taking the pan on and off the heat so the butter softens and thickens creamily without melting to oil. Taste for seasoning.

Serve the duck on a warmed platter or plates and pass the sauce separately.

The panelled dining room at Schoppenwihr.

CHOUCROUTE DU BARON

SAUERKRAUT WITH SAUSAGE, BACON AND PORK LOIN

The Watteville-Berckheims serve this choucroute *with Alsatian beer or the same white wine as they use in cooking. Note that some cured meats are saltier than others. To remove excess salt, blanch the meat by putting it in a pan of cold water, bringing it to the boil and simmering it for 5 minutes. Drain it and proceed with the recipe.*

8 servings

90 g/3 oz GOOSE FAT OR LARD
4 LARGE ONIONS, CHOPPED
1.8 kg/4 lb UNCOOKED SAUERKRAUT, RINSED AND SQUEEZED DRY
1 LARGE DESSERT APPLE, PEELED, CORED AND SLICED
1 × 500 g/1 lb PIECE OF UNSMOKED STREAKY BACON
1 × 500 g/1 lb PIECE OF SMOKED BACK BACON
500 g/1 lb SMOKED PORK SAUSAGES
500 g/1 lb SMOKED LOIN OF PORK
SALT AND PEPPER
2 BOTTLES (750 ml/1¼ PINTS EACH) WHITE WINE, PREFERABLY RIESLING
2 tsp JUNIPER BERRIES, TIED IN MUSLIN
125 ml/4 fl oz SCHNAPPS
16 MEDIUM NEW POTATOES
8 CURED PORK CHOPS
8 FRANKFURTER SAUSAGES
DIJON MUSTARD FOR SERVING

MUSLIN

Melt two-thirds of the fat in a large flameproof casserole, add the onions and cook them over low heat, stirring occasionally, until soft, 6 to 8 minutes. Spread half the sauerkraut over the onions. Place the apple, both kinds of bacon, the smoked sausages and smoked pork loin on top. Season very lightly. Cover the meat with the rest of the sauerkraut and add the wine. Cut a piece of greaseproof paper to fit inside the casserole and press it directly on top of the sauerkraut. Cover and simmer on top of the stove until the sauerkraut is tender, $1\frac{1}{2}$ to 2 hours. Add the juniper berries and schnapps halfway through cooking.

Half an hour before the end of the cooking time, put the potatoes in a pan of salted water, bring to the boil and cook until tender, 15 to 20 minutes. Drain them and keep warm; peel them just before serving.

Melt the remaining fat in a frying pan and cook the pork chops until well done, 5–7 minutes on each side. Add them to the casserole. Cook the frankfurters in very hot water until heated through, about 1 minute. Drain.

To serve, discard the juniper berries and taste the sauerkraut for seasoning. Carve the bacon and pork loin in generous slices. Drain the sauerkraut well and pile it on a large heated platter with the meats, sausages and potatoes on top. Pass the mustard separately.

'Better too much than too little; choucroute improves when reheated,' is an old family saying.

CHÂTEAUX OF THE

HEART OF FRANCE

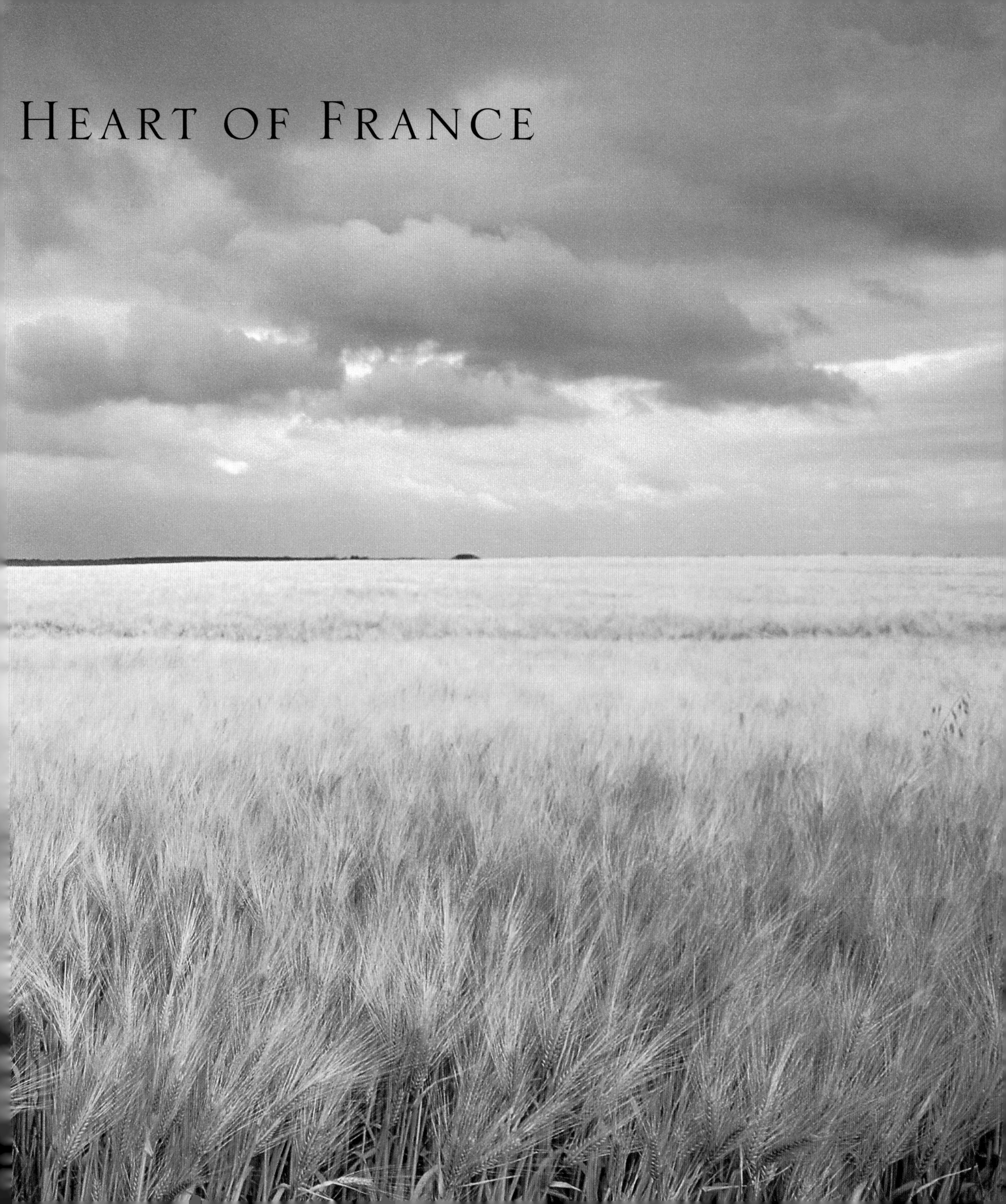

CHÂTEAU DU FEŸ

RESEARCHING AND WRITING *CHÂTEAU CUISINE* HAS BEEN A PLEASURE ON MANY LEVELS, NOT LEAST BECAUSE IT COMBINES TWO OF MY GREATEST LOVES IN LIFE — WRITING ABOUT FRENCH COOKERY AND RESTORING THE CHÂTEAU DU FEŸ IN BURGUNDY, ALONG WITH MY HUSBAND, MARK. WE FIRST BOUGHT LE FEŸ LONG BEFORE WE HAD DECIDED TO OPEN *LA VARENNE* COOKING SCHOOL THERE, CATCHING OUR INITIAL GLIMPSE OF IT IN MARCH 1982 IN A SHEETING MIST OF RAIN. I FEARED IT WOULD BE THE 12TH IN A SAD SERIES OF BEAUTIFUL HOUSES WRECKED BY NEGLECT AND PREDATORS WHO HAD STRIPPED PANELLING AND DRESSED STONE, TAKING ANYTHING PORTABLE OF VALUE. BUT EVEN THROUGH THE DOWNPOUR, THE BEAUTY OF LE FEŸ WAS APPARENT. WE FOUND THAT THE ROOF WAS SOUND, THERE WAS A MODICUM OF BATHROOMS, EVEN SOME CENTRAL HEATING. A WEEK LATER WE HAD OFFERED THE ASKING PRICE AND HAD BEEN ACCEPTED. WE HAD LAUNCHED IRRATIONALLY, IRREVOCABLY, ON THE ADVENTURE THAT THE FRENCH CALL *LA VIE DE CHÂTEAU*.

WE MOVED IN DURING LATE JULY, JUST BEFORE THE FOUR-WEEK AUGUST HOLIDAY WHEN EVERY ARTISAN DISAPPEARS FOR A MONTH. HOWEVER, WE MANAGED TO INSTALL A SMALL FAMILY KITCHEN TO REPLACE THE DERELICT IRON RANGE LEFT OVER FROM THE 19TH CENTURY. NOW, TEN YEARS LATER, THE SAME MAKE-SHIFT OPEN SHELVES AND CEMENT FLOOR ARE STILL IN PLACE. IN USE 12 HOURS A DAY IN THE HOLIDAY SEASON, WHEN FAMILY AND FRIENDS APPEAR FROM NOWHERE. THIS WAS OUR FIRST LESSON IN CHÂTEAU LIFE: THINK AHEAD, AS TEMPORARY SOLUTIONS TEND TO BECOME PERMANENT.

Built around 1640, Château du Feÿ follows the classical style of Louis XIII, with staircases hidden in the wings so as not to interrupt the flow of central rooms, destined for the entertaining of guests. The sturdy towers, linked by a long roof, are typically Burgundian.

The entrance to our vegetable garden (right). At Le Feÿ we conduct a running battle with Monsieur Milbert, the 70-year-old gardener who keeps our one-hectare vegetable garden in apple pie order. He insists on growing all produce to maximum size, regardless of flavour, whereas we like to gather the first babies of the season as soon as they sprout. His leeks are prodigious, their serried rows a protection against winter hunger.

We were aware the water supply was delicate, dating from the 1940s and pumped under the RN 6 – the old trunk road south – up the hill via a kilometre of uncharted private line. It cut out on a public holiday, leaving 15 of us to wash and cook from the swimming pool. Not long after, the power transformer (also private, uninsured and even more decrepit than the water system) was struck by lightning. No electricity, no pump, no water – no nothing. The discovery that a chandelier had parachuted to the floor during the storm seemed trivial until we found that the gale was not to blame, but rather a rotten main beam holding up a substantial part of our investment. Lesson number two: château infrastructure is unique, and expensive.

Inside, Le Feÿ was comfortable but shabby, painted a drab colour called 'Napoleonic grey' and about as dusty as the Emperor in his tomb. The three reception rooms, leading one from another with mirrors at each end in the classic *enfilade*, were transformed when painted cream. Encouraged, we launched on the bedrooms, then bathrooms, then cast an eye on the three abandoned cottages in the outbuildings. The wall surrounding the hectare of vegetable garden was crumbling dangerously. The immense well, 85 metres deep and dating from the time of Saint-Vincent de Paul (an early visitor to Le Feÿ), was firmly sealed under 30 centimetres of cement. What a shame not to display its ancient masonry! Perhaps lesson number three has never really sunk in: an old property such as Le Feÿ offers limitless possibilities for restoration, at limitless cost.

We quickly took to the culinary treats of château life: garden vegetables and fruits, misshapen and bug-ridden but with incomparable flavour; wild strawberries gathered beside the drive in spring; esoteric mushrooms picked under the tutelage of the caretaker's wife, with a quick interview to cross check at the pharmacy to be sure they were edible. It was a year before I wandered into a chicken house and discovered the brick bread oven, which now bakes wonderfully crusty bread and croissants when fired up by the local baker. The old wine and walnut presses stand idle, but the travelling machine comes once a year to crush our apples for cider.

Le Feÿ was bought as a family retreat, but its promise as a culinary haven soon emerged. Starting with a few residential classes, the programme has expanded over nine months of the year, covering French cuisine, cheeses, wines and professional culinary training. Our son has redecorated the gamekeeper's cottage in cheery

People often ask us where the name Feÿ comes from. The name 'Fay' or 'Fays' is common enough in France, probably first used to signal a copse of beeches, but there are no beech trees at Le Feÿ, and the eccentric dots over the 'y', indicating two syllables pronounced Fey-ee, has stuck over the centuries. With a little imagination, 'Feÿ' might be linked to 'Feyturage', a word found in the first French-English dictionary of 1611 meaning 'a charme, or inchantment'.

citrus yellow and our daughter cooks for summer guests. The 20-plus beds in the château are constantly overflowing with chefs, students, trainees, college kids and friends. My husband says the property is busier now than at any time since the French Revolution, and probably he's right. One thing is certain: like so many château owners, having taken possession of this marvellous property, we have found that it has taken possession of us.

OMELETTE BOURGUIGNONNE

SNAIL OMELETTE WITH WALNUTS

This omelette can be made with walnuts and no snails, or the snails can be served on their own with a walnut, garlic and parsley butter. Both are as delicious as the original.

2 servings

125 g/4 oz CANNED SNAILS
45 g/1½ oz BUTTER
2 CLOVES GARLIC, CHOPPED
SALT AND PEPPER
30 g/1 oz COARSELY CHOPPED WALNUTS
2 tbsp CHOPPED PARSLEY
5 or 6 EGGS

23 cm/9 in OMELETTE PAN

Drain and rinse the snails and cut each into 2 or 3 pieces. Melt half the butter in a frying pan, add the snails, garlic, salt and pepper and cook gently for 4 or 5 minutes. Remove from the heat and stir in the walnuts and parsley. (The snails can be prepared up to 8 hours ahead.)

To make the omelette, whisk the eggs with a little salt and pepper until slightly frothy. If necessary, warm the snail mixture over low heat. Heat the remaining butter in the omelette pan until it stops sputtering. Add the eggs and stir briskly with a fork, pulling the cooked egg from the sides to the centre of the pan. After 10 seconds, stir in the prepared snails and continue cooking until the mixture is almost as thick as scrambled eggs, 5 to 10 seconds longer. Leave the omelette on the heat until browned on the base and still soft on top if you like a moist omelette, or almost firm if you prefer it to be well done.

Fold the omelette, tipping the pan away from you and turning the edge with a fork. Slide the omelette on to a warmed platter. Serve it at once, cutting it in half for 2 people.

PAIN AUX NOISETTES

HAZELNUT BREAD

Hazelnut trees grow wild all around Château du Feÿ, a source of the hazelnut oil that is used to moisten the nuts in this bread.

Makes 2 loaves

375 g/12 oz PLAIN WHOLEMEAL FLOUR, MORE FOR SPRINKLING
125 g/4 oz PLAIN FLOUR
1 tbsp SALT
375 ml/12 fl oz LUKEWARM WATER
125 ml/4 fl oz HAZELNUT OIL
1 tbsp HONEY
2 tsp DRY YEAST OR 15 g/½ oz FRESH YEAST*
150 g/5 oz SHELLED HAZELNUTS

2×20–23 cm/8–9 in CAKE TINS

Pile both types of flour on a work surface. Sprinkle with the salt. Make a well in the centre with your hand and pour in one-quarter of the water. Add the hazelnut oil and honey, then sprinkle or crumble the yeast on top and leave until it dissolves, about 5 minutes. Add the remaining water and work with your fingertips, gradually drawing in the flour to make large crumbs. Press them together to make a ball.

Sprinkle the work surface with flour and knead the dough until smooth and elastic, 5 to 10 minutes. (The dough may also be mixed and kneaded in an electric mixer using the dough hook.) Put the dough in a lightly oiled bowl, turn it over so the top is oiled, and cover with a wet cloth. Leave it to rise in a warm place until doubled in bulk, 1 to 1½ hours.

Meanwhile, toast the hazelnuts. Heat the oven to 180°C/350°F/Gas Mark 4. Spread the nuts on a baking sheet and bake them until browned and the skins are loose, 10 to 15 minutes. Leave them to cool slightly, then rub with a coarse cloth to remove the skins. Coarsely chop half the nuts in a food processor or crush lightly with the end of a rolling pin.

Oil the cake tins. Knead the dough lightly to knock out the air, then work in all the hazelnuts. Divide the dough in half and shape it into rounds on a floured surface. Set them, smooth side up, in the prepared tins. Leave to rise again, uncovered, in a warm place until doubled in bulk, about 1 hour. Heat the oven to 220°C/425°F/Gas Mark 7.

Sprinkle the loaves lightly with wholemeal flour and slash the top two or three times with a knife. Bake in the heated oven for 15 minutes. Reduce the temperature to 190°C/375°F/Gas Mark 5 and continue baking for 30 to 40 minutes until the loaves sound hollow when tapped on the base. Transfer them to a rack to cool. The loaves are best eaten the same day.

Le Feÿ is home to a collection of old cookery books which we both began collecting 25 years ago.

Omelette Bourguignonne with Pain aux Noisettes. Snails abound in the woods around Le Feÿ after a shower of rain, but we usually resist the temptation and buy them prepared. Wild snails must be kept for 7 days to purge them of bitterness before you start cooking them – ever had snails escape in your cellar?

CHÂTEAU DE CHÂTEAU-RENAUD

To buy a vast half-ruined château in the province of Berry — the once isolated centre of France — would seem quixotic, not least for Yves and Michèle Halard, interior designers famed for their exquisite fabrics and sophisticated taste. Yet this was the adventure they undertook in 1985. Not for them the glitter of the Midi, nor the chic of the Loire. 'Today the ultimate luxury is unspoilt space,' explains Madame Halard. 'After the confines of life in Paris, we wanted to breathe.'

Châteaurenaud certainly offered plenty of scope. Since the Revolution, its 17th-century structure had been scarcely touched. The Halards found dozens of grey peeling rooms deteriorating from damp, and more recently from lack of inhabitants. 'The original ambiance was still there. That was important for us since no one had bothered to interfere,' says Michèle Halard. Gradually she and her husband began restoration, first of the roof, then of one room after the other (there are at least 50 of them). Transformation would perhaps be a better term, for the Halard touch is everywhere, in the fabrics, the subtle colours of paint mixed with care by Yves himself, and in the curiosities collected in forays to nearby antique fairs and sale rooms. 'We enjoy a touch of fantasy,' Yves whispers.

Yves and Michèle Halard have a passion for objets trouvés that fill every room and add to the sense of relaxed informality.

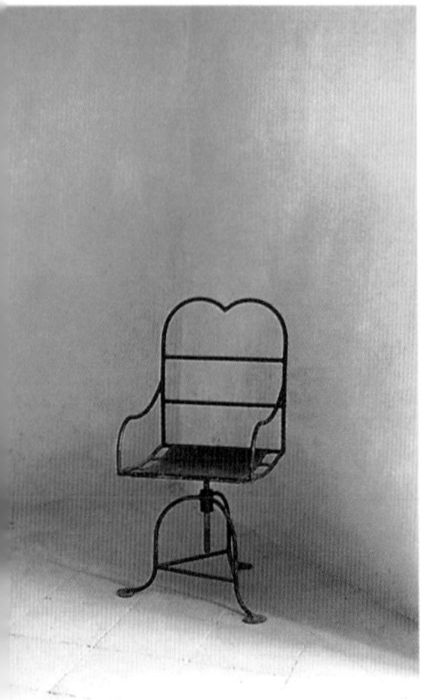

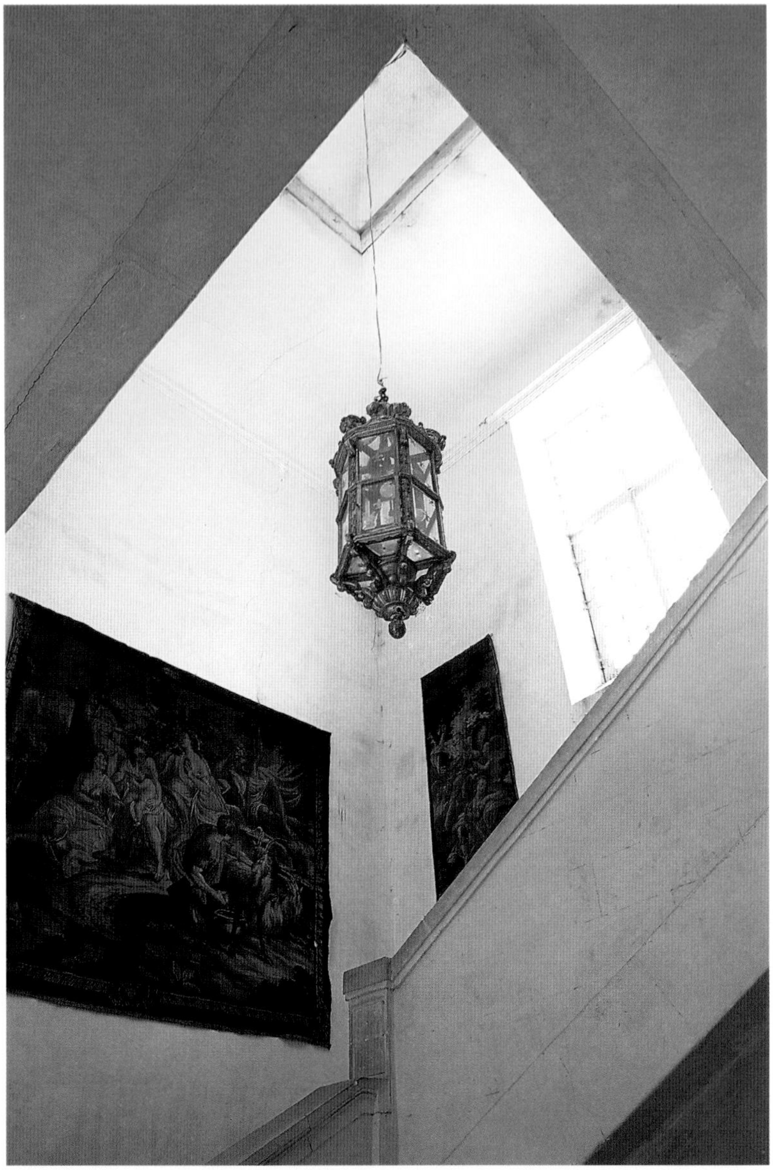

The impressive hallway of Châteaurenaud is dominated by cool, cream stone and decorated very simply with minimal furniture and tapestries in soft, muted colours (right). The library, with its shelves made by the Halards and a distinctive second-hand step-ladder, is an enticing place to while away an afternoon (below right).

Michèle Halard brings the same sense of fantasy to the table, often changing the settings with each meal. A collection of Halard napery is about to be launched with a '*Directoire*' theme, full of deep reds, soft yellows and grey. 'I never add flowers, but instead create a still life on the table,' she remarks. 'It may be rich, sunny, poetic, rustic. And I pick what pleases me – silver, vermeil, vegetables, leaves, baskets. I vary it all the time. Table decoration is unique in that way. How lucky we are – a meal is a celebration three times a day!'

I wondered if Michèle Halard had any time for cooking, and she assured me she is every bit a gourmande. She likes simple country dishes, very much in the current mode, and tries to cut down on the butter and cream. Recipes must be quick to prepare such as salmon *en papillote*, roast veal with baby onions (the Berry is cattle country), veal *blanquette* ('*très snob*' right now) and a flourless chocolate cake spiced with ginger, cinnamon and powdered coffee. Madame Halard's favourite lunch-time menu is even simpler – two or three choice cheeses from the region, a loaf of good bread and a glass of wine from Bordeaux.

Châteaurenaud has once more become a living château. What seemed a blind adventure has proved a brilliant stroke. Berry may seem a world removed from Paris, but nowadays the Halards can drive there in two-and-a-half hours. Back at home, Yves Halard spends much of his time with artisan craftsmen, bringing his brilliant design conceptions to life. 'It would be unthinkable to embark on another château adventure. As it is, we will never finish,' he declares. 'We are here forever,' adds Michèle, speaking for them both.

SOUPE CRÈME DE POIS

CREAMED SPLIT PEA SOUP

Bacon and split peas are a classic pair, but if you do not have a bacon or gammon bone, substitute a piece of smoked back bacon.

6 servings

400 g/13 oz GREEN SPLIT PEAS, RINSED
1 BACON OR GAMMON BONE WITH SOME MEAT
750 ml/1¼ PINTS CHICKEN STOCK (see page 221), MORE IF NEEDED
600 ml/1 PINT WATER, MORE IF NEEDED
1 LEEK, WHITE PART ONLY, FINELY CHOPPED
2 ONIONS, FINELY CHOPPED
1 CARROT, FINELY CHOPPED
3 SPRIGS OF PARSLEY
125 ml/4 fl oz CRÈME FRAÎCHE* OR DOUBLE CREAM
SALT AND PEPPER
GRATED NUTMEG

Combine the peas, bacon bone, stock and water in a large saucepan. Bring to the boil, skimming off the froth occasionally.

Reduce the heat to moderately low, add the chopped vegetables and the parsley and cover the pan. Simmer until the peas are very tender and well flavoured with bacon, 1 to 1½ hours, depending on the age of the peas. Stir from time to time during cooking and add more stock and water if the soup starts to catch.

Discard the bacon bone. Purée the soup in a blender or food processor until smooth. Return the soup to the pan and reheat it. The consistency should be rich but not sticky, so thin it with more stock and water if necessary. (The soup can be refrigerated for up to 2 days.)

To finish, reheat the soup if necessary and stir in the crème fraîche or cream. Season to taste with salt, pepper and nutmeg. Ladle the soup into warmed soup bowls.

A work room full of Halard designs and fabric samples, laid out on trestle tables (top left). Pet rabbits in an old out-building (above). The light and airy staircase (below) is simply and strikingly decorated.

A rich and aromatic stuffing transforms a shoulder of roast lamb.

ÉPAULE D'AGNEAU FARCIE

LAMB SHOULDER FILLED WITH VEAL KIDNEY, SHALLOTS AND MUSHROOMS

This stuffed lamb recipe combines the simplicity of a large joint with a dramatic presentation. The lamb shoulder is boned, then stuffed with a whole veal kidney and a mixture of mushrooms, shallots and parsley. With the lamb, serve sautéed spring onions and a rich potato gratin.

6 servings

1×2 kg/4½ lb SHOULDER OF LAMB, BONED (RESERVE THE BONES)
SALT AND PEPPER
LEAVES FROM A SPRIG OF FRESH THYME, OR ½ tsp DRIED THYME
2 tbsp VEGETABLE OIL
1 ONION, QUARTERED
1 CARROT, QUARTERED
125 ml/4 fl oz WHITE WINE
250 ml/8 fl oz BROWN STOCK (see page 221)

For the stuffing
60 g/2 oz BUTTER
2 SHALLOTS, FINELY CHOPPED
1 CLOVE GARLIC, CRUSHED
250 g/8 oz MUSHROOMS, FINELY CHOPPED
4 tbsp CHOPPED PARSLEY
1 VEAL KIDNEY (ABOUT 300 g/10 oz)
3 tbsp COGNAC OR BRANDY
LEAVES FROM A SPRIG OF FRESH THYME, OR ½ tsp DRIED THYME

TRUSSING NEEDLE AND KITCHEN STRING OR POULTRY SKEWERS

Heat the oven to 240°C/475°F/Gas Mark 9 and lightly oil a roasting tin.

For the stuffing, melt half the butter in a frying pan and add the shallots. Sauté them over moderate heat for about 5 minutes until just golden, stirring often. Add the garlic and stir for 1 minute. Add the mushrooms, salt and pepper and sauté them until they lose all their moisture, about 5 minutes. Stir in the parsley and transfer the stuffing to a bowl. Taste for seasoning.

Skin the kidney, if necessary, and cut out the fat and ducts from the centre with a small sharp knife. Put the kidney cut side down on the work surface. Pressing your hand firmly on top, cut the kidney almost in half lengthways; leave one side joined. Spread the kidney flat. Melt the remaining butter in the frying pan and brown the kidney over high heat for about 1 minute on each side. Add the Cognac or brandy and heat for 20 or 30 seconds, then tip the pan and light the spirit with a match. (Stand back from the flames.) Continue cooking, shaking the pan until the flames subside, for about 30 seconds. Remove the pan from the heat and sprinkle the kidney with salt, pepper and the thyme.

Trim the lamb of excess fat. Sprinkle the cut surface of the lamb with salt, pepper and the thyme. Spread the mushroom mixture in the centre and cover with the kidney. Sew the openings shut with a trussing needle and string or secure with poultry skewers. Roll up the meat and tie it with string to form a neat roll. Brush with oil.

Spread the lamb bones, onion and carrot in the roasting tin and set the lamb on top. Put the tin in the oven and reduce the temperature to 200°C/400°F/Gas Mark 6. Roast for 45 minutes, basting often, until the meat is medium rare: a skewer inserted in the meat should be warm to the touch when withdrawn after 30 seconds, or a meat thermometer should register 54°C/130°F.

Transfer the meat to a carving board with a juice catcher, cover loosely with foil and leave it to rest for 15 minutes.

To make a gravy, pour off the fat from the roasting tin. Add the wine to the tin and bring it to the boil, scraping to dissolve the browned roasting juices. Add the stock and simmer for 5 to 10 minutes to concentrate the flavour. Strain the gravy into a small saucepan and season.

To finish, remove the string from the joint and carve it into 6 mm/¼ in slices. Arrange the meat on a warmed platter. Stir the juice from the meat into the gravy. Serve the gravy separately.

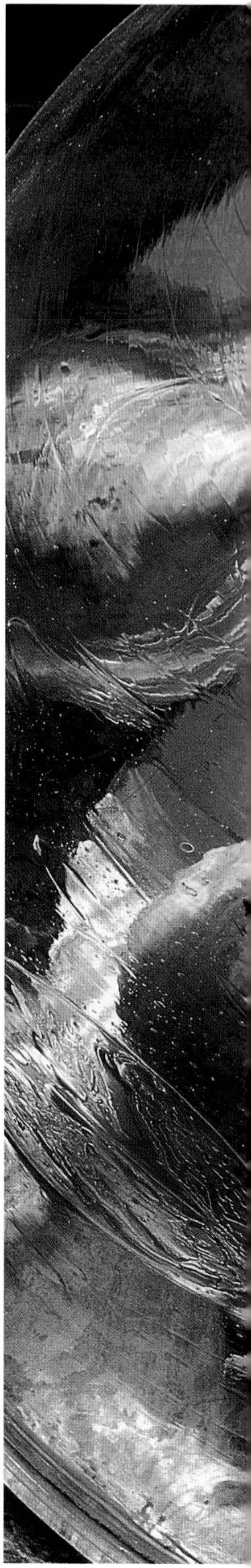

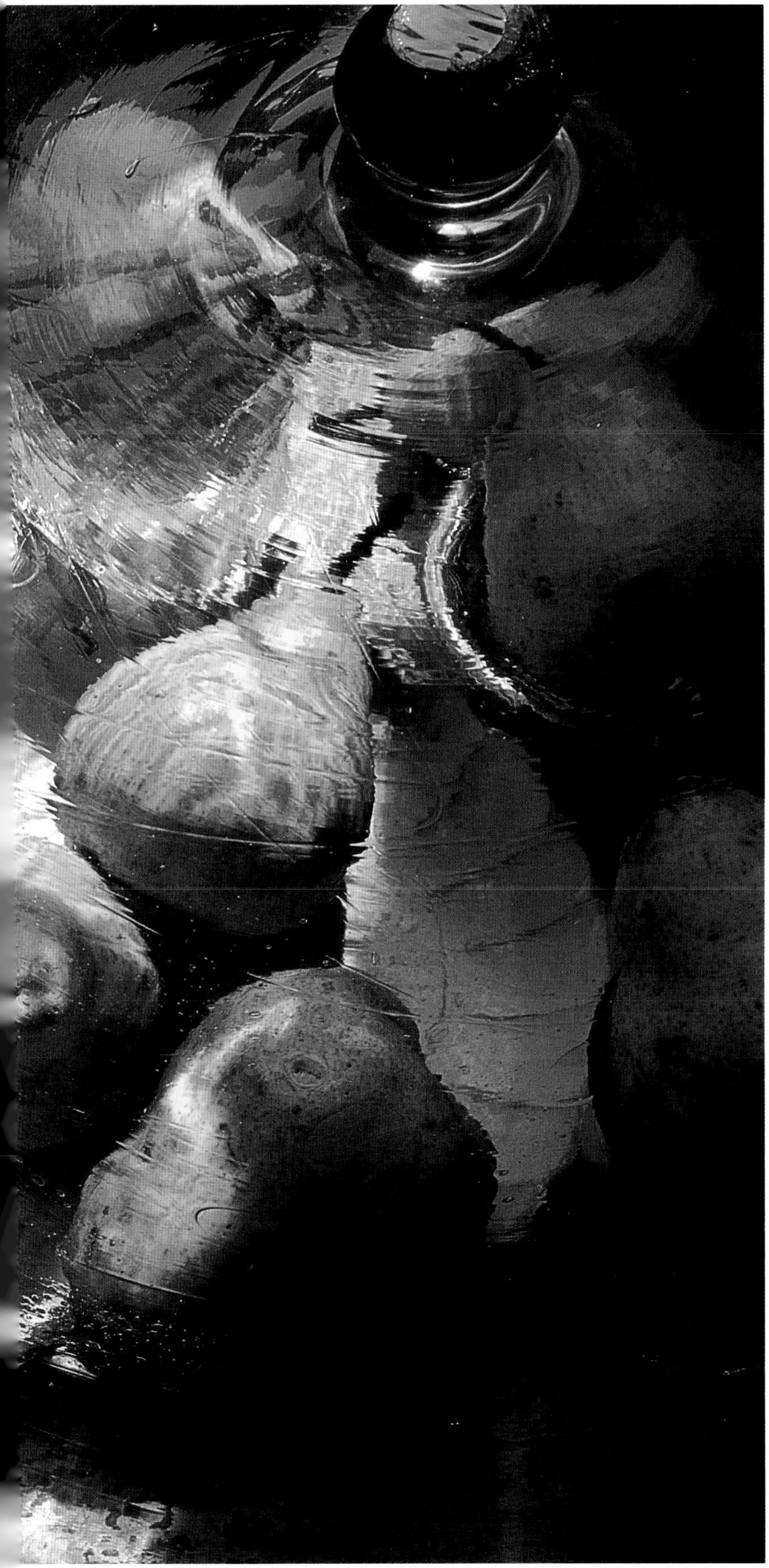

TARTE PAYSANNE AUX POIRES

RUSTIC PEAR TART

Michèle Halard believes a home-made fruit tart is one of life's pleasures. This pear tart is one she makes up quickly for a weekend in the country. You'll find that Comice pears will keep their shape well during cooking.

8 servings

375 g/12 oz PUFF PASTRY DOUGH
(see page 221)
5 FIRM PEARS (ABOUT 1 kg/2 lb
TOTAL WEIGHT)
JUICE OF 1 LEMON
60 g/2 oz UNSALTED BUTTER
50 g/1¾ oz CASTER SUGAR

25 cm/10 in FLAN TIN WITH A REMOVABLE BOTTOM

Sprinkle the flan tin with water. Roll out the dough to a round about 5 cm/2 in larger than the tin and use to line the tin*, leaving about 1 cm/⅜ in extending above the rim. Fold over this dough inside the tin, pressing to make a sturdy-sided shell. Chill until firm, about 15 minutes. (The tart case can be shaped up to 2 days ahead and kept in the refrigerator.)

Heat the oven to 190°C/375°F/Gas Mark 5. Prick the bottom of the tart case with a fork. Bake the tart case blind*.

Meanwhile, peel, halve and core the pears. Cut each pear half into 6 wedges. Toss them in a bowl with the lemon juice to prevent discoloration. Melt the butter in a large frying pan. Add the pears, sprinkle them with the sugar and sauté for about 15 minutes, tossing the pears often so they cook and caramelize evenly.

Spoon the pears into the part-baked tart case. Return to the oven and bake the tart for 15 to 20 minutes until the pastry is golden and the pears are tender.

A simple pear tart – 'one of life's pleasures', says Michèle Halard.

Bastion des Dames

'My husband suffers from restoration fever,' confides Monique Boisseaux. 'He always has to be building, or rebuilding!' She and her husband, André, have just completed work on the Demeure Saint-Martin, a charming 18th-century townhouse in the centre of the Burgundian wine town, Beaune. Their first project, and the one still closest to their hearts, was the family house, the Bastion des Dames de la Tour Bussière. The Bastion is unique, built into the massive Renaissance walls of Beaune itself, and named for the Cistercian nuns who lived there until the Revolution.

The Château de Meursault vineyard, which is 5 kilometres from Bastion des Dames, is part of André Boisseaux's domain. The vineyard covers 55 hectares.

At the base of the Bastion is a guard house, its walls seven metres thick — ideal insulation for wine cellars. Above them, the Boisseaux have perched a spacious modern house. 'We live right on top of our wines,' says Monique Boisseaux. And what wines! As a grower and *négociant*, André Boisseaux is a household name. His empire, Le Domaine du Château de Meursault, includes some of the most prestigious names on the aptly named Côte-d'Or (slope of gold) — Puligny-Montrachet, Savigny-lès-Beaune, Volnay, Pommard, Beaune and Aloxe-Corton, as well as Meursault itself.

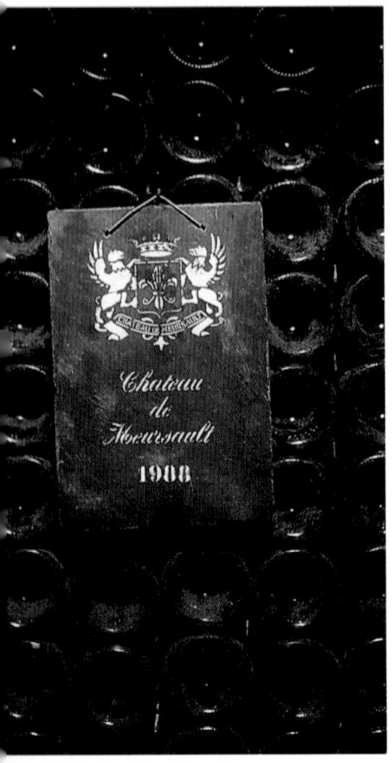

The vineyard is magnificent, but the real showpiece is below ground, where there are 400,000–500,000 bottles and 2000 casks of fine wine.

André Boisseaux told me that he has three passions – hunting, fishing and fine wine. In the forest of Cîteaux, not far from home, he raises deer, wild boar and even a few mountain goats. More than once the Boisseaux family has rescued an abandoned baby boar and raised it in the Bastion kitchen. The beasts are notoriously savage, but 'Coco' remained tame for several months. He delighted André Boisseaux by roaming the house during parties, to the consternation of guests from countries such as Britain where wild boar is unknown.

Many cooks have access to a vegetable garden, but few to home-raised fish and game, and Monique Boisseaux takes full advantage. She enjoys cooking haunch of venison or wild boar, accompanied by whole and puréed chestnuts, apples baked in butter, prunes simmered in red wine, tartlets of cranberry jelly, and of course the best of wine. But no wine is added to the game. 'I don't like to marinate game in the old way,' she told me. 'The sauces are too heavy, masking the flavour of the meat.' So Madame Boisseaux uses a dry marinade, a mixture of olive oil, chopped carrot and onion, thyme, bay leaf and rosemary, rubbing it into the meat before leaving it to stand for up to 48 hours. Then it is roasted *à point*, slightly pink, and served with a simple gravy.

Hospitality is a way of life for Burgundian vintners, culminating in the *Paulées*, the feasts held in November during the famous wine auctions at the Hospices de Beaune. On the third Saturday evening in the month, as a curtain raiser, 250 wine-growers and buyers are invited to a grand dinner at Château de Meursault. Sunday brings lunch for over 100 prepared by Madame Boisseaux at the Bastion. She describes the menu as *ultra rapide*, though it hardly sounds like fast food. First course might be fish *timbales*, or cold poached pike with a herb mayonnaise, followed perhaps by a ham *en croûte* or a Bresse chicken with morel mushrooms, not forgetting the cheese board and a simple dessert such as fruit tart.

On Monday the *Paulée* itself is held when 600 growers, large and small, gather at Château de Meursault for a banquet which lasts all day. Traditional dishes of the region abound – *gougères* or cheese puffs, versions of *coq au vin* made with both red and white wines, piquant *saupiquet* or ham in cream sauce and, of course, snails whose natural habitat is the vine.

Monique Boisseaux unveiled a favourite family recipe to me thus: 'The snails are gathered after a shower of rain and left without food to hibernate in the cellar for several weeks. Then they are lined up on a tin tray in a bed of water and cooked gently for 15 minutes or so. Bottles of vintage white Burgundy are enthroned on the table, then the family gathers, forks and *tastevins* in hand, to savour wine and snails *au naturel*. That's the best way, you know,' she added, with a hint of despair for those nations that do not share the French appreciation for things that creep and crawl.

Traditionally, a 'timbale de brochet' would have been served in a timbale or pastry case. Here the delicate puff pastry garnish recalls the original presentation.

TIMBALE DE BROCHET

POACHED PIKE WITH PASTRY IN A VELVETY SAUCE

The lakes in the forest of Cîteaux are breeding ponds for pike, sandre *(a succulent cousin of pike), carp and crayfish. Pike or any white fish fillets can be used in this recipe.*

6 servings as a main course, 8 to 10 as a first course

250 g/8 oz PUFF PASTRY DOUGH (see page 221)
1 EGG, BEATEN TO MIX TO GLAZE
750 g/1½ lb PIKE FILLET, CUT INTO 3 OR 4 LARGE PIECES
SALT AND PEPPER
2 SHALLOTS, FINELY CHOPPED
175 ml/6 fl oz DRY WHITE WINE
175 ml/6 fl oz WATER
15 g/½ oz BUTTER
1 tbsp PLAIN FLOUR
3 EGG YOLKS
125 ml/4 fl oz CRÈME FRAÎCHE*
OR DOUBLE CREAM

7.5 cm/3 in PASTRY CUTTER

Sprinkle a baking sheet with water. Roll out the puff pastry dough on a floured surface to a sheet 3 mm/⅛ in thick. Stamp out at least 18 crescents with the pastry cutter. Transfer them to the baking sheet and chill for at least 15 minutes. Heat the oven to 220°C/425°F/Gas Mark 7. Brush the crescents lightly with egg glaze and bake until puffed and golden, 8 to 12 minutes. (The crescents can be baked a day or two ahead and kept in an airtight container.)

Sprinkle the fish with salt and pepper. Butter a large frying pan and put in the shallots, wine, water and fish. Press a piece of buttered foil on top. Bring the liquid just to a simmer on top of the stove, then remove the pan from the heat. Allow the fish to cool slightly, then transfer it to a platter using a fish slice. Keep the fish warm while preparing the sauce.

Strain the cooking liquid and make a sauce: Melt the butter in a saucepan. Whisk in the flour and cook, stirring, until foaming. Whisk in the hot cooking liquid. Bring the sauce to the boil, whisking constantly, then simmer for 2 minutes. Mix together the egg yolks and crème fraîche or cream. Whisk in a little of the hot cooking liquid and stir this back into the rest. Heat gently, stirring, but do not boil. (The egg yolks will thicken in the heat but if overcooked they will curdle.) Taste the sauce for seasoning.

To finish, cut the fish into 1 cm/⅜ in diagonal strips. Arrange the fish on a warmed platter and coat with the sauce. Decorate with pastry crescents. Pass the remaining crescents separately.

OEUFS AU VIN DE MEURSAULT

POACHED EGGS IN WHITE WINE SAUCE

Burgundy is famous for poached eggs en meurette, *in a red wine sauce, but Monique Boisseaux prefers this lighter version made with the white wine from her vineyards. A bottle of Chardonnay wine is a less expensive alternative to Burgundian Meursault, but quite acceptable.*

4 servings as a main course, 8 as a first course

500 ml/16 fl oz CHICKEN OR WHITE VEAL STOCK (see page 221)
75 g/2½ oz BUTTER
3 SHALLOTS, FINELY CHOPPED
2 tbsp PLAIN FLOUR
500 ml/16 fl oz FULL-BODIED WHITE WINE
2 CLOVES GARLIC, CRUSHED
SALT AND PEPPER
A BOUQUET GARNI*
250 g/8 oz SMALL MUSHROOMS, QUARTERED
1×45 g/1½ oz PIECE OF STREAKY BACON, CUT INTO *LARDONS**
2 tbsp VINEGAR
8 EGGS
12 OR 24 TRIANGULAR *CROÛTES*, FRIED IN OIL AND BUTTER (see page 220)
2 tbsp CRÈME FRAÎCHE* OR DOUBLE CREAM

Bring the stock to the boil. Melt half the butter in a saucepan and add the shallots. Sauté over moderate heat until golden, 3 to 5 minutes. Stir in the flour and cook until foaming. Whisk in the boiling stock, the wine, garlic and a little salt and pepper; add the bouquet garni. Bring the sauce to the boil, whisking constantly. Reduce the heat and simmer, stirring occasionally, until the sauce thickens enough to coat a spoon, ¾ to 1 hour. Strain and set aside.

Melt the remaining butter in a frying pan. Add the mushrooms with salt and pepper. Toss

Oeufs au Vin de Meursault – poached eggs in a white wine and mushroom sauce tempt the diner at Bastion des Dames in Beaune.

them in the butter over moderately high heat until they lose all their moisture, about 5 minutes, then remove. Fry the bacon gently in the pan until the fat runs, then cook until golden, about 5 minutes. Drain it on kitchen paper.

Fill a large shallow pan two-thirds full of water, add the vinegar and bring to the boil. Break 4 eggs, one at a time, into a patch of bubbling water. Regulate the heat so the water barely simmers and poach the eggs until the white sets but the yolk is still soft, 3 to 4 minutes. Remove the eggs with a slotted spoon to a pan of cold water to stop the cooking, then drain them. Poach the remaining eggs.

(The sauce, garnish and eggs can be cooked up to 2 hours ahead and kept at room temperature. Rub the surface of the sauce with a knob of butter to prevent a skin forming.)

To finish, wrap the *croûtes* in foil and reheat them in a low oven if necessary. Reheat the sauce, stir in the mushrooms, bacon and crème fraîche or cream and taste for seasoning. Transfer the eggs to a bowl of very hot water. Leave for 2 or 3 minutes to warm then drain on kitchen paper and trim off any strings of white.

To serve, put the eggs on warmed plates and spoon the sauce over them. Add the *croûtes* as a final decoration.

LES GOUGÈRES BOURGUIGNONNES

BURGUNDY CHEESE PUFFS

During the vendanges *at Château de Meursault, the grapes are picked by hand, with the bunches clipped whole so that the juice inside each grape cannot oxidise. Workers take their lunch amongst the vines, but on the last day of the harvest, long tables laden with food are set up in the old kitchen of the château, and everyone gathers to taste* vin doux, *the first fresh juice pressed from the white grapes. The wine has a rich bouquet and already a light sparkle.*

Light Burgundian gougères are traditionally served with the first wine pressing after the harvest at Château de Meursault.

Makes about 24×7.5 cm/3 in puffs

250 ml/8 fl oz WATER
90 g/3 oz BUTTER, CUT INTO PIECES
¾ tsp SALT
175 g/6 oz PLAIN FLOUR
4 EGGS
150 g/5 oz GRUYÈRE CHEESE, GRATED

PIPING BAG AND 1 cm/⅜ in PLAIN TUBE (OPTIONAL)

Heat the oven to 220°C/425°F/Gas Mark 7 and butter one or two baking sheets.

Heat the water, butter and salt in a saucepan until the butter melts. Bring just to the boil and then remove the pan from the heat. Add the flour all at once and beat with a wooden spoon until the mixture is smooth and comes away from the sides of the pan in a ball, about 1 minute. Beat over low heat for 1 minute. Off the heat, beat in 3 of the eggs, one at a time. Whisk the last egg until mixed. Now beat enough of this egg into the mixture to make a dough that is soft and very shiny. Stir in the cheese.

Either put the dough in a piping bag and pipe 5 cm/2 in mounds on a baking sheet, spacing them well apart, or use two spoons to shape the dough. Bake in the heated oven until golden and crisp, 25 to 30 minutes.

Château d'Ainay-le-Vieil

The Château d'Ainay-le-Vieil lies on the borders of Berry, a province hotly disputed by the kings of England and France during the Hundred Years War. With its nine turrets, moat and classic drawbridge, Ainay was a key fortress besieged many times — it belonged briefly to the controversial Jacques Coeur, a man of such power and means in 15th-century France that today in Berry you can visit a whole string of imposing châteaux along the route named after him.

Princesse Georges-Henri's father, Geraud d'Aligny, was a distinguished poet and wrote of Ainay's walls as 'an immutable witness, omnipresent, unchanging.'

A single family, the Bignys, have owned Ainay for over 500 years and they count Jean-Baptiste Colbert, Louis XIV's brilliant minister, among their illustrious forebears. An ancestor of his installed a Renaissance palace within Ainay's rugged walls, and a 19th-century descendant restored its grandeur after many of the rooms were ransacked during the Revolution. Today Ainay is owned by six brothers and sisters in the Bigny line of descent, including Princesse Georges-Henri de la Tour d'Auvergne, or Marie-Sol as she is known to her friends.

With her brothers and sisters, Marie-Sol was brought up at Ainay – their remarkable mother, the very soul of the property, turned the château into a refuge for nuns during World War II, then kept the children at home for a while so that she could personally instruct them in the three R's before they left for school. In those days, Ainay was an oasis – not so today to judge by the village soirées held in the vaulted barracks beside the main gate, or the attraction of the folk museum set up with the help of village craftsmen. Ainay is also now famous for its roses – there are over 200 rare varieties, including a new deep pink rose named Colbert in honour of the family's heritage.

As a child, Marie-Sol was steeped in country customs and the life that revolves around a château – an education that has proved to be of special value now that she is President of Friends of Vieilles Maisons Françaises. Marie-Sol vividly described to me the activities of the pea season in the one-hectare kitchen garden, with the women of the village helping to gather in the harvest. Then, a few weeks later it would be the back-breaking challenge of *haricots verts*. 'It is so sad, the disappearance of communal village life,' she told me when we first met at Ainay. 'Now work is solitary and against the clock. Local farms here used to be proud of their butter, stamping each mound with a distinctive crest such as a rose or thistle. Recently the last dairy near Ainay closed, and now there's only one farm that still supplies unpasteurised milk fresh from the cow.'

In the old days at Ainay, fruit picking tended to be a family affair in the *chartreuse* – a formal orchard of espaliered trees which still yields a dozen fruits including luscious *pêches de vignes*, the wild purple peaches for which the region is justifiably famous.

There was an elderly gardener in charge of table grapes, Marie-Sol recalls. He would wrap them in sacking to protect them from wasps until ripe, then suspend them in a *fruitière* in the base of a tower. By trimming withered patches from time to time, the bunches could be kept until Christmas. For Marie-Sol, nothing has ever quite taken their place.

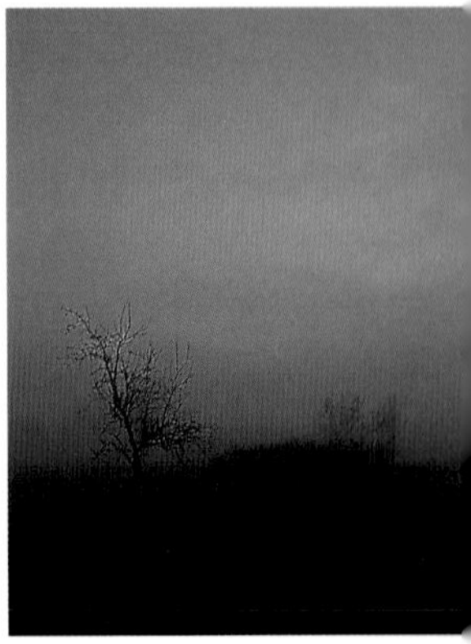

The defensive moat at Ainay is purely decorative today. The original wooden drawbridge has been replaced with a stone bridge.

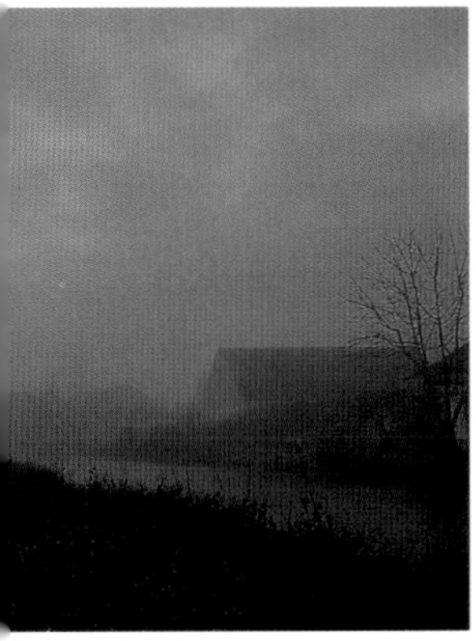

BLANQUETTE DE VEAU

VEAL IN CREAM SAUCE WITH CARROTS

The best way to cook a veal blanquette *is a bone of contention in Berry, where many farms raise fat Charolais cattle. Should the meat first be browned in butter, adding flavour but darkening the sauce? Onions are obligatory, but are carrots correct? They too detract from a* blanquette*'s essential creamy whiteness. 'Bones are important,' insists Ainay's caretaker Catherine Meillant, 'and a bit of cartilage too, to add body to the sauce.' Catherine is only 20 but she cooks* blanquette *with a master hand, serving it with the classic accompaniment of boiled rice.*

6 servings

1 kg/2 lb BONELESS VEAL SHOULDER OR BREAST
30 g/1 oz BUTTER
500 g/1 lb CARROTS, CUT INTO 2.5 cm/1 in LENGTHS ON THE DIAGONAL
1 MARROW BONE, CRACKED INTO PIECES
1 ONION, HALVED
SALT AND PEPPER
2 LITRES/3½ PINTS WATER, MORE IF NEEDED

For the sauce
20 g/¾ oz CORNFLOUR MIXED TO A PASTE WITH 5 to 6 tbsp WATER
2 EGG YOLKS
250 ml/8 fl oz CRÈME FRAÎCHE* OR DOUBLE CREAM

Cut the meat into 5 cm/2 in pieces, discarding any sinew. (Gelatinous pieces will dissolve during cooking and enrich the sauce.) Heat the butter in a heavy flameproof casserole and lightly brown the pieces of meat a few at a time. Put them all in the casserole with the carrots, bone, onion, salt, pepper and enough water to cover all the pieces generously.

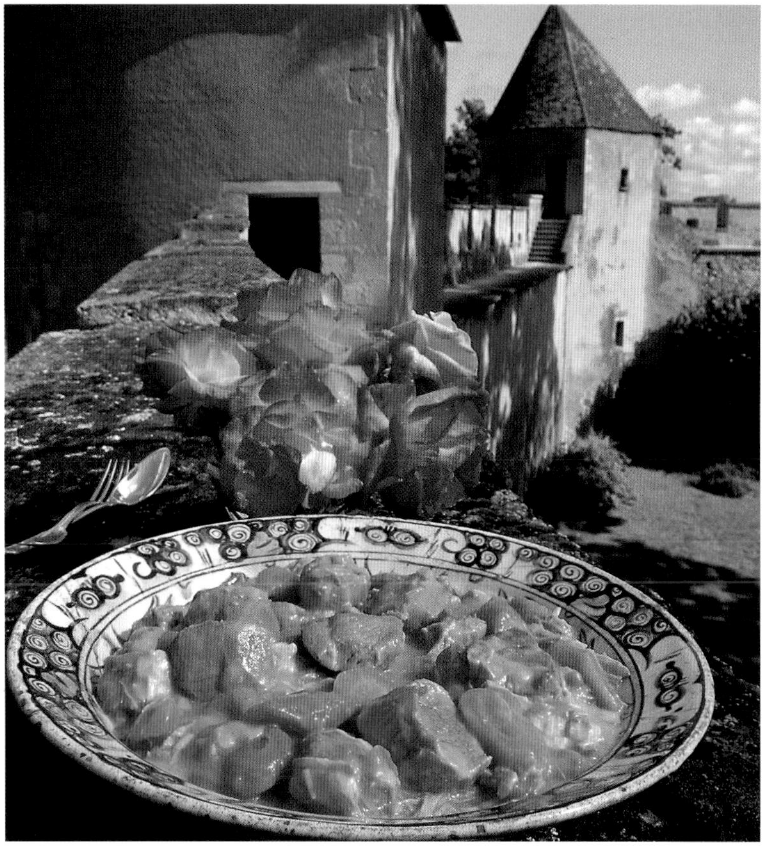

Blanquette de Veau, one of the classics of French cuisine.

Cover the casserole and bring the water to the boil. Lower the heat and simmer until the meat is tender enough to crush between your fingers, about 2 hours. Skim off the scum that rises during the first 30 minutes. Stir occasionally and add more water during cooking if necessary so the meat remains moist. When the meat is tender, discard the onion. (The *blanquette* can be cooked up to 2 days ahead and refrigerated in the cooking liquid.)

Reheat the *blanquette* if necessary. It should be slightly soupy, but if the meat is drowned in liquid, remove the solids and boil the liquid to reduce it. Slowly pour the cornflour paste into the simmering liquid, stirring; it will thicken at once. Add just enough paste to thicken the liquid lightly. Mix together the egg yolks and cream and, off the heat, stir them into the *blanquette*. (The heat of the mixture will cook and thicken the egg yolks.) Taste the sauce for seasoning. (If you need to warm the *blanquette* at this point, do so with care as the sauce may curdle if boiled.) Serve with a separate dish of boiled rice.

PÂTE DE POMMES DE TERRE

CREAMY SLICED POTATOES IN PUFF PASTRY

This dish of thinly sliced potatoes baked in a pastry crust, then topped with cream, exemplifies the hearty cooking of Berry. The pâte *usually accompanies a main dish with plenty of sauce, such as* coq en barbouille, *the local version of* coq au vin. *A simple green salad dressed with walnut oil would complete the meal. 'I like to lighten the* pâte *with herbs,' says Marie-Sol. 'But many people prefer it plain. Either way, be sure to serve it very hot.'*

8 servings

500 g/1 lb PUFF PASTRY DOUGH (see page 221)
1 EGG, BEATEN TO MIX WITH
½ tsp SALT TO GLAZE
750 g/1½ lb POTATOES, PEELED AND THINLY SLICED
3 SHALLOTS, FINELY CHOPPED
3 to 4 tbsp CHOPPED MIXED FRESH HERBS, SUCH AS PARSLEY, TARRAGON, CHERVIL AND CHIVES
SALT AND PEPPER
175 ml/6 fl oz CRÈME FRAÎCHE* OR DOUBLE CREAM

25 cm/10 in FLAN TIN WITH A REMOVABLE BOTTOM

Sprinkle the flan tin with water. Divide the dough in half. Roll out one piece and use to line the tin*, overlapping the edges of the tin. Brush the dough edges with egg glaze.

Arrange a layer of potatoes, so that the slices overlap each other, in a neat pattern in the bottom of the pastry case. Sprinkle with some of the shallots, herbs, salt and pepper. Continue to layer the potatoes, shallots, herbs, salt and pepper, finishing with a layer of seasoning, until all the ingredients are used.

Roll out the remaining dough to a round 5 cm/2 in larger than the flan tin and cover the potatoes with it. Trim the edges and seal the pastry lid to the case with a fork, or scallop with the back of a knife. Brush the *pâte* with egg glaze. Using a sharp knife, mark a design on the lid, being careful not to cut through to the filling, or decorate it with pastry trimmings. Chill the *pâte* until firm, about 15 minutes. Heat the oven to 220°C/425 F/Gas Mark 7 and put in a baking sheet to heat.

Bake the *pâte* on the hot baking sheet until the pastry starts to brown, 15 to 20 minutes. Reduce the temperature to 180°C/350°F/Gas Mark 4 and continue baking the *pâte* for 35 to 45 minutes until it browns and the potatoes are tender when pierced with a knife. If the pastry browns too quickly, cover it with foil. (The *pâte* can be baked a day ahead and then reheated in a low oven.)

To finish, warm the crème fraîche or cream. Cut a 10 cm/4 in round in the lid and remove it. Spoon in the crème fraîche or cream, replace the round of pastry and serve at once.

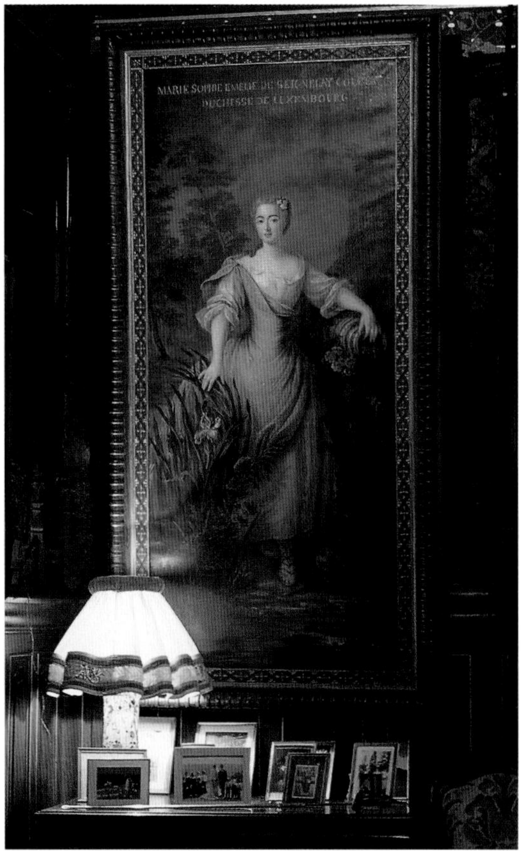

Portraits of family ancestors adorn the walls and silently record the prominent royal and historical connections of Ainay.

A bowl of Princesse Georges-Henri's truffles stands beside a glass engraved with the Colbert coat of arms – a serpent (top right). 'In that glass, we always say wine tastes quite different!' she laughs. The interiors of Ainay are exquisitely decorated in grand French style with ornate ceilings and richly decorated fireplaces (bottom right).

TRUFFES DE NOËL AU CHOCOLAT

CHOCOLATE CHRISTMAS TRUFFLES

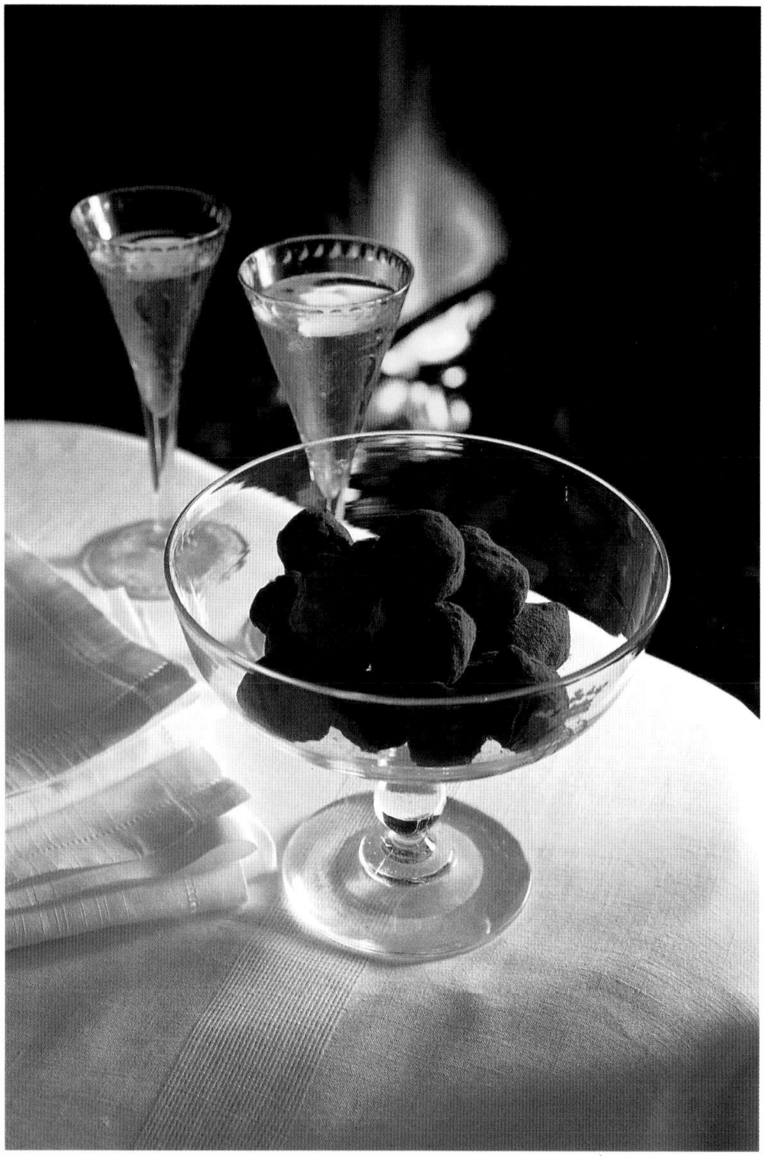

At Christmas time, Marie-Sol's family looks forward to these delectable morsels, affectionately called 'baby Jesus in velvet trousers'. Truffles are commonly served after dessert with coffee or, for a special occasion, with Champagne.

Makes about 500 g/1 lb truffles

250 g/8 oz BITTERSWEET CHOCOLATE, CHOPPED
4 tbsp WATER
250 g/8 oz UNSALTED BUTTER, CUT INTO PIECES
60 g/2 oz CASTER SUGAR
6 EGG YOLKS
125 g/4 oz UNSWEETENED COCOA POWDER

Warm the chocolate in the water in a heavy pan over very low heat without stirring. When the chocolate softens, add the butter and sugar all at once. Stir gently with a wooden spoon until the chocolate and butter melt completely and the mixture is smooth.

Remove the pan from the heat and leave the mixture to cool for 2 or 3 minutes. Add the egg yolks, one by one, stirring vigorously. (The heat of the mixture will cook and thicken the egg yolks.) Spread the mixture in a shallow baking dish. Put the dish, uncovered, in the freezer to chill until the mixture is firm, 1 to 2 hours.

Sift the cocoa on to a tray. Dust your hands with cocoa to discourage sticking. Scoop out the chocolate mixture with a teaspoon and shape it into 2.5 cm/1 in balls by rolling them in your hands. Roll them, a few at a time, in the tray of cocoa until well coated. Transfer them to a baking sheet lined with greaseproof paper. Put them in the freezer to firm, about 30 minutes. Note: they will be soft and may flatten slightly.

Château de Caïx

His Royal Highness Henrik de Monpezat, Prince Consort of Denmark bought the Château de Caïx quite simply to be at home, on his own *terroir*. The Prince is French by birth and much of his family, the Monpezats, still live in the stony, picturesque region of Quercy, with its medieval capital Cahors. Queen Margrethe feels equally at home, and for 25 years the royal couple has come here each summer on holiday.

The vineyards stretch along the hillside, carpeting the land up to Caïx. The distinctive Château de Caïx wine is typical of the black wines of the region (below).

When the Prince bought the Château de Caïx he had in mind 'a comfortable country house'. He has indeed created one. In the mid-1970s Caïx was hardly a prize, despite its view over the scenic river Lot. The walls were crumbling and the garden was overgrown. But Prince Henrik's sharp eye looked beyond the rotten roof and the broken windows, past the 14th-century pepperpot towers, to the work of clever 18th-century owners who had so skilfully converted the medieval shell to an elegant, livable home. 'It needed to be saved,' he told me. 'As we say in French, I caught my crayfish and turned it into a lobster!'

On a warm summer's evening, Queen Margrethe and Prince Henrik of Denmark are often to be found on the garden terrace.

Now not just the house but also the surrounding vineyard has been reclaimed, clustering almost to the front terrace. After ten years of growth, the vines are mellowing and the rich red Château de Caïx they produce is typical of the black wines of the region, so dark as to be virtually opaque, although the district is also becoming known now for some lighter wines.

Much enjoyed in medieval times and probably as far back as 600 A.D., the *vins noirs* of Cahors are enjoying a comeback enthusiastically supported by Prince Henrik. 'We grow three grape varietals to produce the wine,' he explains. 'The bulk is Malbec, with some Merlot for softness, and Tannat for tannin, just as it sounds.' The château has extensive cellars, but for the moment the wine is vinified by a local producer. Much of the 120,000 bottles go to Denmark. 'It's much appreciated at Court,' the Prince notes with some satisfaction.

When at Caïx, life for the Danish royal family is relaxed. Protocol is abandoned and Prince Henrik and Queen Margrethe drop in on their neighbours like everybody else in the holiday season. On market day in Cahors, the Queen can be seen with her shopping basket, and she particularly appreciates being accepted as one of the locals 'with open arms'. 'To be honest, this is my only real holiday,' she says. 'There are a thousand things to do, as in any holiday home. But we enjoy nothing so much as watching the sunset and dining with a few friends on the terrace, overlooking the vines which slope down to the river.'

Back in Denmark, the Prince maintains a personal interest in fine cooking by keeping in close touch with the three royal chefs. 'I like to keep a good table, in the traditional sense, and we sometimes send the chefs *en stage* for a week or two to top restaurants such as Haeberlin in Alsace and Baumanière in Provence. They come back with excellent ideas.'

Other ideas come from Prince Henrik himself, such as the following wonderfully rich *tourte*, a luxurious combination of snails, sweetbreads, *foie gras*, mushrooms and truffles evoking Renaissance *béatilles*, so called because of their heavenly, beatific qualities. The *tourte* should be served, instructs His Royal Highness, with the dark, mellow wine of Château de Caïx!

LA TOURTE DU PRINCE HENRIK

PRINCE HENRIK'S TOURTE WITH SWEETBREADS, SNAILS AND FOIE GRAS

Truly regal, this grand confection contains some of the world's most valued ingredients.

8 servings

375 g/12 oz VEAL SWEETBREADS
45 g/1½ oz BUTTER
4 SHALLOTS, FINELY CHOPPED
SALT AND PEPPER
1 CLOVE GARLIC, FINELY CHOPPED
125 g/4 oz *PÂTÉ DE FOIE GRAS* OR FRESH CHICKEN LIVERS, DICED
250 g/8 oz MUSHROOMS, QUARTERED
175 g/6 oz CANNED SNAILS, DRAINED
1 CANNED TRUFFLE, DICED, WITH ITS LIQUID (OPTIONAL)
500 g/1 lb PUFF PASTRY DOUGH (see page 221)
1 EGG, BEATEN TO MIX WITH ½ tsp SALT TO GLAZE

For the sauce suprême
375 ml/12 fl oz CHICKEN STOCK (see page 221)
60 g/2 oz MUSHROOMS, CHOPPED
SALT AND WHITE PEPPER
90 g/3 oz BUTTER
100 g/3¼ oz PLAIN FLOUR
4 tbsp CRÈME FRAÎCHE* OR DOUBLE CREAM
A SQUEEZE OF LEMON JUICE
2 tbsp CHOPPED PARSLEY

25 cm/10 in FLAN TIN WITH A REMOVABLE BOTTOM

Soak the sweetbreads in cold water for 2 hours to clean them, then cut away any discoloured parts. Blanch the sweetbreads*: put in cold water, bringing to the boil and simmer for 10 minutes. Drain. Pull away the ducts and discard the skin. Dice the sweetbreads.

To make the *sauce suprême*, combine the stock, mushrooms, salt and pepper in a saucepan. Bring to the boil and simmer for 15 minutes. Strain the stock. Melt the butter in a heavy saucepan. Whisk in the flour and cook until it foams, 1 or 2 minutes. Remove the pan from the heat and allow to cool slightly, then whisk in the stock. Bring to the boil, whisking constantly until it thickens. Add the crème fraîche or cream. Boil again. Add the lemon juice and parsley, and set aside.

Heat half the butter in a large frying pan. Add the shallots and cook them for 3 to 5 minutes, stirring often, until soft. Add the sweetbreads, salt and pepper and cook for 4 to 6 minutes, stirring often, until tender and golden. Transfer the sweetbreads and shallots to a bowl with a slotted spoon. Add the remaining butter, the garlic, chicken livers, if using, and mushrooms to the pan with salt and pepper and cook briskly for 2 to 3 minutes, stirring often, until the livers brown but are still pink on the inside. Add them to the sweetbreads. If using *pâté de foie gras*, dice it and add to the mixture. Also add the snails and truffle with its liquid, if using. Pour in the *sauce suprême* and mix thoroughly.

Sprinkle the flan tin with water. Divide the pastry dough in half. Roll out one piece of dough and use to line the tin*, draping it over the edges of the tin. Brush the dough edges with egg glaze. Spoon the filling into the pastry case.

Roll out the remaining dough to a round 5 cm/2 in larger than the flan tin and cover the *tourte* with it. Trim the edges and seal the pastry lid to the case with a fork, or scallop with the back of a knife. Brush the *tourte* with egg glaze. Using a sharp knife, mark a design on the top or decorate it with pastry trimmings. Chill the *tourte* until firm, about 30 minutes.

To finish, heat the oven to 220°C/425°F/Gas Mark 7 and put in a baking sheet to heat. Set the *tourte* on the hot baking sheet and bake until the pastry starts to brown, 10 to 15 minutes. Reduce the temperature to 180°C/350°F/Gas Mark 4 and continue baking until the *tourte* is brown and very crisp, 30 to 40 minutes. If the pastry browns too quickly, cover it with foil. Serve very hot.

This temple d'amour ancien (above) nestles among trees in the château grounds. Jacques Le Franc de Pompignan, an 18th-century French writer and owner of Caïx, used this tranquil building whilst writing.

Truffe en Aumonière – a truly aristocratic dish. The puff pastry wrapping traps the aroma of the truffle. This wonderful chronometer, shaped like a crown, is one of the treasures of Caïx. Made by a Provençal artisan, it was given to the royal couple when they bought the château, and it bears a Latin inscription meaning 'May the hours be happy' (far right).

TRUFFE EN AUMONIÈRE

WHOLE BAKED TRUFFLE IN PASTRY

The garden at Château de Caïx is less orderly than the vineyard, for the royal family can spare only a few weeks in the year to visit. However, Prince Henrik has great hopes for some hazelnut trees seeded with truffles which he planted nine years ago. 'Next year they should start to produce,' he explains. 'This is great truffle country, just next to Périgord, so we might be lucky.' If so, he will be able to make this recipe, a favourite of his, with his own harvest – an aumonière *is a coin purse.*

4 servings

250 g/8 oz PUFF PASTRY DOUGH (see page 221)
4 FRESH TRUFFLES (ABOUT 30 g/1 oz EACH)
OR CANNED TRUFFLES WITH THEIR JUICE
60 g/2 oz BUTTER
1 SMALL ONION, FINELY DICED
½ CARROT, FINELY DICED
½ STICK CELERY, FINELY DICED
SALT AND PEPPER
175 ml/6 fl oz VEAL STOCK (see page 221)
2 tbsp PORT
125 g/4 oz *PÂTÉ DE FOIE GRAS*
CUT INTO 4 SLICES
1 EGG, BEATEN TO MIX WITH
½ tsp SALT TO GLAZE

Sprinkle a baking sheet with water. Roll out the dough to a 28 cm/11 in square and trim the edges. Cut out four 10 to 12 cm/4 to 5 in squares. Transfer them to the baking sheet and chill until firm, about 15 minutes.

If using fresh truffles, brush each one gently under cold running water to remove earth, then peel it with a small knife. Reserve the peelings to cook with the vegetables.

Melt half the butter in a frying pan. Add the onion, carrot, celery, salt and pepper and cook over moderate heat for 5 to 8 minutes, stirring often, until just tender. Add the stock, port and truffle peelings or canned truffle juice and simmer until the vegetables are tender, about 15 minutes. Taste for seasoning. Remove the pan from the heat and leave to cool. Drain the vegetables, reserving the cooking liquid.

Put a slice of *foie gras* in the centre of each pastry square and set a truffle on top. Surround the truffle with a tablespoon of vegetables. Sprinkle with salt and pepper.

Brush the four corners of each pastry square with egg glaze, bring up the corners to the top of the truffle and seal the pastry edges. Brush the *aumonières* with egg glaze. Chill them for at least 30 minutes. (They can be refrigerated for up to 24 hours.)

Heat the oven to 240°C/475°F/Gas Mark 9. Bake the *aumonières* in the heated oven until puffed and brown, about 15 minutes.

Meanwhile, make a *jus*: reheat the vegetable cooking liquid and boil to reduce it to 125 ml/4 fl oz, to concentrate the flavour. Lower the heat and gradually whisk in the remaining butter. Taste the *jus* for seasoning. Serve the *aumonières* immediately they are cooked, with the *jus* passed separately.

PASTIS

LAYERED FLAKY PASTRY TART WITH PRUNES AND ARMAGNAC

Prepared phyllo dough works very well here if you want to save time. You will need 6 sheets of it for this recipe.

8 servings

500 g/1 lb PLAIN FLOUR, MORE IF NEEDED
1 EGG
¼ tsp SALT
250 ml/8 fl oz WATER
½ tsp LEMON JUICE
4 tbsp WALNUT OIL

For the filling

250 g/8 oz PRUNES, STONED
75 ml/2½ fl oz ARMAGNAC
125 g/4 oz BUTTER, MELTED
100 g/3½ oz CASTER SUGAR

25 cm/10 in FLAN TIN WITH A REMOVABLE BOTTOM

For the filling, soak the prunes in the Armagnac for 2 to 3 hours or overnight. Before using, drain the prunes, reserving the Armagnac.

Sift the flour into a large bowl and make a well in the centre. Add the egg, salt, water, lemon juice and oil and work them together with your fingertips until thoroughly mixed. Quickly work the flour into the other ingredients to make a pliable, slightly sticky dough.

Flour a work surface and knead the dough for 5 to 7 minutes, picking it up and throwing it down, until it is shiny and very smooth. Alternatively, work it in an electric mixer with a dough hook. Cover the dough with an upturned bowl to keep it moist and leave to rest for at least 30 minutes. Meanwhile, heat the oven to 190°C/375°F/Gas Mark 5. Butter the flan tin.

Cover a table with a sheet and lightly flour it. Divide the dough into three equal pieces. Roll out each piece of dough to as large a square as possible. Cover each one with a damp towel and leave it to rest for 15 minutes. Flour your hands

Pastis is traditionally made by the women of Quercy. This flaky tart melts away in your mouth, leaving a delicious hint of prunes, Armagnac and butter.

and gently insert them under one piece of dough. Starting at the centre and working outwards, carefully stretch the dough with both hands, making as few holes as possible. It should eventually form a rectangle about 38×75 cm/15×30 in. Brush the dough with melted butter. Pull, stretch and butter the remaining pieces of dough. Alternatively, butter the sheets of phyllo dough, if using.

Cut each rectangle of home-made dough into two rounds 5 cm/2 in larger than the flan tin, or cut each sheet of phyllo dough into one round of the same size. Press three of the rounds into the tin, sprinkling each one with sugar and Armagnac. Arrange the drained prunes in an even layer on the bottom of the pastry case. Sprinkle with more sugar. Cover the prunes with the three remaining dough rounds, again sprinkling each one with sugar and Armagnac.

Fold the overlapping dough up around the edges of the tart. Cut the dough trimmings into 5 cm/2 in strips and arrange them on top, pleating them to form ruffles. Sprinkle with sugar, Armagnac and melted butter.

Bake the tart in the heated oven until brown and crisp, 30 to 40 minutes. Serve it lukewarm.

CHÂTEAU DE LA VERRERIE

THE '*PAYS FORT*' NEAR SANCERRE IS ONE OF THE FORGOTTEN PARTS OF THE LOIRE. 'IT WAS ALWAYS A MYSTERIOUS LAND OF WOLVES AND FORESTS, FAR OFF THE BEATEN TRACK,' EXPLAINS COMTE ANTOINE DE VOGÜÉ, AS HE RECOUNTS THE PROPERTY'S ROMANTIC PAST AND ITS CONNECTION WITH THE ROYAL STUART FAMILY OF SCOTLAND. FIRST, IN THE EARLY 15TH CENTURY, CHARLES VII OF FRANCE GAVE THE STUARTS LAND IN RECOGNITION OF THEIR SUPPORT DURING THE HUNDRED YEARS WAR AGAINST THE ENGLISH. CONSTRUCTION OF THE PRESENT CHÂTEAU BEGAN THEN, AND WAS COMPLETED IN RENAISSANCE STYLE WITH A MAGNIFICENT ARCADED GALLERY WHICH STILL LINES ONE SIDE OF THE COURTYARD. A COUPLE OF CENTURIES LATER, LA VERRERIE REVERTED TO THE FRENCH CROWN, ONLY TO BE DONATED ONCE AGAIN, THIS TIME TO LOUISE DE KEROUALLE, DUCHESS OF PORTSMOUTH AND FAVOURITE OF ENGLAND'S CHARLES II.

A dreamy and romantic view of La Verrerie across the lake. Construction of the château began in the early 1400s. An elegant Renaissance arcade lines one side of the courtyard (below).

16th-century frescoes have recently been uncovered in the chapel at La Verrerie.

Since then the château has changed little. It is still tucked away in peaceful woods abundant with game, fronting a placid lake. 'It's not a fortress but a *château de plaisance*,' says Françoise de Vogüé. 'Despite its size, La Verrerie is intimate, full of gaiety and light. In season we hunt wild duck, partridge and pheasant,' the Comtesse continues, 'and ride with a couple of dozen hounds in the traditional *chasse à courre* for deer.' Visitors are welcome at La Verrerie and can dine with the family in an international atmosphere – the staff must speak at least two languages. 'We like to receive our guests as friends,' says the Comte, whose son, Béraud, runs Vie de Château, an international agency that receives guests and rents château accommodation throughout France.

In August, when children and grandchildren gather, the Vogüés may be 30 or more at table, with the Comtesse in charge in the kitchen. She often likes to start with a cold first course, using pretty plates and imaginative presentation. A summer favourite is sliced melon interleaved with country ham, decorated with celery and tomatoes from the garden. The main course is likely to be local leg of lamb with garden peas, *haricots verts* and fried baby potatoes. Unusual sauces are her trademark, such as gravy flavoured with truffle oil, and fresh English-style mint sauce with cider vinegar and honey.

Françoise de Vogüé cooks with aplomb because for ten years she acted as chef and manager of La Maison d'Hélène, the charming little restaurant in a half-timbered cottage overlooking the lake. Here, too, the cuisine is *du pays*, with Loire salmon served with white butter sauce, and noisettes of venison with apples. The recipes that follow are from her grandmother's collection, a book headed with a typically acid quote from Oscar Wilde: 'All men are monsters. The only thing to do is to feed the wretches well. A good cook works wonders!'

SABLÉS AU FROMAGE

BUTTERY CHEESE WAFERS

The Comtesse de Vogüé passes around these crumbly, butter-rich wafers with drinks. Any well-flavoured mature cheese can be used for sablés *– tangy Cantal from France's Massif Central makes an unusual alternative to Gruyère.*

Makes about 35

250 g/8 oz PLAIN FLOUR
SALT AND PEPPER
175 g/6 oz UNSALTED BUTTER, CUT INTO PIECES
100 g/3½ oz GRUYÈRE CHEESE, GRATED
1 EGG, BEATEN TO MIX WITH ½ tsp SALT TO GLAZE

5 cm/2 in PASTRY CUTTER (OPTIONAL)

Sift the flour into a bowl with ¼ tsp salt and a pinch of pepper. Add the butter and rub it in with your fingers until the mixture resembles fine crumbs. Stir in the cheese and press the dough together with your fist. Turn the dough on to a floured surface and knead it, pushing it away with the heel of the hand and gathering it up with your fingers. Wrap the dough and chill it until firm, at least 30 minutes.

Butter one or two baking sheets. Roll out the dough on a floured surface to a sheet about 3 mm/⅛ in thick. Stamp out rounds with the pastry cutter and put them on a baking sheet. Alternatively, cut the dough into triangles. Brush the *sablés* with egg glaze. Chill them for at least 15 minutes before baking.

Heat the oven to 190°C/375°F/Gas Mark 5. Bake the *sablés* until golden, about 15 minutes. Leave them on the baking sheet for 3 or 4 minutes before carefully removing to a rack to cool completely.

They can be stored in an airtight container for up to a week.

Magnificent frescoes also adorn the cool arcades.

A great fireplace with flaming logs is a welcoming sight for guests at La Verrerie.

OEUFS A LA MIRABEAU

CREAMY MOULDED EGGS WITH TOMATO SAUCE

Named for the family of the Comte de Mirabeau, the 18th-century revolutionary, this unusual recipe is excellent as a first course or for brunch. The eggs are simply whisked with Parmesan cheese, cream, butter and seasonings, then baked in the oven to a creamy texture. Fresh tomato sauce is the ideal accompaniment.

4 servings

4 EGGS
3 tbsp DOUBLE CREAM
2 tbsp GRATED PARMESAN CHEESE
15 g/½ oz BUTTER, MELTED
SALT AND PEPPER
GRATED NUTMEG
TOMATO SAUCE (see below)

4 RAMEKINS (125 ml/4 fl oz EACH)

Heat the oven to 180°C/350°F/Gas Mark 4. Generously butter the ramekins. Put the ramekins in the freezer until the butter is firm, then butter them again.

Break the eggs into a bowl and whisk to mix them. Whisk in the cream, cheese, butter, ¼ tsp salt, a pinch of pepper and a grating of nutmeg.

Pour the egg mixture into the prepared ramekins. Put them in a *bain-marie** and bring the water to the boil on top of the stove. Transfer them to the oven and bake just until the eggs set and puff slightly, 12 to 15 minutes.

Meanwhile, heat the tomato sauce. Run a knife around the eggs and turn out on to warmed plates. Spoon the tomato sauce in a ribbon around the edge of the plates. Pass the remaining sauce separately.

SAUCE A LA TOMATE

TOMATO SAUCE

The flavour of this tomato sauce is incomparable when made with vine-ripened tomatoes as found in the de Vogüé garden.

Makes about 250 ml/8 fl oz

750 g/1½ lb FRESH TOMATOES OR
1×400 g/14 oz CAN TOMATOES,
WITH THE JUICE
1 ONION, HALVED
60 g/2 oz BUTTER, CUT INTO PIECES
SALT AND PEPPER

Quarter fresh tomatoes and cook them, covered, in a saucepan over low heat until soft, about 10 minutes. Work fresh tomatoes or canned tomatoes with their juice through a food mill, or purée them in a food processor and then work them through a sieve to remove the seeds.

Combine the puréed tomatoes in a saucepan with the onion, butter and salt to taste. Bring to the boil, then simmer, uncovered, over moderate heat, until the sauce thickens, about 45 minutes. Stir the sauce occasionally during cooking. Discard the onion. Taste the sauce for seasoning. (This sauce will keep for 3 days, covered, in the refrigerator. It also freezes well.)

Juicy red raspberries flourish at La Verrerie. Here they are served with 'Crottin de Chavignol' – locally made goat cheese.

Gâteau Fondant au Chocolat

Rich Chocolate Gâteau with Caramel and Vanilla Custard

This recipe tolerates a wide range of cooking times. In under an hour you will have a creamy cake which needs to chill for at least a day so it's firm enough for slicing. Increase the cooking time to $1\frac{1}{4}$ or $1\frac{1}{2}$ hours for a drier, firmer result.

10 servings

250 g/8 oz BITTERSWEET CHOCOLATE, CHOPPED
250 g/8 oz UNSALTED BUTTER, CUT INTO SMALL PIECES
200 g/$6\frac{1}{2}$ oz CASTER SUGAR
3 tbsp PLAIN FLOUR
3 EGGS

For the vanilla custard
500 ml/16 fl oz MILK
1 VANILLA POD, SPLIT, OR FEW DROPS VANILLA ESSENCE
5 EGG YOLKS
60 g/2 oz CASTER SUGAR

For the caramel sauce
4 tbsp COLD WATER
100 g/$3\frac{1}{4}$ oz CASTER SUGAR
125 ml/4 fl oz WARM WATER

23×12.5×10 cm/9×5×4 in LOAF TIN OR TERRINE

Line the bottom of the tin with greaseproof paper and heat the oven to 180°C/350°F/Gas Mark 4.

Melt the chocolate in a heavy saucepan over low heat, stirring constantly. Add the butter and sugar, a little at a time, stirring until the butter is incorporated and the sugar dissolves. Stir in the flour. Heat the mixture until it is very hot, but do not boil. Allow to cool slightly then, off the heat, beat in the eggs, one by one. (The heat of the mixture will cook and thicken the eggs.)

Pour the mixture into the prepared loaf tin. Set the tin in a *bain-marie** and bring the water to the boil on top of the stove. Transfer to the oven and bake the cake until a thin crust forms, 40 to 50 minutes. The cake will rise slightly but will fall again as it cools. Leave it to cool to room temperature, about 1 hour. Cover and refrigerate the cake for at least 24 hours.

Make the vanilla custard (see page 222).

For the caramel sauce, heat the cold water and the sugar until the sugar dissolves, then boil steadily to a golden brown caramel. Remove from the heat and at once add the warm water. (Stand back because the caramel will sputter.) Heat gently until the caramel melts, then leave it to cool. (The caramel sauce can be kept, refrigerated, for a day.)

To finish, run a knife around the cake and turn it out of the tin. Peel off the lining paper. Cut the cake into very thin slices. Set the slices on plates and spoon vanilla custard around the edge. Spoon the caramel sauce around the cake, letting the caramel drip into the vanilla custard.

Gâteau Fondant au Chocolat is a versatile cake allowing a wide range of cooking times, depending on your taste.

Châteaux of the Mountains

La Roche-Froide

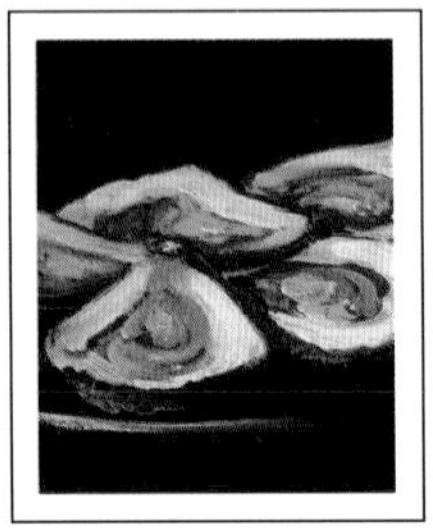

La Roche-Froide – 'Cold Rock' – is aptly named. The house stands in the village of Aixe-sur-Vienne near Limoges, a tall grey mass dating from the 16th century. This is '*La France profonde*', a region so far from the capital that 18th-century courtiers lived in dread of the word *limoger*, which came to mean banishment (forced retirement or redundancy in today's jargon). In winter, snow is frequent, icing the roofs and weighing down the surrounding firs, but in summer La Roche-Froide comes to life, thanks to the vivacity of its owners, Robert and Christiane Desproges-Gotteron.

'Entertaining is no bother to me,' smiles Christiane Desproges-Gotteron. 'I've cooked all my life, first as a child by watching my mother and grandmother.' Madame Desproges-Gotteron treasures a turn-of-the-century cookery book, passed down through three generations of women in her family, and once used for instructing young girls at a local convent. Family dinner for 30 is still commonplace. 'I like to cook with the seasons,' she says. 'For example, last weekend we had roast beef, with small tomatoes baked very slowly with olive oil, a bit of sugar, salt and pepper until they wrinkled and were almost *confit*.'

An image of La France profonde. La Roche Froide is a tall, grey mass dating from the 16th century.

A family wedding is celebrated with a huge cake, decorated with sparklers (below), a celebration echoed 300 years earlier in the dining scene (far right) which hangs on the walls of La Roche-Froide.

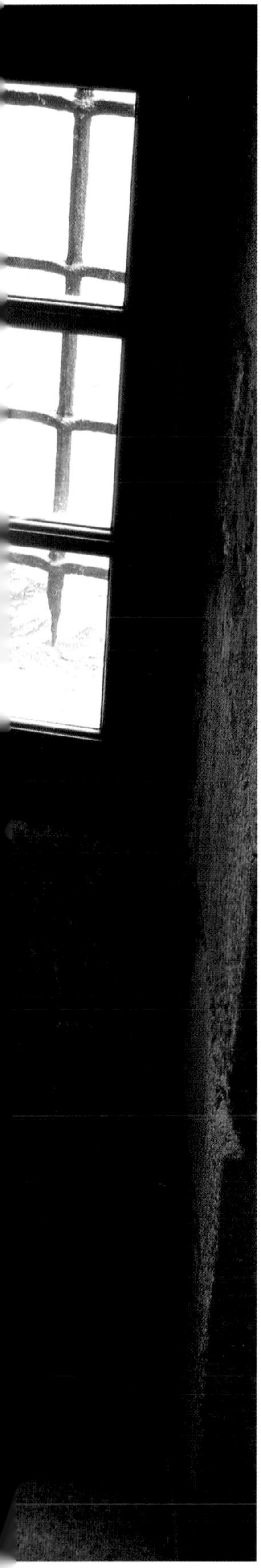

Christiane Desproges-Gotteron also likes to live off the countryside. In the old days, a Limousin farmer's rent was often paid partly in *foie gras* with the farmer's wife first presenting the fattened birds for family approval. Today, a young woman in the village fattens geese, so a favourite Desproges-Gotteron first course is fresh *foie gras*, served with a contrasting pâté of courgette and onion, briskly flavoured with lemon. An alternative might be chicken terrine layered with aspic and baby vegetables, marinated beef *carpaccio*, or perhaps a three-melon soup flavoured with mint. All are inspirations of the châtelaine, Christiane Desproges-Gotteron. 'I cook by instinct,' she says.

She and her husband divide their time between La Roche-Froide and a house nearby at Pompadour, home of the national stud. Officers from the stud are frequent guests and on 15 August, the night of the annual horse trials, the garden is filled with riders in and out of uniform. Robert Desproges-Gotteron traditionally likes to collect his daily newspaper and *baguette* by horse-drawn carriage. 'We are still 100 years behind the times,' says Madame Desproges-Gotteron.

Oeufs aux Truffes

Eggs *en Cocotte* with Truffles

In her cooking at La Roche-Froide, Madame Desproges-Gotteron mixes richness and simplicity. She may elevate a modest egg to luxury by adding a slice of precious black truffle, but just a pinch of freshly chopped tarragon or chives gives a memorable taste too.

4 servings

2 tbsp FINELY DICED COOKED HAM
SALT AND PEPPER
4 EGGS
4 tbsp CRÈME FRAÎCHE* OR DOUBLE CREAM
4 TRUFFLE SLICES
12 BREAD STICKS, FRIED IN OIL AND BUTTER (see page 220)

4 RAMEKINS (125 ml/4 fl oz EACH)

Heat the oven to 190°C/375°F/Gas Mark 5. Butter the ramekins. In each ramekin, put ½ tablespoon of ham and a little salt and pepper. Break in an egg and add a tablespoon of crème fraîche or cream. Top with a truffle slice.

If the bread sticks were made ahead of time, wrap them in foil and reheat them in the oven while cooking the eggs.

Set the ramekins in a *bain-marie** and bring the water to the boil on top of the stove. Transfer the eggs to the oven and bake them until the whites are almost set, about 10 minutes; the eggs will continue to cook in the heat of the ramekins after they are removed from the oven.

Serve the eggs at once – the whites should be just set and the yolks soft. Pass the fried bread sticks separately.

In Pot-au-Feu, the cooking liquid is reduced to make a well-flavoured broth which can be served as a first course.

POT-AU-FEU A LA ROYALE

BEEF TOP RIBS, VEAL SHIN AND CHICKEN SIMMERED WITH VEGETABLES

This pot-au-feu *has been a family recipe for generations and made the reputation of an epi curean great-uncle. Apparently he always returned to the ancestral home after a spell of good eating for a 'cure' based on the old cook's special* pot-au-feu. *Christiane Desproges-Gotteron likes to serve her deluxe version with poached duck or goose liver. If you have access to this treat, tie it up in muslin and poach it in the broth for 3 to 4 minutes for the duck liver; 10 to 12 minutes for the goose. To serve, discard the muslin, slice the liver and arrange with the meats on a platter.*

10 to 12 servings

5 LITRES/8 PINTS WATER
1 ONION, STUDDED WITH 2 CLOVES
A LARGE BOUQUET GARNI*
SALT
10 BLACK PEPPERCORNS
1.4 kg/3 lb VEAL SHIN, TIED IN A NEAT BUNDLE
1 kg/2 lb BEEF TOP RIBS, TIED IN A NEAT BUNDLE
750 g/1½ lb CARROTS, CUT INTO 5 cm/2 in PIECES
½ BUNCH CELERY, CUT INTO 5 cm/2 in PIECES
500 g/1 lb TURNIPS, QUARTERED
1 kg/2 lb LEEKS, CUT INTO 5 cm/2 in PIECES

For the stuffed chicken
60 g/2 oz FRESH BREADCRUMBS
125 ml/4 fl oz MILK
1 tbsp VEGETABLE OIL
1×2 kg/4½ lb OVEN-READY CHICKEN WITH GIBLETS, GIBLETS CHOPPED
SALT AND PEPPER
175 g/6 oz CURED HAM, CHOPPED
1 CLOVE GARLIC, FINELY CHOPPED
4 tbsp CHOPPED PARSLEY
1 EGG, BEATEN TO MIX
¼ tsp GROUND ALLSPICE

For the garnishes and condiments
1 SMALL LOAF FRENCH BREAD, SLICED INTO THIN ROUNDS AND TOASTED
COARSE SALT
MUSTARD
CORNICHONS OR GHERKINS

TRUSSING NEEDLE AND KITCHEN STRING

Combine the water, onion, bouquet garni, salt and peppercorns in a large pot and bring to the boil. Add the veal shin and top ribs to the pot, reduce the heat to low and simmer, uncovered for 1 hour, skimming occasionally.

Meanwhile, make the stuffing. Soak the breadcrumbs in the milk until soft, then squeeze dry. Heat the oil in a frying pan and add the chopped chicken giblets with salt and pepper. Fry them, stirring, until brown, 2 to 3 minutes. Mix them with the soaked breadcrumbs, ham, garlic, parsley and beaten egg, and season with pepper and allspice. (Salt may not be needed if the ham is salty.) Beat very well until thoroughly mixed. Sauté a small piece of the stuffing and taste it for seasoning. Stuff the chicken and truss the bird*.

Add the stuffed chicken to the pot with enough water to cover all the ingredients. Continue simmering for another hour, adding more water as necessary.

Add the carrots, celery and turnips with more salt if needed, and continue to simmer until the meat, chicken and vegetables are very tender, about another hour. Add the leeks 20 minutes before the end of cooking. Be sure there is always enough liquid to cover the meats and vegetables. (*Pot-au-feu* can be kept in the refrigerator for up to 3 days.)

Reheat the *pot-au-feu* if necessary. Transfer the meats, chicken and vegetables to a carving board with a juice catcher and discard the string. Boil the broth to reduce it by one-third or until well flavoured. Meanwhile, cut the meats into

The pot-au-feu itself, is a delicious assortment of tender meats and vegetables served with a rich stuffing. Madame Desproges-Gotteron also adds a generous slice of foie gras.

medium-thick slices and arrange them on a large warmed platter. Carve the chicken, pile the stuffing on the platter and arrange the pieces of chicken on top. Arrange the vegetables around the meats and chicken. Cover the platter and keep the meats and vegetables warm.

To serve, strain the broth, taste it for seasoning and skim off the fat. Put the toasted bread in warmed soup bowls, pour the broth over them and serve it as a first course. Serve the meat platter as a main course, with the salt, mustard and *cornichons* as condiments.

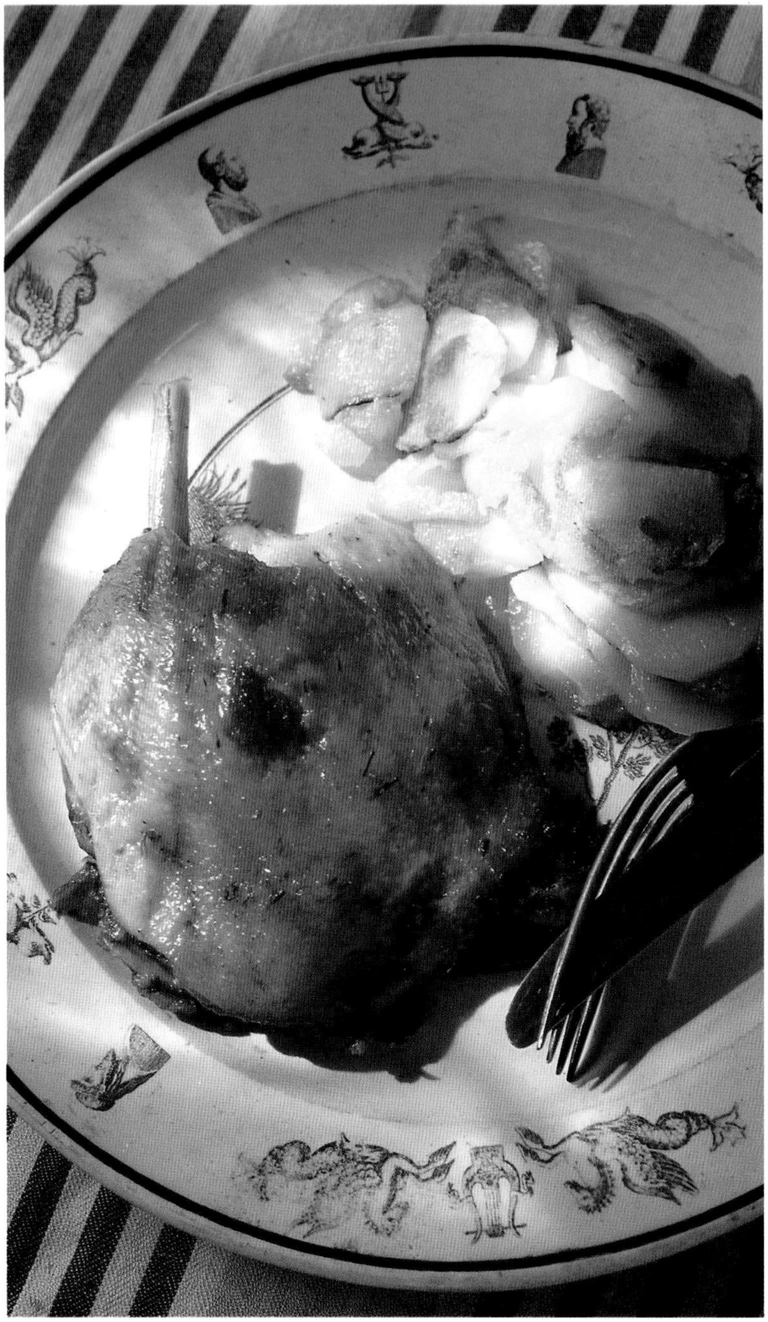

Salted and then baked in rich fat, this crisp duck melts in the mouth.

CONFIT DE CANARD CROUSTILLANT

CRISP DUCK CONFIT

Madame Desproges-Gotteron likes to serve this tender, crisp-skinned duck with garlic potatoes sautéed in the fat drained from the confit. *Lately, when heating the pieces of duck for serving, she has been basting them with a spoonful (or 'tear-drop' as she puts it) of honey so it caramelizes on the crisp skin.*

4 servings

1×1.8 kg/4 lb OVEN-READY DUCK, JOINTED INTO 8 SERVING PIECES*
45 g/1½ oz COARSE SALT
1 tsp GROUND BLACK PEPPER
3 SPRIGS OF FRESH THYME
3 BAY LEAVES, CRUMBLED
750 g/1½ lb LARD OR GOOSE FAT, MORE IF NEEDED

Rub each piece of duck with some of the coarse salt and put it in a bowl. Sprinkle with the pepper and the remaining salt and add the thyme and bay leaves. Cover and leave in a cool place for 6 to 12 hours, depending on how strong a flavour you want.

When ready to cook, wipe the excess salt from the duck pieces. Heat the oven to 150°C/300°F/Gas Mark 2. Put the duck pieces, skin side down, in a heavy flameproof casserole and cook over low heat for 15 to 20 minutes until the fat runs and the duck skin turns golden. Add enough melted lard or goose fat to cover the duck, then cover the casserole tightly and transfer it to the heated oven. Cook until the duck is very tender and has rendered all its fat, about 2 hours. Tradition has it the duck should be tender enough to pierce with a straw.

Pour a layer of the rendered fat into the bottom of a terrine or bowl and leave it until set. Pack the pieces of duck on top and pour over enough fat to cover them completely, adding melted lard if necessary. Cover the bowl and keep it in a cool place for at least a week for the flavour to mellow. (If sealed with a cloth sprinkled with salt and then covered with paper, *confit* will keep for several months in a cool place.)

To serve the *confit*, leave it in a warm place until the fat runs. Drain the duck pieces, then fry them in a little of the fat until they are very hot and the skin is crisp and brown. Transfer the *confit* to a warmed platter and serve it very hot. Keep the leftover fat for frying potatoes.

FRAMBOISES A LA MERINGUE ET CHANTILLY

RASPBERRIES WITH BAKED MERINGUE AND WHIPPED CREAM

'The Limousin is raspberry country,' notes Christiane Desproges-Gotteron. 'All summer they are ridiculously cheap in the market, less than the cost of picking!' When pressed for time, she buys 125 g/4 oz of baked meringues, then layers them with the berries and sauce in a dish. It can even be prepared a day ahead, with the topping of whipped cream added just before serving. 'Impossible to bungle!' she says.

4 servings

3 EGG WHITES
150 g/5 oz CASTER SUGAR
CASTER SUGAR FOR SPRINKLING
250 g/8 oz RASPBERRIES
RASPBERRY SAUCE (see below)

For the Chantilly cream
250 ml/8 fl oz DOUBLE CREAM
1 tbsp ICING SUGAR
FEW DROPS VANILLA ESSENCE

1 LITRE/2 PINT SOUFFLÉ DISH (OPTIONAL)

Heat the oven to 120°C/250°F/Gas Mark ½. Butter and flour a baking sheet.

Whisk the egg whites until very stiff. Add 3 tablespoons of the caster sugar and continue whisking until glossy to make a light meringue, about 30 seconds longer. Fold in the remaining caster sugar using a large metal spoon.

Shape the meringue into ovals with two large spoons, dropping them on the baking sheet. Sprinkle them with caster sugar and bake in the heated oven until dry and pale beige in colour, 1½ to 1¾ hours. Transfer them to a rack and cool completely. (Baked meringues will keep up to 3 weeks in an airtight container.)

To finish, make the Chantilly cream (see page 220) and chill it. Spoon the berries into the soufflé dish or a serving bowl. Pour in the raspberry sauce and crumble the baked meringues over the top. Spread the Chantilly cream over all.

COULIS DE FRAMBOISES

RASPBERRY SAUCE

Sweet raspberry sauce is a wonderful accompaniment to a variety of desserts and cakes.

Makes 300 ml/½ pint

250 g/8 oz RASPBERRIES
2 tbsp CASTER SUGAR, MORE IF NEEDED

Purée the raspberries in a food processor or blender with the sugar. Sieve the sauce to remove the pips. Taste it and add more sugar if needed, then chill. The sauce can be kept 1 or 2 days in the refrigerator.

Summer brings a profusion of raspberries to the area around La Roche-Froide.

Château d'Anjony

The medieval fortress of Anjony looms grim and forbidding in a lost corner of Auvergne. On the summer day that I first introduced myself to Comte and Comtesse de Léotoing d'Anjony, the telephone was intermittently cut off by thunder and storm and the river below was in flood. Unlike most fortresses, Anjony was never intended to ward off invaders. 'The château was built as a symbol of power,' explains the Comte, 'and the Léotoing d'Anjonys have lived here since the beginning.' The present châtelain is the Comte's father, the Marquis de Léotoing d'Anjony.

As a close companion to Joan of Arc, Louis d'Anjony was granted permission to build this five-storey, rectangular keep in 1439, a direct challenge to the local lords of Tournemire whose own fort was scarcely a bow shot distant. Such an affront could not pass unchecked. Starting with a petty dispute about the right to bake bread in the communal oven, the quarrel climaxed a century later in a double murder, with a corpse disinterred from holy ground and thrown down before the gates of the château, to be found the next morning, half eaten by dogs. The Tournemires had gone too far. Both King and Pope refused to countenance body-snatching, and the family of Anjony triumphed.

The Château d'Anjony dominates a remote valley in the Auvergne (page 144). Inside, the Salle des Preux, the room of the Nine Knights, is a magnificent fresco-covered hall. The murals were painted in the 16th century for a grand wedding, and they feature historical and biblical figures, as well as life-size effigies of the bride and her groom.

The famous Black Virgin in the castle chapel. The 35 centimetre high statue, Notre Dame d'Anjony, is thought to date back to the 1400s (above right). The chapel ceiling is decorated with scenes from Christ's life (right). The Anjony crest can be seen in the centre of the frescoes.

The fertile Doire valley where Anjony stands majestic on a rocky promontory.

The fruits of their success can be seen in the château which is a storehouse of treasures – throughout its history, Anjony has never been ransacked. Anjony is home to one of the finest of the medieval black virgins of Auvergne, sculpted in darkened wood, the holy child on her knees clothed in gold. But the virgin is overshadowed by an astonishing gothic chapel, painted with 16th-century biblical scenes stretching right up to the keystone of the vaulted roof. The '*Salle des Preux*' (Warriors' Hall) is equally animated, a Renaissance Hollywood, starring Judas Maccabaeus, Hector of Troy, King David and Alexander the Great on his elephant gambolling under the gaze of Charlemagne on the opposite wall. At one side of the great fireplace stands Michel d'Anjony, who commissioned the frescoes to honour and impress his wife, Germaine de Foix, cousin of the future King Henri IV. Such grandeur might overwhelm, but not Robert de Léotoing d'Anjony who adores his cosy study. 'In winter these rooms stay wonderfully warm. *Dieu merci* for thick walls!'

I talked with Edith de Léotoing d'Anjony about the countryside surrounding the château, so bleak to a stranger's eye. 'We are in the heart of Cantal here,' she says. 'Fifty years behind the times, from the plumbing upwards.' However inhospitable the land may seem, cattle of the sturdy rust-coloured Salers breed thrive – 100 or more range on the property. Their milk goes to make cheese: Cantal and Salers, a variation of Cantal made only with the milk from cattle grazed in mountain pastures from May to late September. Both are legally protected with *appellation contrôlée* status. The best resemble a mature Cheddar, smooth but dry with a touch of bite, the result of at least three months of ageing at over 900 meters. The cheeses are shaped by moulds into huge 45 kilogram discs which can be rolled along like a wheel. Cantal cheese turns up in local dishes like *tourte de Salers*, a cheese pie, and *gannat* or cheese brioche. Other local specialities include stuffed cabbage and *le pounti*, a meat and vegetable loaf layered with plump prunes. 'We get hungry in these climes,' remarks the Comtesse.

By no means all of Edith de Léotoing d'Anjony's dishes are Auvergnat. She collects antiquarian cookery books, like those written nearly 200 years ago by the great Carême. Recently she tried one of his recipes for wild duck with a stuffing of apples and redcurrants. 'Very modern, don't you think?' she remarks. Escoffier's *pudding de cabinet* (layers of sponge fingers and glacé fruits baked in custard) is another favourite with an established pedigree (see page 94). Out here in the mountains, fashions change slowly. Châteaux like Anjony and the food that is served there are intended to be good for all time.

Local cheese being made in Salers from the milk of Salers cows by Henri Rouchy at the Domaine Fouey. This traditional and time-consuming process is increasingly rare today.

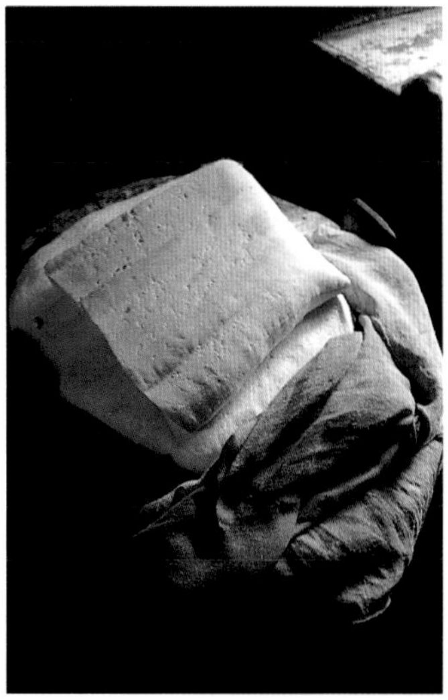

The austere towers of Anjony (see page 144) contrast with the living quarters and the opulence of the Comtesse's table.

LE POUNTI

MEAT AND VEGETABLE LOAF WITH PRUNES

Not all château cooking requires truffles and foie gras*. The Comtesse de Léotoing d'Anjony prefers the rustic dishes of the Auvergne highlands such as this traditional loaf layered with prunes. Serve it as a first course or brunch dish. It also makes a good accompaniment to plain roast meat or chicken. 'Be sure to add plenty of seasoning,' says the Comtesse.*

8 to 10 servings

12 STONED PRUNES
3 tbsp COGNAC OR BRANDY
250 g/8 oz COOKED HAM OR LEFTOVER ROAST BEEF OR PORK
250 g/8 oz STREAKY BACON, RINDED, CUT IN PIECES
250 g/8 oz SWISS CHARD LEAVES OR SPINACH
2 ONIONS, CUT IN PIECES
3 tbsp CHOPPED MIXED FRESH HERBS, SUCH AS PARSLEY, TARRAGON AND CHIVES
1½ tsp DRY YEAST OR 10 g/⅓ oz FRESH YEAST*
250 ml/8 fl oz LUKEWARM MILK
45 g/1½ oz PLAIN FLOUR
4 EGGS
SALT AND PEPPER

1.5 LITRE/2½ PINT SHALLOW BAKING DISH

Heat the oven to 180°C/350°F Gas Mark 4. Butter the baking dish. Cut the prunes in half and soak in the Cognac or brandy. Chop together the ham or meat, bacon, Swiss chard, onions and herbs in a processor or by hand.

Sprinkle or crumble the yeast over the milk and leave to dissolve, about 5 minutes. Sift the flour into a bowl and gradually stir in the yeast mixture. Whisk in the eggs to make a batter and add a little salt and plenty of pepper.

Stir the batter into the ham mixture. Pour half this batter into the prepared dish. Cover with the soaked prunes and any liquid. Pour the rest of the batter on top of the prunes, spreading it evenly. Bake in the heated oven for 50 to 60 minutes until browned and a skewer inserted in the centre is hot to the touch when withdrawn after 30 seconds. Serve lukewarm or at room temperature, cut in slices. (*Pounti* can be kept covered in the refrigerator for up to 3 days.)

A simple sauce of wine, cream and mushrooms is the perfect way to enjoy the taste of fresh trout (right).

TRUITES AUX MORILLES

SAUTÉED TROUT WITH MOREL MUSHROOMS

At the foot of Anjony, weekend fishermen sit patiently, rod in hand, hoping to catch the trout that swim through the Doire river. The Comtesse de Léotoing d'Anjony simply pan fries the trout with fresh morels during their short season, or otherwise with field mushrooms, stirring in a ladle of cream at the end for a sauce.

4 servings

125 g/4 oz FRESH MORELS OR 30 g/1 oz DRIED MORELS
4 TROUT (ABOUT 250 g/8 oz EACH), CLEANED AND TRIMMED
SALT AND PEPPER
100 g/3½ oz SEASONED FLOUR
125 g/4 oz CLARIFIED BUTTER (see page 220)
175 ml/6 fl oz WHITE WINE
375 ml/12 fl oz CRÈME FRAÎCHE*
OR DOUBLE CREAM

Pick over fresh morels and trim the stalks. Shake and gently brush them to remove any earth, splitting the stalk to remove any soil inside. Soak dried morels in warm water for 1 to 2 hours until fairly soft, stirring occasionally to loosen any grit. Rinse the morels in cold running water to remove any remaining grit and pat dry. Cut them into thin slices.

Sprinkle the fish with salt and pepper. Coat them with seasoned flour.

Heat the butter in two large frying pans. Add the fish and brown them over moderate heat, 2 to 3 minutes on each side. Add the morels to the pans with a little salt and pepper. Continue cooking over fairly low heat for 5 to 7 minutes until the fresh morels are tender and the flesh of the trout can just be pulled from the bone with a knife. Transfer the fish and fresh morels to a warmed platter and keep warm. If using dried morels, leave them in the pans.

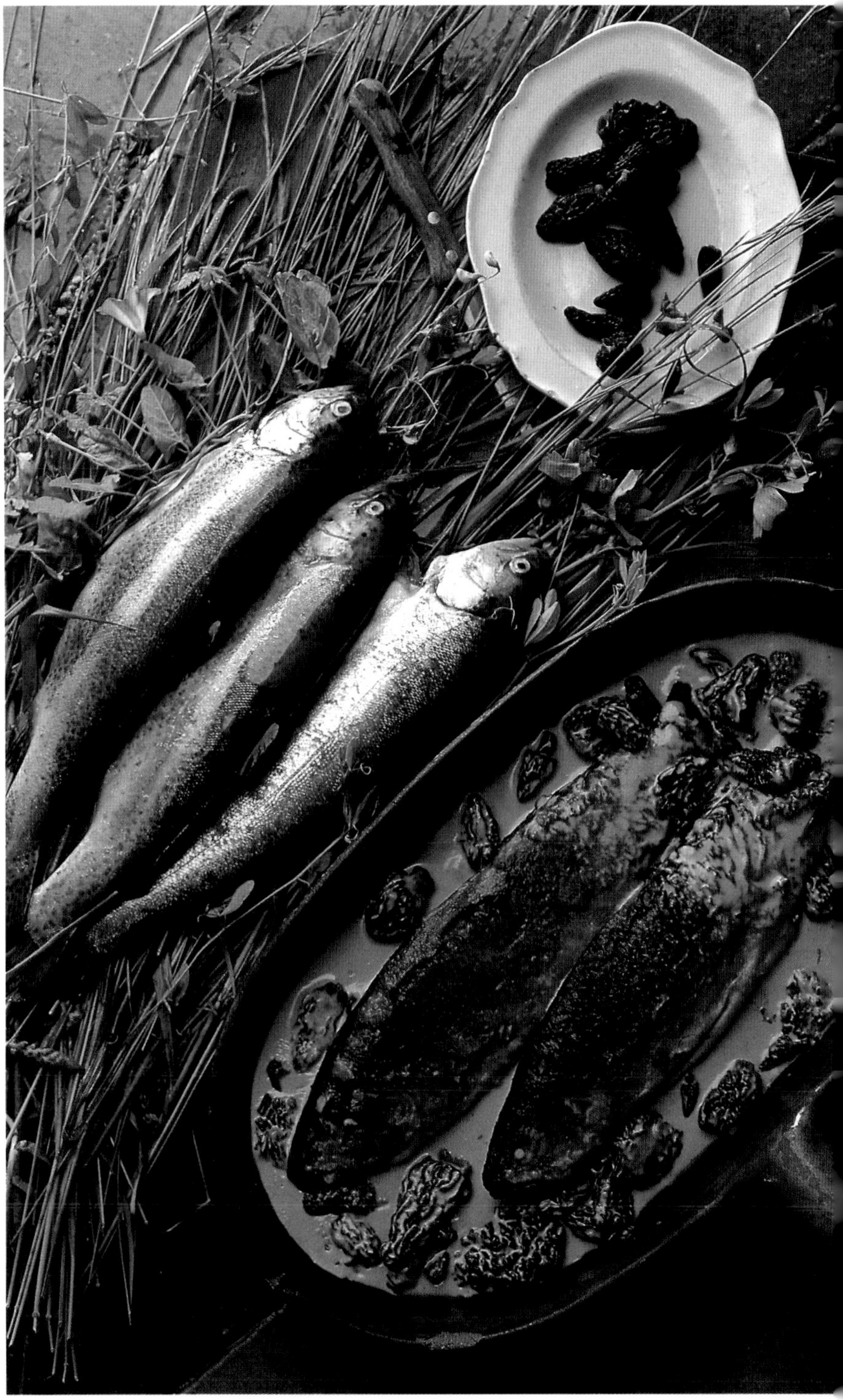

Pour off the butter. Add the wine to the pans and bring to the boil, scraping to dissolve the browned pan juices. Simmer until reduced by half. Combine all the juices in one pan. Add the crème fraîche or cream and simmer to concentrate the flavour, 5 to 10 minutes. Taste for seasoning. Pour the sauce over the fish and serve immediately.

Château de Jozerand

For Joy de Rohan-Chabot, the Château de Jozerand is both family home and artist's *atelier*. The château has been in her husband's family since the early 1700s, and she was born nearby. 'I adore the countryside,' she says. 'The changing seasons, the ice in winter, the view of the mountains from my window.' Icy indeed, for the Château de Jozerand stands in northern Auvergne at an altitude of 500 metres. 'At Christmas we may have 20 or 30 degrees of frost, or the sun may be shining and we can eat outdoors.'

Comtesse Joy de Rohan-Chabot is a noted artist, but the limitations of paint on canvas are not for her. She loves to experiment with surfaces, decorating doors, furniture, fabric, anything that comes to hand. Just now she is decorating an old enamelled bath. 'It's exciting. Each time I must to some extent invent a new technique. She draws very much on nature – 'this seems to be the year of snails,' she confides. Joy has just completed a portrait of her husband in a rocking chair, surrounded by a forest of trees and potted plants.

The Château de Jozerand is in a remote spot of northern Auvergne. A ghost is mandatory. In the days of the present Comte's grandfather, the children's tutor complained of a presence that each night shook his bed. A few years later, central heating was installed in the old tower and a skeleton was revealed, buried in the wall. Tests showed the bones to be 15th-century. In the archives it was found that of the three Rochefort d'Ailly brothers who lived in Jozerand at that time, one had disappeared after returning from the wars to claim his inheritance. In 1902 the skeleton was buried in the cemetery, and hauntings ceased.

In the grounds at Jozerand, box hedges and topiary predominate. Joy de Rohan Chabot has made the old orangery into her studio. Its calm atmosphere and good light make it ideal for working on her painted screens and decorated furniture.

Life at Jozerand revolves around the ancient vaulted kitchen, which does double duty as the family room. 'In summer we'll have 30 guests or more, and laughter seems to start at eight in the morning and continue into the small hours.' The kitchen is heated from the great open fireplace and the copper pots are put to good use. 'I walk for kilometres from cupboard to cupboard when I am cooking,' says the Comtesse. Vegetable soups are her forte, based on leeks, sorrel or whatever else is in season. In summer, she finds chilled cucumber soup refreshing. The day we talked together she had roast chickens to serve with Chinese black mushrooms and a spicy oriental sauce. 'I love to invent,' she says. 'I may read a cookery book for ideas, but I never follow it exactly.'

Jozerand is an historic monument, but unusually it is listed less for its 14th- and 15th-century shell than as a showcase for its Neoclassical renovations. Today Jozerand blooms with flowered wallpapers and the glowing colours that brought a fresh breeze to salons and bedchambers over 150 years ago. A modern and individual touch is also in evidence: Joy de Rohan-Chabot loves to decorate screens with collages of roses, trailing vines and vegetables.

The ambiance at Jozerand is international: Joy's mother was Scottish, and in summer she calls on young British or American cooks to take charge in the kitchen. The current chef is Korean. At any time the language may be English or French, the speaker aged seven to seventy-seven.

The warmth of the Rohan-Chabots, and the relaxed and cosmopolitan atmosphere at their château, are an instant welcome: 'Jean is nonconformist, and so am I. Jozerand is a reflection of the two of us.'

POTAGE DES COMBRAILLES AUX ORTIES

NETTLE SOUP WITH SORREL

In spring, before the nettles flower, Joy de Rohan-Chabot dons gardening gloves and long trousers to gather nettle tops in the Combraille hills for this special soup. The leaves are simmered with home-grown sorrel in beef stock, and, just before serving, a dollop of fresh cream is added to smooth out the grassy flavours. Nettle soup without the sorrel is good too.

6 to 8 servings

1 kg/2 lb TENDER NETTLE TOPS
60 g/2 oz BUTTER
500 g/1 lb SORREL, STALKS REMOVED
1 LARGE ONION, FINELY CHOPPED
20 g/¾ oz PLAIN FLOUR
1 LITRE/1⅔ PINTS BEEF STOCK (see page 221)
SALT AND PEPPER
125 ml/4 fl oz CRÈME FRAÎCHE*
OR DOUBLE CREAM

Wash the nettle tops and discard the stalks, wearing rubber gloves. Bring a large pan of salted water to the boil. Add the nettle leaves, bring the water back to the boil and cook, stirring often, until the leaves are very tender, 15 to 30 minutes, depending on the age of the nettles. Drain them.

Purée the nettle leaves in a blender or food processor until mostly smooth, then work the purée through a drum sieve or food mill to remove the fibres.

Melt one-quarter of the butter in a big saucepan. Add the sorrel and cook over moderate heat, stirring often, until it softens to a purée, 3 to 5 minutes. Combine the cooked sorrel with the nettle purée.

Melt the remaining butter in a saucepan and add the onion. Sauté it over moderate heat until soft, 3 to 5 minutes. Stir in the flour and cook until foaming. Whisk in the stock, vegetable purées and a little salt and pepper. Bring the soup to the boil, whisking constantly. Reduce the heat and simmer, stirring occasionally, until the soup is well flavoured, about 30 minutes. (The soup can be made ahead and refrigerated for up to 2 days.)

To finish, reheat the soup if necessary, stir in half the crème fraîche or cream and season the soup to taste with salt and pepper. Spoon it into warmed soup bowls and add a spoonful of the remaining crème fraîche or cream to each bowl, swirling to create a marbled effect if you like.

Joy de Rohan-Chabot's nettle soup with sorrel is a delicious and original way to use the first wild plants of spring.

Gigot Brayaude

Slow-Braised Lamb from Auvergne

A leg of mature mountain sheep was once traditional for this recipe, braised for 7 hours until the meat began to fall off the bone. Today, the dish is often prepared with younger lamb, but several hours' cooking is still the key. 'We eat the meat without a knife, it's so tender,' notes Joy de Rohan-Chabot. With the gigot, *the Comtesse serves a tart redcurrant jelly or blackberry jam, made with berries gathered at Jozerand.* Truffade *(see page 175) would make a perfect accompaniment.*

8 servings

1×2 kg/4½ lb LEG OF LAMB OR MUTTON
2 ONIONS, SLICED
2 CARROTS, SLICED
A SPRIG OF FRESH THYME,
OR ½ tsp DRIED THYME
1 BAY LEAF
500 ml/16 fl oz WATER, MORE IF NEEDED
SALT AND PEPPER
125 ml/4 fl oz COGNAC OR BRANDY

KITCHEN STRING

Heat the oven to 120°C/250°F/Gas Mark ½. Trim the meat of all excess fat. Tie the meat tightly with string and put it in a large casserole with the onions, carrots, thyme, bay leaf, water, salt and pepper. Cover and cook in the heated oven for 5 hours, turning the meat occasionally. The water should scarcely bubble; if it simmers, reduce the heat. Add more water if necessary so the casserole doesn't dry out during the long cooking. After 5 hours, add the Cognac or brandy, return the casserole to the oven and continue cooking until the meat is very tender, about 1 hour longer. (The meat can be refrigerated for up to 3 days; reheat it before proceeding.)

Remove the strings from the meat and carve it in thick slices. Strain the cooking liquid and skim off the fat. This gravy should be rich and concentrated, so boil to reduce it if necessary. Alternatively, add a little water if you do not have enough. Serve the lamb with the unthickened cooking liquid.

The secret to the perfect Gigot Brayaude is slow cooking at a low temperature.

Shady pathways and forgotten corners abound on the property.

Rhubarbe Meringuée

Rhubarb Meringue Gratin

In this seasonal dessert, the Comtesse de Rohan-Chabot blends the tart flavour of rhubarb with sweetened whipped cream and airy meringue, echoing the combination so popular in lemon meringue pie.

4 to 6 servings

1 kg/2 lb RHUBARB, PEELED AND FINELY DICED
375 g/12 oz GRANULATED SUGAR
250 ml/8 fl oz DOUBLE CREAM, CHILLED
1 tbsp ICING SUGAR, SIFTED
3 EGG WHITES
150 g/5 oz CASTER SUGAR

1 LITRE/2 PINT GRATIN OR BAKING DISH; PIPING BAG AND LARGE STAR TUBE (OPTIONAL)

Butter the gratin dish. Combine the rhubarb and granulated sugar in a saucepan. Heat gently, stirring, until the sugar dissolves, then boil, stirring occasionally, for 20 to 30 minutes until the rhubarb softens to a purée with a few whole pieces in it. (Watch the mixture carefully towards the end of cooking so it doesn't caramelize.) Spread the rhubarb mixture in the prepared dish. (It can be refrigerated for a day.)

For the Chantilly cream, put the cream in a bowl set in another bowl containing ice and water, then whip until stiff. Add the icing sugar and continue whipping until the cream stiffens again. Cover the bowl and set it aside in the refrigerator to chill.

Heat the oven to 190°C/375°F/Gas Mark 5. For the meringue, whisk the egg whites until they are very stiff. Add 3 tablespoons of the caster sugar and continue whisking until glossy to make a light meringue, about 30 seconds longer. Lightly fold in the remaining caster sugar using a large metal spoon.

Either scoop the meringue into the piping bag and pipe rosettes over the rhubarb to cover it completely, or spread the meringue with a spatula. Bake the gratin in the heated oven until golden, 8 to 12 minutes. Serve at once with the Chantilly cream.

Château du Chassan

'We were forced to make a choice: should we hold on to the inheritance handed down by 16 generations, despite all it would cost and the demands it would make on our family? Or should we move out? It was painful even to think about that possibility.' Général Gonzague and Madame de Jenlis are realists. When, nearly 20 years ago, they decided to bring the Château du Chassan back to life, they knew it would be hard.

Sheltered close to the village of Faverolles, Le Chassan commands a sweeping view of the chilly uplands of Auvergne near Saint-Flour. The château itself, built in classic 18th-century style, has an endearing country atmosphere. The panelled rooms lack the florid carving of more sophisticated houses, while the curving staircase and stone floors, cut from the local grey granite, lend a rustic air. Le Chassan may be a château, but it is also clearly a working farm, where sheep and angora goats are raised in the nearby fields, and hay is gathered right up to the front door of the château.

Chassan was originally a mountain fortress, but by the mid-1700s, it was uninhabitable so the owners demolished the property, using the old masonry to construct a traditional Auvergnat manor house.

The 16th-century tapestries date from the old château and were apparently cut up in the 1750s to fit the smaller dimensions of the new manor house (right). The vast stone staircase dating from 1764 is decorated with the family crest (below right).

Very early on, the Jenlis family realised that farming was not enough. For their commitment to succeed in this remote upland countryside with its long winters, the village inhabitants must be involved as well. Thus was born the Buffadou cooperative – a *buffadou* is a blowpipe used to kindle a fire, and this is one of the first items the cooperative produced. The concept was simple: farmers and villagers could spend the quiet winter months fashioning artisan products to sell to summer visitors. Jams and jellies made from wild fruit – bilberries, raspberries, redcurrants and crab apples – were among the first ventures, as were baskets, wrought-iron work and knitted sweaters.

Soon, urged by Suzanne de Jenlis, an enterprising villager began fattening *foie gras* geese and ducks, raising two flocks a year between the busy seasons of grass-cutting (for silage and hay) and the grain and potato harvests. Reluctant husbands were persuaded to let their wives – some had never left home – take a ten-day course in porcelain decoration at a convent in the Alps. Now Buffadou porcelain, along with other crafts, is sold in Paris and has been on exhibition in Los Angeles.

Recently a ruined farmhouse was renovated as a summer hotel, while the cooperative restaurant in Faverolles, l'Auberge du Dinadou,

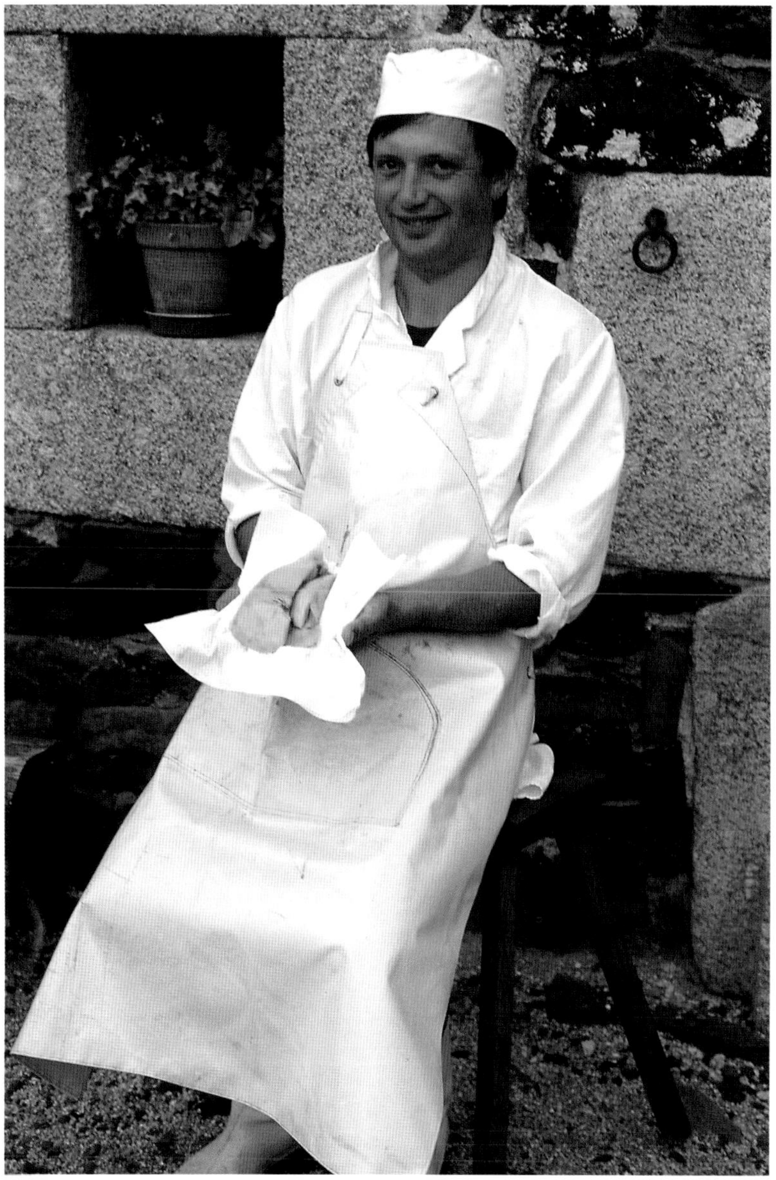

serves country dishes like beef *daube* with prunes and *croustade* of wild mushrooms, locally picked and dried in the sun. Madame de Jenlis' speciality of chilled home-made terrine of *foie gras* – with a hot fricassée of wild mushrooms sautéed in goose fat, the two divided by a 'frontier' of salad greens – would do a Parisian restaurant proud.

The way was not always easy, but by now the cooperative is no longer an uncertain idealistic experiment but a showpiece with over 300 members. Suzanne de Jenlis finds herself called on to help with similar ventures in other parts of France. Finances remain precarious but as members come to realise the value of their work, the cooperative should go from strength to strength. 'It is sometimes hard to convince simple country folk of their own gifts,' Madame de Jenlis told me.

Meanwhile, the Château du Chassan has recaptured past glories. The salon panelling is freshly painted in a blue which harmonises perfectly with the splendid 16th-century tapestries. Antique furniture gleams with polish. Outside, the formal lawns are neatly tonsured. The Jenlis commitment to the renewal of the family château has been amply rewarded. Their ancestors, who include thinkers like de Tocqueville and doers like de Lesseps, of Suez canal fame, and Vauban the great military architect, would be proud. Not just a château, but a whole village has come back to life.

In the local village of Faverolles, the agricultural co-operative founded by Madame de Jenlis produces a range of foie gras and home-made preserves.

A hearty winter salad of robust greens, walnuts and locally-produced duck breast is a favourite at the cooperative restaurant in Faverolles.

SALADE AU MAGRET DE CANARD CONFIT

DUCK BREAST CONFIT WITH WALNUTS AND WINTER GREENS

At the Château du Chassan, the confit *comes from Le Buffadou, the agricultural cooperative run by Madame de Jenlis. She likes to pair the rich and meaty duck breast with slightly bitter winter greens, and when they are available she adds a special touch with a few wild mushrooms sautéed in duck fat.*

4 servings

2 *CONFIT* DUCK BREASTS (see page 150)
500 g/1 lb MIXED WINTER GREENS, SUCH AS CURLY ENDIVE (FRISÉE) AND ESCAROLE
2 tbsp MAYONNAISE (see page 221)
70 g/2¼ oz CHOPPED WALNUTS

For the vinaigrette
2 tbsp VINEGAR
SALT AND PEPPER
75 ml/2½ fl oz VEGETABLE OIL

Leave the duck breasts in a warm place until the fat runs.

Meanwhile, trim the greens, wash them and tear into bite-size pieces. Dry them thoroughly and put in a bowl.

Make the vinaigrette (see page 222) and whisk in the mayonnaise and walnuts. A short time before serving, toss the greens lightly with the vinaigrette and divide amongst the four individual plates.

Just before serving, drain the duck breasts, then fry them in a little of the melted fat until they are very hot and the skin is crisp and brown. Pull the duck breasts into slices with two forks and arrange the slices on top of the greens. Serve at once.

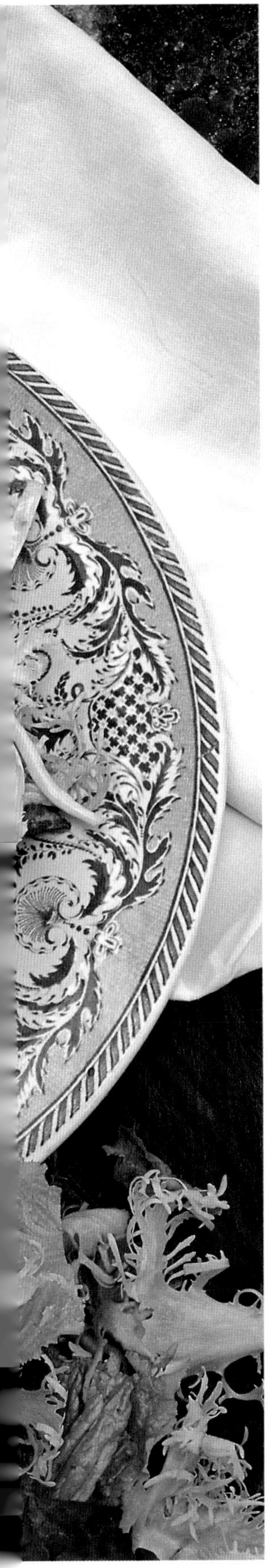

Daube aux Pruneaux

Beef Stew with Prunes

For Madame de Jenlis, a daube *with beef and prunes spells home cooking, because cattle are a mainstay in Auvergne, raised both for beef and for milk. Auvergnat prunes, though less celebrated than those from the Garonne and Lot river valleys in South-western France, are still much appreciated locally. With the* daube, *serve boiled potatoes or buttered noodles.*

10 to 12 servings

2 kg/4½ lb BEEF CHUCK OR TOPSIDE, CUT INTO 5 cm/2 in CUBES
500 g/1 lb CARROTS, CUT INTO 3.75 cm/1½ in PIECES
500 g/1 lb ONIONS, QUARTERED
3 LITRES/4¾ PINTS ROBUST RED WINE, MORE IF NEEDED
1 BAY LEAF
SALT AND PEPPER
375 g/12 oz STONED PRUNES

Combine the meat, carrots, onions and wine in a heavy flameproof casserole. Bring the wine to the boil, then reduce the heat and simmer, covered, over very low heat for 3 hours.

Remove the casserole from the heat and add the bay leaf and salt. Add more wine if needed; the wine should barely cover the meat. Allow to cool to room temperature, then leave to marinate, covered, in the refrigerator for about 24 hours, stirring the meat occasionally.

The next day, add the prunes to the casserole. Bring the wine to the boil, then reduce the heat. Cover the casserole and simmer over very low heat until the meat and prunes are very tender, about 1 hour. (The *daube* can be cooked up to 2 days ahead and refrigerated in the cooking liquid. The flavour mellows on keeping.)

To finish, reheat the *daube* if necessary. If the sauce is thin, remove the solids and boil until it lightly coats a spoon. Season the *daube* with pepper; it should be peppery. As you prefer, skim off the fat, or leave to enrich the meat.

Beef stew is enhanced with dark, mellow prunes, a product of Auvergne.

CHÂTEAU DE VIRIEU

EVER SINCE IT WAS BUILT NEARLY 1000 YEARS AGO, THE CHÂTEAU DE VIRIEU HAS BEEN A REFUGE. LAST TIME WAS IN THE SECOND WORLD WAR, WHEN VIRIEU WAS A RESISTANCE HIDEOUT. IN 1943 THE GERMANS CONDUCTED A RIGOROUS SEARCH, BUT ALL THEY FOUND IN AN OBSCURE CLOSET WAS A LITTLE BOX OF JADE JEWELLERY, MISLAID BY THE MARQUISE DE VIRIEU THREE YEARS EARLIER. 'I WAS DELIGHTED IT TURNED UP,' SHE SAID. THE INVADERS TOTALLY OVERLOOKED THE MEDIEVAL CACHETTE UNDER THE TERRACED BATTLEMENT, ORIGINALLY DESIGNED TO STOCK GRAIN IN TIME OF SIEGE. IT WAS FILLED WITH 40 TONS OF GUNS AND AMMUNITION, CRAFTILY CONCEALED BY PLANTINGS OF POTATOES.

The massive walls of Virieu have withstood assault over the centuries and sheltered arms caches for the Resistance in World War II.

DESPITE ITS NAME, THE CHÂTEAU DE VIRIEU HAS NOT ALWAYS BEEN IN THE HANDS OF THE VIRIEU FAMILY. ONE BRANCH BUILT THE CHÂTEAU, BUT AS PART OF A MARRIAGE SETTLEMENT IT PASSED TO ANOTHER FAMILY IN THE 13TH CENTURY. THE PRESENT BRANCH RE-ACQUIRED VIRIEU IN 1874 BUT HAS ONLY MADE A SERIOUS HOME THERE SINCE THE 1920S, WHEN RESTORATION BEGAN. SEVENTY YEARS ON, AND THE WORK STILL CONTINUES. THIS YEAR'S PROJECT, UNDERTAKEN BY AN EXPERT FROM YALE UNIVERSITY, IS THE PRESERVATION AND CATALOGUING OF THE LIBRARY, WHICH INCLUDES MEDIEVAL MANUSCRIPTS AND SOME NOTABLE 16TH- AND 17TH-CENTURY ENGRAVINGS. NEXT YEAR MARIE-FRANÇOISE DE VIRIEU HOPES TO RESTORE THE 16TH-CENTURY DOVECOTE WITH ITS PEPPERPOT ROOF. SHE ALSO SPEAKS WISTFULLY OF PLANS FOR CREATING A MAZE, TO BE PLANTED IN HEDGES OF BOX.

Just recently, the Marquise turned her attention to the vegetable garden. Faithful to an old map of the property, it is now laid out in diagonals like those of the British flag, with a great basin and fountain in the centre. Adjacent is a formal French garden, in perfect harmony with the rolling hills of the surrounding province of Dauphiné. In essence it is a countrified version of the great gardens along the Loire.

The cooking favoured by Marie-Françoise de Virieu is indigenous – potatoes, baked in native *dauphinois* fashion, with milk and cream in a dish rubbed with a cut garlic clove. '*Gratin dauphinois* does not contain cheese,' she told me with authority. 'If it does, it becomes *savoyard* and is usually cooked in veal stock.' Desserts draw on fruit from the local orchards – peaches, pears, currants and plums, often cooked in a tart with a lattice topping. The Marquise loves cheese – little rounds of Saint-Marcellin made of half goat's, half cow's milk; melting Reblochon, which traditionally uses the extra-rich milk drained from the udder last of all; tomme de Savoie with its greyish rind and nutty flavour. 'It's made quite far away from here now,' she says, '20 kilometres or more.' Then she laughs. '*Nous pensons petit*' – in mountain districts a kilometre is still a considerable distance!

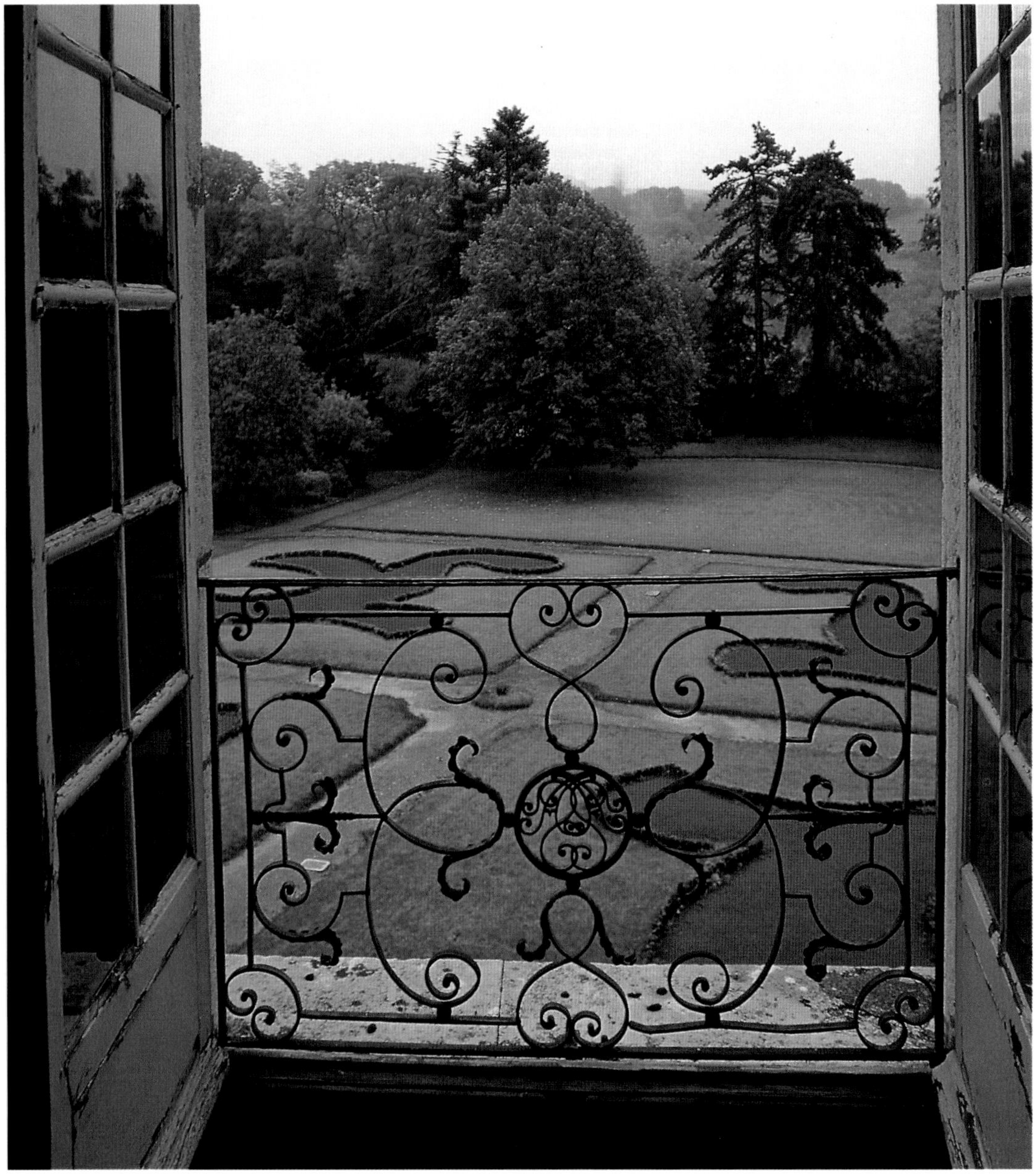

The garden, full of parterres and manicured lawns, has been restored according to original 18th-century plans.

FAISANS A LA CHARTREUSE

PHEASANTS *EN COCOTTE* WITH CHARTREUSE LIQUEUR

The Dauphiné is the home of Chartreuse and of the Carthusian monks who make it. At a distillery in Voiron, near the present monastery, monks work with 130 mountain plants and herbs to produce this famous green or yellow liqueur according to their secret recipe. For centuries the Virieu family had close links with the order, with the right to be buried in a nearby monastery. In this dish, the liqueur, enriched with a little cream, beautifully complements the pheasant meat.

The triumphant restoration of the original gardens provides Virieu with an exhaustive range of fresh vegetables.

4 servings

75 ml/2½ fl oz GREEN CHARTREUSE LIQUEUR
2 YOUNG OVEN-READY PHEASANTS (ABOUT 1 kg/2 lb EACH)
SALT AND PEPPER
2 STRIPS OF BARDING FAT* (optional)
60 g/2 oz CLARIFIED BUTTER (see page 220)
1 LARGE ONION, FINELY CHOPPED
3 CLOVES GARLIC, FINELY CHOPPED
1 STICK CELERY, FINELY CHOPPED
A SPRIG OF FRESH THYME
A SPRIG OF FRESH ROSEMARY
1 BAY LEAF
125 ml/4 fl oz WHITE WINE
250 ml/8 fl oz CHICKEN STOCK (see page 221)
3 tbsp CRÈME FRAÎCHE* OR DOUBLE CREAM
1 tsp ARROWROOT DISSOLVED IN 1 tbsp COLD WATER

TRUSSING NEEDLE AND STRING

Working over a large bowl, pour half the liqueur into the cavities of the birds and shake gently to coat the insides. Set the birds in the bowl and pour over the remaining liqueur. Leave them to marinate at room temperature for 15 minutes, turning them two or three times.

Lift the birds out of the liqueur, letting excess drain into the bowl. Reserve the liqueur. Pat the birds dry with kitchen paper. Season the cavities with salt and pepper. Truss the birds*. If using barding fat, drape it over the breasts and tie it in place with string.

Heat the butter in a large flameproof casserole and brown the birds on all sides over moderate heat, about 10 minutes. Add the onion, garlic, celery and herbs. Cover the pot and cook over low heat for 15 minutes.

Heat the reserved liqueur in a small saucepan for 20 or 30 seconds. Tip the pan and light the liqueur with a match. (Stand back from the flame.) Pour it flaming over the birds and continue cooking, basting the birds with the liqueur, until the flames subside, about 30 seconds. Cover the pot again and continue cooking for about 15 minutes until the birds are just done: the juice from the cavity should run slightly pink when a bird is lifted with a two-pronged fork if you like meat pink at the bone. For well done meat, continue cooking for 5 to 10 minutes longer.

Transfer the birds to a carving board, cover loosely with foil and leave them to rest for 15 minutes. Pour off the fat from the casserole, leaving the cooking juices. Add the wine and stock to the pot and bring to the boil, stirring to dissolve the juices. Simmer until reduced by half, 10 to 15 minutes.

Strain the sauce into a saucepan. Add the crème fraîche or cream and simmer 1–2 minutes to thicken slightly. Gradually whisk in enough of the arrowroot so the sauce thickens a little more. Taste it for seasoning.

Remove the string and barding fat from the birds, carve them and arrange on a warmed platter or plates. Pour the sauce over the birds.

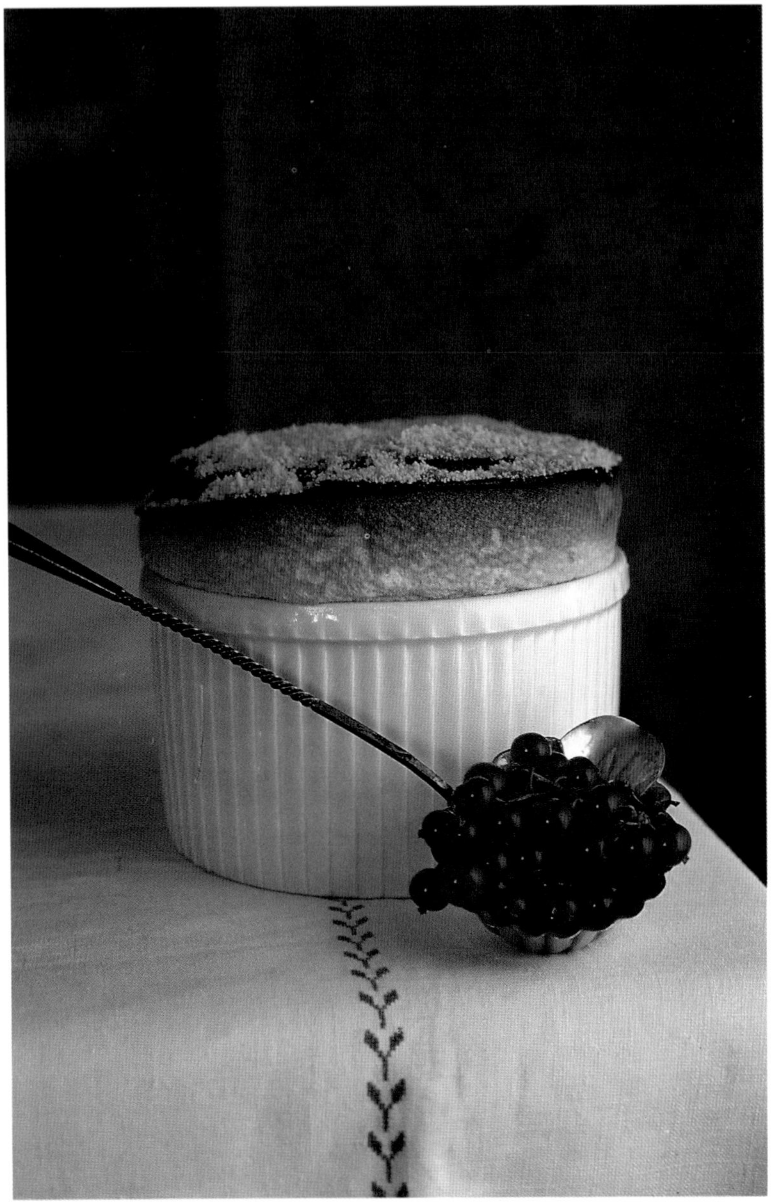

A delicate soufflé captures the taste of summer fruits.

SOUFFLÉ AUX CONFITURES

APRICOT JAM AND ALMOND SOUFFLÉ WITH REDCURRANT SAUCE

The Marquise de Virieu's soufflé, layered with apricot jam and served with a redcurrant sauce, recalls the luscious summer harvest of Dauphiné fruits. Made without milk or flour, it's exceptionally light. You can vary the recipe, if you like, by using a different jam – perhaps peach, strawberry or cherry. This dessert is endlessly flexible as other flavours of seedless jam or jelly such as apricot can be used for the sauce too.

4 servings

150 g/5 oz APRICOT JAM
2 to 3 tbsp WATER
3 EGGS, SEPARATED
75 g/2$\frac{1}{2}$ oz CASTER SUGAR
1 EGG WHITE
PINCH OF SALT
2 tbsp GROUND ALMONDS

For the redcurrant sauce
100 g/3$\frac{1}{4}$ oz REDCURRANT JELLY
2 to 3 tbsp WATER

1 LITRE/2 PINT SOUFFLÉ DISH

Heat the oven to 180°C/350°F/Gas Mark 4. Generously butter the soufflé dish. Put the dish in the freezer until the butter is firm, then butter it again.

Thin the apricot jam so it is pourable by heating it with the water; allow it to cool.

Whisk the egg yolks and half the sugar in a bowl by hand or with a electric mixer until the mixture falls from the whisk in a thick ribbon and it will hold a slowly dissolving trail, about 5 minutes.

Whisk the 4 egg whites with the salt until stiff. Add the remaining sugar and continue whisking until glossy to make a light meringue, about 30 seconds. Gently fold the meringue into the egg yolk mixture.

Transfer half the soufflé mixture to the prepared dish. Spoon the apricot jam over the top. Add the remaining mixture and smooth the surface with a rubber spatula. Run your thumb around the edge of the dish so the soufflé will rise in a hat shape. Bake the soufflé in the heated oven until puffed and golden, 20 to 25 minutes.

Meanwhile, make the redcurrant sauce. Melt the jelly in a small pan with the water, stirring gently until smooth.

Serve the soufflé as soon as it is baked, sprinkled with the ground almonds. Pass the redcurrant sauce separately.

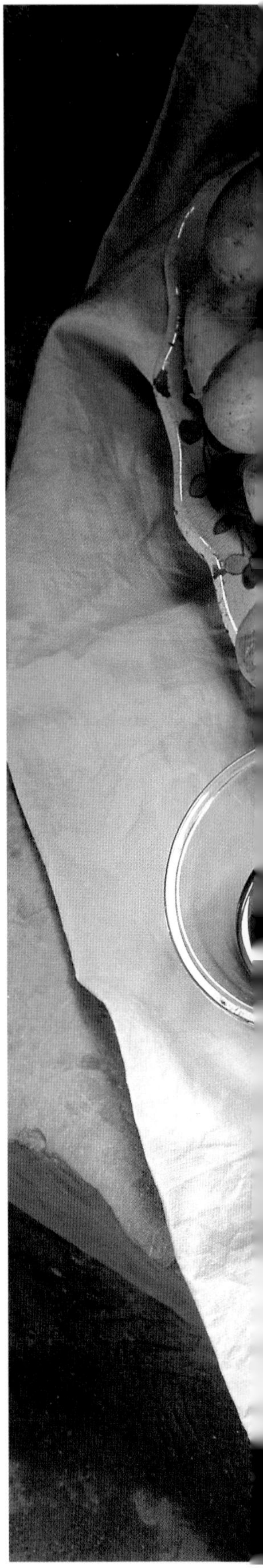

TRUFFADE

CRUSHED POTATOES WITH CHEESE

Hearty truffade *comes from a rugged patch of France, where potatoes and the dependable pig sustain body and soul during the cold winter months. In this variation from the Dauphiné, the Marquise de Virieu uses olive oil, a reminder that sunny Provence is not far away, and the local tomme, a cow's or goat's milk cheese with a musty grey rind. Cantal and Gruyère cheese are also good, especially as they authenticate the mountain origins of the dish.*

4 servings

1 × 175 g/6 oz PIECE OF SMOKED STREAKY BACON, CUT INTO *LARDONS**
2 tbsp OLIVE OIL
1 kg/2 lb POTATOES, PEELED AND THINLY SLICED
SALT AND PEPPER
250 g/8 oz TOMME, CANTAL OR GRUYÈRE CHEESE, CUT INTO THIN STRIPS

25 cm/10 in NON-STICK FRYING PAN

Heat the bacon in the frying pan, stirring, until the fat runs and the bacon is tender; do not brown it. Remove it with a slotted spoon and drain it on kitchen paper.

Add the oil to the pan and heat it. Add the potatoes and sprinkle them lightly with salt and pepper, remembering the bacon and cheese are salty. Cover and cook over low heat for 5 minutes. Return the bacon to the pan. Continue to cook, uncovered, over low heat for 20 to 30 minutes, stirring the potatoes from time to time and crushing them when they begin to soften, until very tender. Stir in the cheese until it melts into threads. Taste for seasoning.

Raise the heat to high and leave the mixture to cook for 5 to 8 minutes, without stirring, to brown the base. Press on the potato cake occasionally to hold it together. When it is golden on the base, run a spatula around it and turn it out on to a warmed platter. Serve hot.

Truffade, a satisfying dish which is a meal in itself, or try it as a superb accompaniment to Gigot Brayaude (see page 162).

Châteaux of the Sun

Chartreuse de Bonpas

The Chartreuse de Bonpas was originally a Carthusian foundation. Set on the banks of the Durance river, it was a popular rest house for travellers on the busy route from Avignon to Aix-en-Provence ('*bon pas*' means 'happy step' in French). Thick stone walls provided relief from the searing summer sun as well as protection from bandits who roamed the countryside. Apparently the food was also good, for after breaking her journey there in November 1675, the diarist Madame de Sévigné quipped that the monastery should be called '*bon repas*'. 'You will recall,' she wrote to her daughter, 'the fine repast we enjoyed there with the monks.'

Today Bonpas thrives in the hands of Jérôme and Yveline Casalis, whose family has owned it for three generations. The property is still dedicated to the production of wines and olive oil, as it was under the monks. Red and white Chartreuse de Bonpas wines, classified Côtes-du-Rhône, are exported to Britain and the United States. Olive oil production is more modest, limited to a few hundred litres a year and consumed with appreciation on the spot. 'We like to freeze a small bowl of oil so it sets almost to a jelly,' Madame Casalis told me, 'then we spread it on toast. Delicious!'

A smiling Madonna welcomes visitors to Bonpas, a haven of refuge for over 600 years. Within the grounds, shady stone gardens and cool ponds provide relief from the intense southern sun (far right).

The walls and chapel of the Chartreuse de Bonpas date back to the time of Pope John XXII in the 14th century.

Aïgo boulido, or garlic soup, is a summer favourite with the Casalis family. It is said to assuage colds and high blood pressure. To make it, heads of mild fresh garlic are simmered in salted water with some sprigs of sage, then poured over toasted *croûtes* that have been moistened with olive oil. Other summer dishes include fish terrine and *pistou*, a fresh vegetable soup with basil pesto sauce. 'We eat according to the seasons,' says Yveline Casalis. 'No hot-house tomatoes in December or melons in March for us! Just now we're bottling preserves, tomatoes, pears in syrup, and green and purple plums for tarts in the winter.'

Winter also brings a robust Provençal *pot-au-feu* with some marrow bones, flavoured with garlic, juniper and 'quantities of herbs'. Just as *bouillabaisse* is flavoured with the garlic mayonnaise, *aïoli*, so *pot-au-feu* is served with a light herb mayonnaise. To make it, Madame Casalis crushes a whole hard-boiled egg, mixes it with a raw egg yolk, a chopped shallot and 2 or 3 tablespoons of chopped fresh herbs, then whisks in a cup or so of her olive oil. The result is light and aromatic, excellent with cold or hot meats.

Add to this culinary abundance the beauties of the Lubéron landscape: picturesque villages tumbling down from pinnacled hillsides, sloping groves of grey-green olive trees and the fertile orchards of the rich Durance valley. Bonpas was built as a haven, and so it remains.

Fricot d'Artichauts de Provence

Artichokes Simmered in Olive Oil and White Wine

Little mauve artichokes the size of a child's hand are a speciality of Provence. Those in the Bonpas garden are often eaten raw, leaves and all, à la croque de sel *– with sea salt and butter. Or they may be simmered in this* fricot *or stew. Common globe artichokes, while too tough to eat uncooked, can also be used in the* fricot. *Serve these artichokes as a first course, or pair them with a meat dish that doesn't repeat the tomato theme.*

4 servings

8 BABY GLOBE ARTICHOKES OR
4 MEDIUM ARTICHOKES
1 LEMON, HALVED
4 tbsp OLIVE OIL
1 ONION, THINLY SLICED
175 ml/6 fl oz WATER, MORE IF NEEDED
1 tsp TOMATO PURÉE
500 ml/16 fl oz WHITE WINE
1 CARROT, CUT INTO JULIENNE STRIPS*
½ tsp DRIED HERBES DE PROVENCE*
SALT AND PEPPER

For baby artichokes, snap off the tough outer leaves. Trim the stalk with a stainless steel knife and cut off the tops of the remaining leaves. Cut the artichokes in half through the stalk.

While you're working, rub the cut surfaces of the artichokes with a lemon half. As you finish each artichoke, drop it into a bowl of cold water to which the juice from the remaining lemon half has been added.

For medium artichokes, break off the stalk. Using a very sharp stainless steel knife, cut off all large bottom leaves, leaving a cone of small soft leaves in the centre. Trim the base to an even round shape, slightly flattened at the base. Quarter the artichokes and cut each quarter into two wedges. Cut out the fuzzy choke, leaving the small soft leaves attached. (If the leaves are tough, cut them all away.)

Blanch* the artichokes in boiling salted water for 10 minutes, then drain them.

Heat the oil in a sauté pan and add the onion. Sauté it over moderate heat until soft, 3 to 5 minutes. Stir the water into the tomato purée. Add the tomato water, blanched artichokes, wine, carrot, herbs, salt and pepper to the pan. Bring the liquid to the boil, then reduce the heat and simmer, covered, until the artichokes are tender and the liquid is almost absorbed, ½ to 1 hour, depending on the age of the artichokes. If the pan becomes dry, add more water during cooking. Taste for seasoning. Serve warm.

Olive oil, white wine and fresh vegetables, all produced at Bonpas, come together in this Provençal stew (left). The kitchen garden is still enclosed by the monastery's original walls, with its recesses for beehives (above).

SOUPE AU PISTOU

VEGETABLE SOUP WITH GARLIC AND BASIL

The garden at Bonpas provides Yveline Casalis with fresh haricot beans for her soupe au pistou, *so she can dispense with the preliminaries of soaking and parboiling, and just simmer the beans with the other vegetables for an easy seasonal treat. (Later in the year, the dried beans must be parboiled first, as here.) In her variation of the time-honoured garlic and basil* pistou *sauce, Madame Casalis blends in tomatoes, adding a fresh bite to her base of long-simmered vegetables and beans.*

Soupe au Pistou is served throughout the year at Bonpas, using fresh or dried beans as the season dictates.

6 servings

150 g/5 oz DRIED RED KIDNEY BEANS
150 g/5 oz DRIED WHITE KIDNEY BEANS (HARICOT BEANS)
175 g/6 oz FRENCH BEANS, CUT INTO 1.25 cm/½ in PIECES
3 CARROTS, CUT INTO 1.25 cm/½ in PIECES
3 POTATOES, CUT INTO 1.25 cm/½ in PIECES
2 LITRES/3½ PINTS WATER
SALT AND PEPPER
1 MEDIUM COURGETTE, CUT INTO 1.25 cm/½ in PIECES

For the pistou
4 CLOVES GARLIC
2 TOMATOES, SKINNED AND SEEDED*
60 g/2 oz FRESH BASIL LEAVES
175 ml/6 fl oz OLIVE OIL
1 tsp SALT

Soak the dried red and white beans separately overnight in cold water; drain. Put them in separate large saucepans and cover them generously with water. Bring the water to the boil, then reduce the heat and simmer the beans until they are tender but still a little firm, 1 to 1½ hours, depending on the age of the beans. Drain the beans thoroughly.

Combine the red and white beans with all the vegetables, except the courgette, in a saucepan. Add the water and a little salt and pepper. Bring the water to the boil, then reduce the heat and simmer over low heat until the vegetables are very tender, 1¼ to 1½ hours. Add the courgette 15 minutes before the end of cooking. (The soup can be made ahead to this point and refrigerated for up to 2 days.)

To make the *pistou*, purée the garlic, tomatoes, basil, oil and salt in a food processor or blender until smooth. Taste it for seasoning.

Reheat the soup if necessary and stir in the *pistou*. Taste the soup for seasoning and add salt and pepper if needed. Ladle the soup into warmed soup bowls.

VIN D'ORANGE

FORTIFIED ORANGE WINE

Yveline Casalis always has bottles of home-made orange wine on hand to offer as an aperitif to friends. At the end of July following the peach harvest, she also prepares a vin de pêche, *made with the peach tree leaves. Forty is the magic number associated with that fortified wine – Madame Casalis computes 40 peach leaves and 40 sugar cubes for every litre of wine and half-litre of eau-de-vie. Leave this brew to macerate for 40 days and –* voilà! . . . *perfection.*

Makes about 2 litres/3½ pints

1.5 LITRES/2½ PINTS WHITE WINE
250 ml/8 fl oz NEUTRAL EAU-DE-VIE OR VODKA
200 g/6½ oz CASTER SUGAR
1 LEMON, SLICED
2 ORANGES, SLICED
A STRIP OF DRIED BITTER ORANGE PEEL
½ STICK OF CINNAMON

2.5 LITRE/4 PINT PRESERVING JAR

Sterilize the preserving jar*. Combine the wine, eau-de-vie or vodka and sugar in the jar and seal it. Leave it in a cool place overnight, shaking the jar thoroughly from time to time or as often as possible during this period.

The next day, add the lemon, oranges, orange peel and cinnamon to the jar. Seal the jar again and leave it for at least 6 weeks, shaking it once a week.

Strain the liquid through muslin into a jug. Pour the liquid back into the jar or into four wine bottles and seal.

This wine can be kept for 3 or 4 months, stored in a cool, dark place. It is best enjoyed served well chilled.

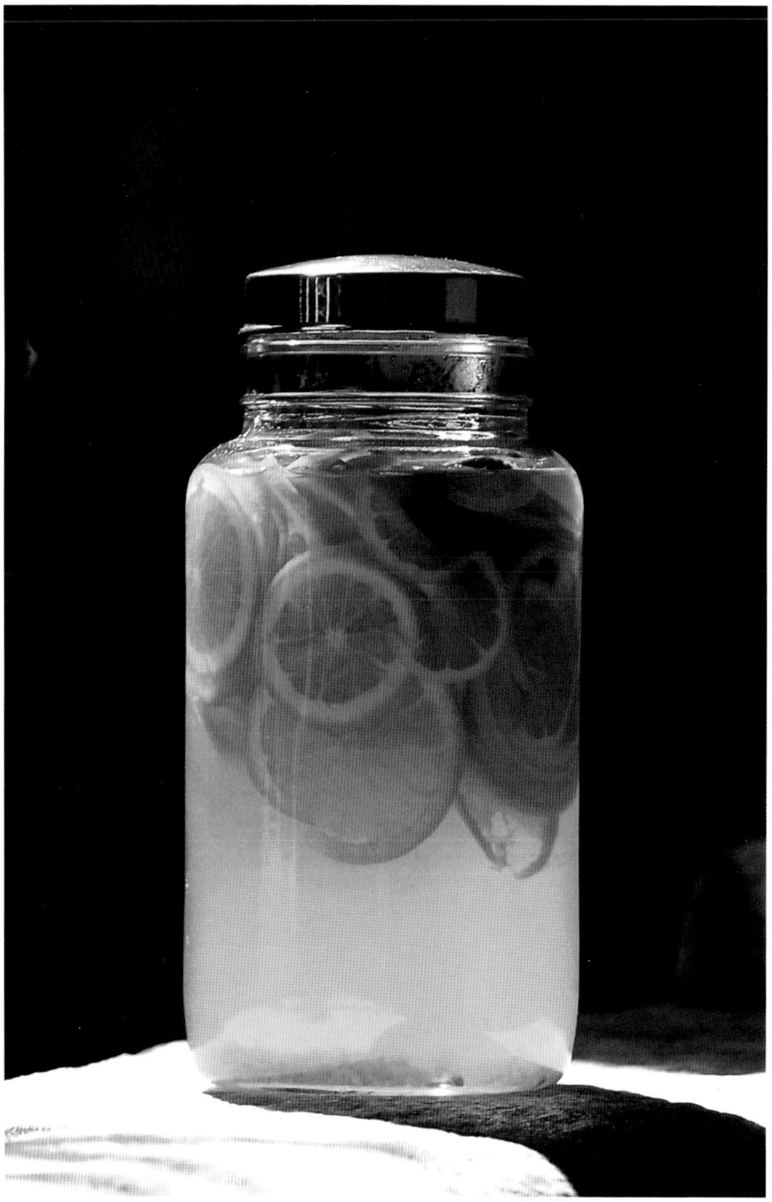

NOUGAT NOIR

HONEY AND ALMOND NOUGAT

Christmas is a great celebration in the Casalis household, with Provençal customs such as the 13 desserts of Christmas followed with enthusiasm. Desserts are likely to include dried figs, raisins and sultanas, stuffed dates and walnuts, almonds, calissons *(almond paste diamonds), glacé melon, clementines,* oreillettes *(pastry fritters), white nougat and this black nougat, a confection of caramelized honey and toasted almonds.*

Makes about 500 g/1 lb

250 g/8 oz HONEY
250 g/8 oz WHOLE UNBLANCHED ALMONDS
GRATED ZEST OF 1 ORANGE

2× 23×12.5×10 cm/9×5×4 in LOAF TINS; RICE PAPER OR NON-STICK SILICONE PAPER

Oil one loaf tin and line the bottom with rice paper or with non-stick silicone paper.

Have ready a basin of cold water. Put the honey in a heavy saucepan and cook over fairly low heat, stirring constantly, until the honey begins to bubble, about 5 minutes. Add the almonds and orange zest and continue to stir for about 15 minutes until the honey turns deep brown and the almonds make a popping sound, showing they are toasted.

Remove the pan from the heat and plunge the base briefly in the basin of cold water to stop the honey from cooking further. Stir until the nougat cools slightly, about 1 minute, then spoon it into the prepared loaf tin. Flatten the nougat with the back of an oiled spoon. Press a piece of rice paper or non-stick silicone paper the size of the inside of the tin on top. Flatten the nougat with the second loaf tin and cans of food or other weights. Refrigerate until firm, about 4 hours.

Peel off silicone paper, but leave on rice paper. Cut the nougat into 2.5 cm/1 in squares. This nougat will keep for several weeks in an airtight container.

Madame Casalis' orange wine is served as part of the Christmas festivities, a reminder of Mediterranean summer sun.

CHÂTEAU DE SAINT-VINCENT

'A PINE FOREST GLITTERING WITH SUNLIGHT, CASCADING DOWN THE HILLSIDE BEFORE MY VERY EYES. ON THE HORIZON, THE MOUNTAINOUS OUTLINE OF THE ALPILLES . . . NOT A MURMUR, YET FAINTLY, EVER SO FAR AWAY, THE PIPING OF A FLUTE, THE CALL OF A CURLEW IN THE LAVENDER, A TINKLE OF MULE BELLS ON THE ROAD. THIS BEAUTIFUL LANDSCAPE OF PROVENCE LIVES BY THE LIGHT OF THE SUN.' SO WROTE THE NOVELIST ALPHONSE DAUDET SHORTLY AFTER HIS FIVE-MONTH STAY AT JONQUIÈRES-SAINT-VINCENT DURING 1866.

THE CHÂTEAU DE SAINT-VINCENT REMAINS UNCHANGED FROM HIS TIME. ITS GOLDEN SANDSTONE TOWERS, VERY PROVENÇAL IN STYLE, STILL GREET THE VISITOR. 'SAINT-VINCENT IS A HOUSE OF MANY FACES,' EXPLAIN ITS CURRENT OWNERS, THE COMTE AND COMTESSE JEAN DE DEMANDOLX-DEDONS. BEHIND THE 18TH-CENTURY FAÇADE IS HIDDEN THE TRADITIONAL CLOSED COURTYARD, WHOSE CELLARS ARE NOW USED FOR STORING WINE AND AS A *CAVEAU DE DÉGUSTATION*. 'THE FOUNDATIONS PROBABLY DATE BACK TO THE 13TH CENTURY,' SAYS CHANTAL DE DEMANDOLX-DEDONS. 'WE KNOW THAT IN THE 17TH CENTURY THERE WAS ALREADY A SUBSTANTIAL PROVENÇAL *MAS*, OR COUNTRY HOUSE, HERE. YOU CAN SEE THE DATE ON THE LINTEL OVER THE DOOR.'

The Provençal property of Saint Vincent has always been primarily a working farm. The buildings have been modified over the centuries with the earliest dating back to the 1400s and the latest being the gracious 18th-century main house (left). The glass covering the ancient map of the property reflects the sunny gardens (below).

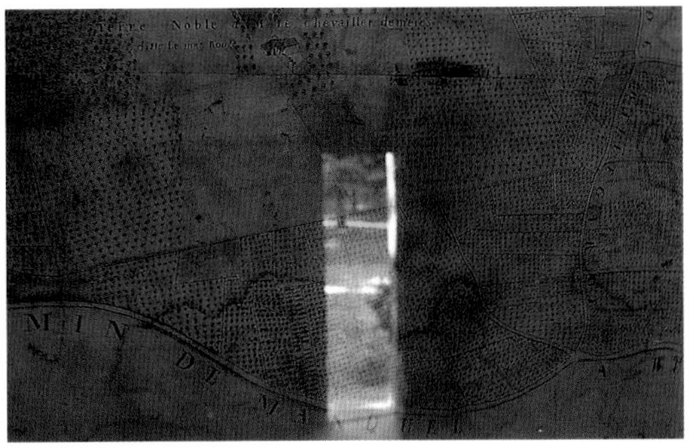

Now, as then, Saint-Vincent remains a flourishing agricultural property, though in extent it is reduced to about 40 hectares of vines and cherries, a fraction of the 18th-century domain. The sun so appreciated by Daudet ripens fruit in record time, so that the Muscat table grapes of Saint-Vincent – the prized Hambourg variety – reach the market the first week in August. At the other extreme of the season, in January, the village marks the festival of Saint-Vincent with the usual mass in a chilly 12th-century chapel, followed by a rather more enjoyable lunch which lasts five hours – because, I was told, the congregation mainly comprises local winemakers, who gather together in honour of their patron saint and sample their produce.

The robust red and rosé wines made around Jonquières-Saint-Vincent are classified 'Costières de Nîmes'. One might describe them as like the wines of Côtes-du-Rhône, but less famous. Likewise the countryside. Just over the Rhône in the Lubéron, second homes abound and tourists proliferate. Here in the Gard, the scene is much as Daudet found it – silent, sunbaked, its own land.

Cherry time – the bright red 'Burlat' variety grows on the estate and is harvested by migrant workers who come from Algeria every year (right and below).

Firm, juicy cherries are essential for Les Cerises Saint-Vincent so that they keep their shape during cooking.

Les Cerises Saint-Vincent

Cherries Flamed with Kirsch

At the Château de Saint-Vincent, May ends in a flurry of activity. The cherry trees begin to droop under the weight of their fruit, and cherry pickers, here for the harvest, work at a feverish pace to gather the ripe Burlat cherries at their peak. The crisp-textured Burlats are perfect for this recipe because they are simmered briefly, before redcurrant jelly and kirsch are added, but hold their shape well. Juicy cherries and best-quality jelly make all the difference in this dessert. Serve it with vanilla ice cream and you have a cousin to cherries jubilee.

4 servings

1 kg/2 lb CHERRIES, STONED
500 ml/16 fl oz WATER
2 tbsp SUGAR, MORE IF NEEDED
300 g/10 oz REDCURRANT JELLY
4 tbsp KIRSCH OR BRANDY

Combine the cherries, water and sugar in a large frying pan. Add more sugar if the cherries are sour. Bring to the boil, then reduce the heat and simmer, stirring occasionally, until the cherries are just tender, about 5 minutes.

Remove the pan from the heat and stir in the redcurrant jelly until melted. Allow the cherries to cool to lukewarm.

Heat the kirsch or brandy in a small saucepan for 20 or 30 seconds. Tip the pan and light the spirit with a match. (Stand back from the flame.) Pour it flaming over the cherries. Stir lightly to mix and serve at once.

Bourride, the traditional Mediterranean fish stew is a celebration of Provençal flavours from land and sea.

BOURRIDE

MEDITERRANEAN FISH STEW WITH GARLIC MAYONNAISE

Less famous than its colourful cousin bouillabaisse, bourride *is a white fish stew, always served with the garlic mayonnaise* aïoli. *It is native to western Provence and Languedoc, where fishmongers sell a mixture 'for* bourride' *without bothering to detail the different fish. A good* bourride *should contain some white fish such as sea bass, bream, John Dory and whiting, some firm fish like monkfish and conger eel, and some richer fish such as mackerel. On the Mediterranean, the bony but full-flavoured scorpion fish, or* rascasse, *is always included but it is hard to find elsewhere. Serve the stew with crusty bread for mopping up the wonderful sauce.*

8 to 10 servings

1.8 kg/4 lb SALT-WATER FISH, CLEANED, TRIMMED AND CUT INTO THICK STEAKS, WITH THE BONE
1 ONION, SLICED
½ BULB FENNEL, SLICED
A SPRIG OF FRESH THYME
1 BAY LEAF
A PARED STRIP OF ORANGE ZEST
SALT AND PEPPER
1 LITRE/1¾ PINTS WATER, MORE IF NEEDED
6 EGG YOLKS

For the aïoli
6 TO 8 CLOVES GARLIC
2 EGG YOLKS
SALT AND WHITE PEPPER
250 ml/8 fl oz OLIVE OIL
JUICE OF 1 LEMON
1 tsp LUKEWARM WATER

For the *aïoli*, purée the garlic, egg yolks and seasoning in a food processor or blender. With the blades still turning, add the oil in a thin stream. Add the lemon juice and water at the end. Season if needed. (*Aïoli* can be made 3 days ahead and kept refrigerated.)

Prepare the fish up to 4 hours ahead, if you like, and keep it in the refrigerator. However, cook the *bourride* only just before serving.

Pack the firm fish, onion, fennel, thyme, bay leaf, orange zest, salt and pepper in a large saucepan and add the water. Bring the water to the boil, then simmer briskly for 5 minutes. Add the remaining fish, putting the more delicate, tender pieces on top. The water should just cover the fish so add more if needed. Simmer until the fish just flakes easily, 8 to 12 minutes.

Transfer the fish to a platter and, if you like, remove the bones and skin. Cover with foil and keep it warm. Strain the broth and keep it hot.

Whisk the *aïoli* with the egg yolks in a heavy

saucepan. Gradually whisk in the hot broth. Set the pan over low heat and stir constantly until the sauce thickens to the consistency of thin cream. (The heat of the mixture will cook and thicken the egg yolks. Don't boil the sauce or it may curdle.) Taste it for seasoning.

To serve, divide the fish among warmed shallow bowls. Ladle the sauce on top and serve.

GRATIN DE COURGETTES

GOLDEN COURGETTE GRATIN

For Chantal de Demandolx-Dedons, Pentecost brings a stream of visitors for the fériade *in Nîmes – the annual festivities inspired by a week of bullfights here – as does the summer music festival at Aix-en-Provence. She looks towards cold dishes, terrines, baked fish, little* tellines *or cockles steamed open with garlic, and this gratin of courgettes, which can be served hot or cold.*

6 servings

1.4 kg/3 lb COURGETTES, GRATED
SALT AND PEPPER
4 tbsp OLIVE OIL
2 LARGE ONIONS, CHOPPED
125 ml/4 fl oz CHICKEN STOCK (see page 221)
2 CLOVES GARLIC, POUNDED TO A PASTE
125 ml/4 fl oz CRÈME FRAÎCHE*
OR DOUBLE CREAM
100 g/3½ oz GRUYÈRE CHEESE, GRATED

2 LITRE/3½ PINT GRATIN OR BAKING DISH

Pack a layer of grated courgette in a colander set over a bowl and sprinkle it generously with salt. Continue layering courgettes and salt until all the courgettes are in the colander, pressing well. Leave for 30 minutes, then rinse and squeeze out all the liquid by handfuls.

Heat the oven to 190°C/375°F/Gas Mark 5 and butter the gratin dish.

Heat half the oil in a large frying pan and add the onions. Sauté them over moderate heat until soft, 6 to 8 minutes, then remove. Add the remaining oil to the pan and sauté the courgettes in batches over high heat, tossing and stirring constantly, until just tender, 2 to 3 minutes. Add all the courgettes to the pan with the onions and pepper. Stir the stock into the garlic paste, then add it to the courgettes. Cook over high heat, stirring often, until the liquid evaporates, 3 to 4 minutes. Stir in the crème fraîche or cream. Taste for seasoning.

Transfer the courgette mixture to the prepared dish. Smooth the top and sprinkle over the cheese. Bake the gratin in the heated oven until hot and golden, 15 to 20 minutes.

'Drippings' from the wine-making process are collected and stored in wooden casks, and eventually transformed into vinegar (above). Tradition is very much alive in Jonquières with Provençal songs, processions and a lively celebration of the feast of Saint-Vincent, patron saint of vignerons, held in January every year. Local wines, of course, are sampled (below left).

CHÂTEAU DE FLAUGERGUES

THE CHÂTEAU DE FLAUGERGUES WAS BUILT AS A *FOLIE*, A WORD THAT IN FRENCH ALSO CARRIES A HINT OF LEAFY FOLIAGE. AT THE TURN OF THE 17TH CENTURY, THE WEALTHY FINANCIERS OF MONTPELLIER BUILT A STRING OF SUCH WOODED COUNTRY RETREATS, WHERE THEY COULD ESCAPE FROM THE BUSTLE AND HEAT OF THE TOWN. DATING FROM 1696, FLAUGERGUES IS ONE OF THE FIRST AND MOST BEAUTIFUL OF THESE HOUSES, AND HAS REMAINED SINCE THE BEGINNING WITH DESCENDANTS OF ITS CREATOR, ETIENNE DE FLAUGERGUES.

'WHEN MY HUSBAND INHERITED FLAUGERGUES IN 1973,' SAYS BRIGITTE DE COLBERT, 'WE HAD LITTLE IDEA HOW MUCH WORK WOULD BE INVOLVED. BUT WE WERE LUCKY, WE WERE YOUNG — I WAS SCARCELY 30. I SUPPOSE YOU COULD SAY IT WAS OUR PERSONAL FOLLY. BUT WE'VE NEVER REGRETTED IT.' SHE HERSELF OVERSAW THE RESTORATION OF THE INTERIOR, WITH ITS ANTIQUE CARPETS AND FURNITURE AND NOTABLE COLLECTION OF PAINTINGS. THE WORK DONE IN ONE OF THE BEDROOMS, COMPLETED WITH WALL HANGINGS FEATURING THE TREE OF LIFE, HAS RECENTLY WON A RESTORATION AWARD. WHEN THE MAYOR OF MONTPELLIER ENTERTAINS VIPS, A VISIT TO THE CHÂTEAU DE FLAUGERGUES IS OFTEN PART OF THE PROGRAMME.

Italianate in style, the cream stone walls of the Château de Flaugergues rise proudly above a classic balustraded terrace. From the windows a splendid view stretches over the city of Montpellier to the sea. Housing has engulfed the vineyards to the south of the estate, but the château and grounds are now protected as an historic monument.

A glimpse of the superb staircase with its wrought-iron balustrade and vaulted stonework hung with Brussels tapestries (above). The salon with elegant 18th-century furniture (right).

Flaugergues is a wine property of some 40 hectares, and the Colberts at once embarked on a programme of modernisation. Two old-master paintings were sold to the Louvre to finance equipment so that the wine could be bottled in the château cellars instead of being sold in bulk. Gradually all the old vines were replaced, until in 1990 the vineyard won *appellation d'origine contrôlée* status as 'Coteaux du Languedoc' from the Méjanelle district. Now the Colbert wines are distributed in the United States and Germany, with sales in the rest of the European Community in prospect. 'Always better than yesterday, but not as good as tomorrow', is Comte Henri de Colbert's motto. To develop local tourism, he finally won recognition for a signposted '*route historique*' which takes the traveller past the finest châteaux and abbeys of Languedoc-Roussillon.

The garden of Flaugergues had been randomly planted with trees by an overzealous 19th-century châtelain, so the Colberts enlisted the help of their four children to recreate the original formal plans, using 10,000 wild box plants culled from the *garrigues* or scrub which carpets the Languedoc hillsides.

Olive trees are equally native, and Brigitte de Colbert pickles the green fruit each year, soaking them overnight in a concentrated brine – 'It's not easy to find the right balance of salt,' she says. 'If it is too strong, the olives "scorch".' Then they must be rinsed with water twice a day for two weeks before being ready to eat. Locals like to add garlic or some of the *garrigues* herbs such as thyme and rosemary, but the Comtesse leaves hers plain. She makes quince compote too, and lemon jam, all from her own trees. Undaunted by the sight of Montpellier's high-rise buildings on the horizon, Brigitte de Colbert reminds me that 'Flaugergues is an agricultural property and we are determined to keep it so'.

COQ AU VIN ROUGE DE FLAUGERGUES

CHICKEN IN LANGUEDOC WINE

The mayor of Montpellier sometimes asks the de Colberts to entertain foreign guests. The Comtesse finds that traditional recipes like blanquette de veau *(see page 129) and* coq au vin *made with their own wine are particularly appreciated.*

4 servings

1 × 1.8 kg/4 lb OVEN-READY CHICKEN, JOINTED INTO SERVING PIECES*
1 CARROT, CHOPPED
1 ONION, CHOPPED
2 SHALLOTS, CHOPPED
1 CLOVE GARLIC, CHOPPED
A LARGE BUNCH OF PARSLEY, TIED WITH STRING
1 BOTTLE (750 ml/$1\frac{1}{4}$ PINTS) ROBUST RED WINE
2 tbsp RED WINE VINEGAR
3 tbsp VEGETABLE OIL
45 g/$1\frac{1}{2}$ oz PLAIN FLOUR
750 ml/$1\frac{1}{4}$ PINTS BROWN STOCK (see page 221)
SALT AND PEPPER

For the garnish
150 g/5 oz BABY ONIONS
45 g/$1\frac{1}{2}$ oz BUTTER
PINCH OF SUGAR
175 g/6 oz SMALL MUSHROOMS, QUARTERED
1 × 150 g/5 oz PIECE OF STREAKY BACON, CUT INTO *LARDONS**

The south-facing gravelly slopes are said to be the secret to the flavoursome wines of Flaugergues (above).

Combine the chicken pieces, carrot, onion, shallots, garlic, parsley, wine and vinegar in a large bowl (not aluminium). Cover and keep in the refrigerator overnight.

Lift the chicken pieces out of the marinade and pat them dry with kitchen paper. Heat the oil in a sauté pan or flameproof casserole. Brown the pieces of chicken a few at a time over moderate heat. Transfer the marinade vegetables to the pan, using a slotted spoon. Sprinkle the flour over the chicken and vegetables and cook until foaming, 2 or 3 minutes. Stir in the marinade liquid and the stock and bring to the boil. Add the parsley. Reduce the heat to low and simmer, covered, until the chicken is tender, about 40 minutes.

Meanwhile, for the garnish, blanch* the onions in a saucepan of boiling water for 1 minute, then drain and peel them – the skins will strip away easily. Trim the roots and stalks of the onions carefully so they will not fall apart during cooking. Put the onions back in the saucepan and add salt, pepper, one-third of the butter, the sugar and water barely to cover. Bring to the boil and simmer for 10 to 15 minutes until the onions are tender and the liquid has evaporated to a shiny glaze.

Melt the remaining butter in a frying pan. Add the mushrooms with salt and pepper. Toss them in the butter over moderately high heat until they lose all their moisture, about 5 minutes. Remove them from the pan. Fry the bacon gently in the pan until the fat runs, then cook until golden, about 5 minutes. Drain on kitchen paper.

Transfer the chicken to a warmed serving dish and keep warm. If the sauce is thin, boil it until it lightly coats a spoon; strain it and taste for seasoning. Stir the onions, mushrooms and bacon into the sauce and taste for seasoning. Pour the sauce over the chicken and serve.

PAUPIETTES DE DORADE COLBERT

ROLLED FISH FILLETS WITH SMOKED SALMON AND PRAWNS

'I do all the cooking,' says Brigitte de Colbert, 'and I like to experiment – paupiettes Colbert *was one of my new recipes this year.'*

6 servings as a first course, 3 as a main course

150 g/5 oz THINLY SLICED SMOKED SALMON
60 g/2 oz UNSALTED BUTTER
6 EVEN-SIZED SKINLESS FISH FILLETS (750 g/1½ lb TOTAL WEIGHT)
PEPPER
375 g/12 oz COOKED PRAWNS, PEELED
1 BOTTLE (750 ml/1¼ PINTS) DRY WHITE WINE
2 tsp ARROWROOT OR POTATO STARCH MIXED TO A PASTE WITH
2 tbsp COLD WATER
3 EGG YOLKS
125 ml/4 fl oz CRÈME FRAÎCHE* OR DOUBLE CREAM
2 tbsp CHOPPED PARSLEY

KITCHEN STRING

Purée half the smoked salmon in a food processor until smooth. Work in the butter.

Place a fish fillet in between two sheets of greaseproof paper and pound it lightly with the flat of a large knife. With the tip of a knife, score the fillet lightly in parallel diagonal lines on the side that has been skinned. Repeat with the remaining fillets.

Sprinkle the skinned side of each fillet with pepper and spread it with the salmon butter. Cut the remaining smoked salmon into thin strips. On each fillet, arrange strips of smoked salmon and 3 or 4 prawns. Set a fillet on a piece of greaseproof paper 5 cm/2 in larger than the fillet. Using the paper to help and starting with a long side, roll up the fillet into a long roll. Wrap it in the paper and tie the ends with string. Repeat with the remaining fillets.

Pack the fish rolls tightly in a frying pan. Add the wine and press a piece of foil on top. Bring the wine just to a simmer, then lower the heat and poach the fish just until firm and opaque, 3 to 4 minutes. Transfer the fish rolls to a platter. Keep the fish warm while making the sauce.

Strain the cooking liquid into a saucepan. Bring it to the boil, then simmer until it reduces by two-thirds, to about 250 ml/8 fl oz. Whisk the arrowroot or potato starch mixture into the simmering cooking liquid; it will thicken at once. (Add just enough paste to thicken the liquid lightly.) Mix together the egg yolks and cream. Whisk in a little of the hot cooking liquid and stir this back into the rest. Heat gently, stirring, but do not boil. (The heat will cook and thicken the egg yolks but if overcooked they will curdle.) Whisk in the parsley and remaining prawns. Season.

Remove the paper from the fish rolls and cut each one in half on the diagonal. Arrange the paupiettes on warmed plates and coat with the sauce. Serve the remaining sauce separately.

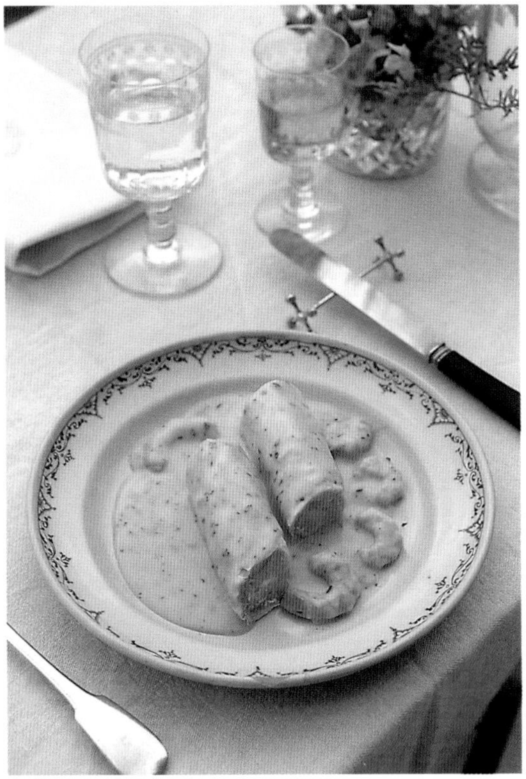

For these stuffed fish rolls, the Comtesse de Colbert favours bream, but any firm white fish such as sole or turbot will do. With the fish, she often serves a rice pilaf.

The Colberts grow their own lemons for this jam. Frost is too frequent in Languedoc for citrus trees to grow outside, so at Flaugergues they are planted in tubs and brought into the greenhouse between All Saints' Day and Easter.

Confiture de Citrons

Lemon Jam

Brigitte de Colbert preserves some of her lemon harvest by making this confiture de citrons *to savour year-round. Somewhat sweeter than lemon curd, the golden jam is a delicious condiment for rich meats like pork and duck, as well as a good spread for breakfast toast.*

Makes about 1.5 litres/2½ pints

2 kg/4½ lb LEMONS
600 ml/1 PINT WATER
1.5 kg/3¼ lb SUGAR

6 PRESERVING JARS (250 ml/8 fl oz EACH)

Scrub the lemons. Cut off the ends and discard them. Cut the lemons into very thin slices. Remove the pips and tie them in a muslin bag. Put the lemon slices and bag of pips in a preserving pan and add enough cold water to cover. Leave to stand overnight.

The next day, bring the lemons and water to the boil. Remove from the heat and leave to stand overnight.

On the third day, drain the lemons and return them to the pan. Add fresh water to cover and again bring the mixture to the boil. Cook the lemons until the peel is tender enough to cut with a spoon. Drain the lemons and set aside.

Heat the measured water and the sugar in the pan, stirring occasionally, until the sugar dissolves, then boil for 5 minutes. Add the lemons and bag of pips and boil as fast as possible for about 40 minutes, stirring from time to time, until setting point is reached. A sugar thermometer should register 105°C/220°F. At this temperature, the jam falls from a spoon in a characteristic 'sheet' of drips. Alternatively, remove the pan from the heat, pour a few drops of jam on to a cold saucer and wait for a moment to see if the drops begin to set. Push them with your finger – if setting point has been reached, the surface of the jam will wrinkle.

Remove the pan from the heat and discard the bag of lemon pips. Allow the jam to cool slightly before pouring it into sterilized jars*. Seal the jars and store in a cool place.

Château de Malle

With its manicured lawns, sleek tiled roofs and hectares of disciplined vines, the Château de Malle radiates the care of a dedicated owner. The Comtesse de Bournazel continues the far-sighted plans begun by her late husband Pierre de Bournazel, always following the strict budgeting needed for a great wine property to flourish. The Château de Malle has long been one of the finest growths of the Sauternes district, besides enjoying one of the most beautiful settings in the entire Bordeaux region.

The château itself was built in the early 17th century by an ancestor, Jacques de Malle. Here is the classic design of the time — the central pavilion flanked by towers, the grand staircase and pedimented façade, in perfectly balanced proportions — without any hint of overwhelming grandeur. For the Château de Malle was conceived as a working agricultural property, and so it remains. The interior *boiseries* and furnishings, striking as they may be, have always come second to the real wealth of the estate, which is in its vineyards, farm buildings and wine cellars.

It was in this courtyard, in March 1814, that the Duke of Wellington camped overnight with his troops. Léontine de Lur-Saluces, an ancestor of the present Comtesse de Bournazel, was aged four at the time and clearly recalled the formidable commander taking her on his lap in a rare moment of relaxation. The château is built in a horseshoe shape, with two wings spanning out from the central pavilion, each ending in a round tower.

Château de Malle is a wine estate with a difference – its 25-hectare vineyard spans two wine areas, so the property produces not only the famous sweet white of Sauternes but also the more traditional red and dry white wines of the Graves district. Nancy de Bournazel likes to cook with them all, adding red wine to game dishes, and Sauternes to fish and fruit punch. Her favourite fruit salad combines strawberries, raspberries, melon, grapefruit and fresh pineapple – 'never apple or banana', she decrees – macerated in Sauternes, then piled in a bowl with overlapping slices of kiwi fruit around the edge. 'Kiwi has become almost a local fruit now,' she tells me.

Châtelaine as well as businesswoman, entertaining is a way of life for Nancy de Bournazel. She is Vice-Grand-Maître of the Commanderie du Bontemps de Sauternes et Barsac, one of the exclusive gastronomic clubs of the Bordeaux region. The yearly feast to celebrate the wine harvest is often held at Château de Malle, bringing as many as 500 'commanders' from all over the world. Last year featured a menu timeless in its simplicity – a salad of lobster and langoustine, salmon fillet, and a rack of lamb with spring vegetables – the better to display the half-dozen prestigious Bordeaux vintages that accompanied it.

FILETS DE SOLE AU SAUTERNES

POACHED SOLE WITH SAUTERNES WINE SAUCE

It may seem a pity to use a great Sauternes such as Château de Malle for cooking, but vignerons *have their privileges, and Nancy de Bournazel does not hesitate to open a bottle and use it to simmer fillets of sole as in this recipe.*

6 servings as a main course,
8 to 10 as a first course

45 g/1½ oz BUTTER
3 SHALLOTS, FINELY CHOPPED
250 g/8 oz MUSHROOMS, FINELY CHOPPED
SALT AND PEPPER
PINCH OF GRATED NUTMEG
750 g/1½ lb SKINLESS DOVER SOLE FILLETS
1 BOTTLE (750 ml/1¼ PINTS) SWEET WHITE WINE
4 EGG YOLKS
250 ml/8 fl oz CRÈME FRAÎCHE* OR DOUBLE CREAM

Melt the butter in a saucepan. Add the shallots and cook over moderate heat until golden, 3 to 5 minutes. Add the mushrooms, salt, pepper and nutmeg. Sauté until the mushrooms lose all their moisture, about 5 minutes.

Place a fish fillet in between two sheets of greaseproof paper and pound it lightly with the flat of a large knife. With the tip of a knife, score the fillet lightly in parallel diagonal lines on the side that has been skinned. Repeat with the remaining fillets. Season the skinned side of each fillet, and spread it with mushroom mixture. Fold it in half, mushrooms inside and tail on top.

The taste of a slightly sweet sauce with fish is unexpected but seems to please everyone who tries Filets de Sole au Sauternes. With it, serve tender spinach sautéed in butter.

Butter a large frying pan or flameproof baking dish. Arrange the fish in the pan, slightly overlapping if necessary, and pour in the wine. Press a piece of buttered foil on top. Bring the wine just to a simmer, then lower the heat and poach the fish just until it is firm and opaque, 3 to 5 minutes. Transfer the fish to a platter and keep it warm while preparing the sauce.

Strain the cooking liquid into a saucepan. Bring to the boil, then simmer until reduced by half. To thicken the sauce, mix together the egg yolks and crème fraîche or cream. Whisk in a little of the hot cooking liquid and stir this back into the rest. Heat gently, stirring, but do not boil. (The heat will cook and thicken the egg yolks but if overcooked they will curdle.) Season.

Arrange the fish on warmed plates and spoon the sauce over it.

CANARD A LA BOURNAZEL

DUCK WITH PEACHES

There is a secret to the moistness of this duck – double cooking. Giselle, the cook at Château de Malle, begins by steaming the duck, a gentle cooking process that keeps the meat tender, while basting it with the melting fat. She completes the process by roasting the duck in a hot oven so the skin becomes lightly browned. For serving, a simple gravy is suggested along with poached peach halves sautéed in butter. As an accompaniment, serve a golden courgette gratin (see page 189) or straw potatoes.

6 servings

2 LITRES/3½ PINTS WATER
2 OVEN-READY DUCKLINGS (ABOUT 2 kg/4 to 5 lb EACH), WITH GIBLETS
SALT AND PEPPER
1 kg/2 lb PEACHES
1 ONION, QUARTERED
500 ml/16 fl oz BROWN STOCK (see page 221)
60 g/2 oz BUTTER

LARGE PAN OR DOUBLE-TIERED STEAMER, TRUSSING NEEDLE AND STRING

Place a rack in the pan, if using. Bring the water to the boil in the pan or steamer. Remove the fat from inside the ducklings. Cut off the wing tips and reserve. Season the cavities of the ducklings with salt and pepper. Truss the birds* and prick the skin so the fat can escape during cooking. Lower the birds on to the rack in the pan or steamer. Cover and steam for 30 minutes.

Meanwhile, heat the oven to 200°C/400°F/Gas Mark 6. Peel the peaches by immersing them whole in boiling water, leaving them for 10 to 30 seconds, depending on the ripeness of the fruit, and then transferring briefly to iced water. Run a knife around the peaches, following the natural division. Twist the halves and remove the stone. With a knife, gently peel the skin from the flesh. Set the peaches aside.

Lift the ducklings from the pan, transfer them to abundant kitchen paper and pat dry. Set the birds in a roasting tin and surround with the wing tips, necks, gizzards and onion. Roast in the heated oven for 20 to 30 minutes, basting often, until the skin is golden and the juice from the centre of the birds runs pink when they are lifted on a two-pronged fork. The birds will be medium rare. If you prefer the meat well done, continue roasting for 10 to 15 minutes longer. Transfer the birds to a carving board, cover with foil and leave to rest for 15 minutes.

To make a gravy, pour all the fat from the tin, leaving the cooking juices. Add the chopped ducks' livers, and stock and bring to the boil, scraping to dissolve the browned cooking juices. Simmer to concentrate the flavour until the gravy coats a spoon, 10 to 15 minutes.

Meanwhile, cook the peaches. Melt the butter in a frying pan. Add the peach halves, salt and pepper and sauté them for 5 to 7 minutes, turning often, until they are very hot.

To finish, remove the string from the ducklings and set them on a warmed platter. Arrange the peaches around the birds. Strain the gravy and check the seasoning. Add more salt and pepper if necessary. Carve the ducklings at the table and serve the gravy separately.

At Château de Malle, a glass of home-produced Sauternes is the natural accompaniment to Canard à la Bournazel.

CHÂTEAU D'URTUBIE

THE ROBUST WALLS, SLATE-ROOFED TURRETS AND RUSTIC SHUTTERS OF THE CHÂTEAU D'URTUBIE ARE SAID TO HOUSE A GHOST, OWING TO A 12TH-CENTURY '*CRIME PASSIONNEL*'. AT THAT TIME THE CHÂTEAU WAS OCCUPIED BY JEAN MONTRÉAL AND HIS WIFE, MARIE. JEAN MADE OFF TO THE COURT OF KING LOUIS XI WHERE HE REMAINED FOR 30 YEARS. DESERTED AND DEPENDENT, POOR MARIE TOOK A YEOMAN AS HER HUSBAND. WHEN JEAN EVENTUALLY RETURNED TO CLAIM BOTH WIFE AND CHÂTEAU, HE FOUND HE HAD NEITHER, SO HE TOOK HIS CASE TO THE JUDGES IN BORDEAUX. MARIE WAS THE LOSER, BUT NOT FOR LONG. IN DEFIANCE, SHE BURNED A LARGE PART OF URTUBIE TO THE GROUND, BEFORE FLEEING WITH HER SUBSTITUTE HUSBAND.

IT IS SAID THAT HER GHOST, IN THE FORM OF A WHITE GOAT, STILL HAUNTS THE CHÂTEAU. 'I REALLY DON'T KNOW,' SMILES THE CURRENT CHÂTELAINE, NICOLE DE CORAL. 'BUT I DO TAKE CARE TO AVOID THAT STAIRCASE!'

An ancient fortified château, with parts dating back to the 14th century, Urtubie is situated in the heart of Basque country. Edward III of England is said to have authorised the building of the château in 1341. The small shepherd boy (inset above) is a motif on the large stone fireplace at Urtubie. The Game Room (right) is decorated with Basque furniture and trophies collected by the Comtesse's forebears in Poitou, north of Bordeaux.

Set in France on the fringes of Spain, the Château d'Urtubie has a foot, as it were, in two nations. The Comte and Comtesse de Coral take advantage of Urtubie's unusually cosmopolitan location. The Comtesse speaks fluent Spanish and does her shopping on both sides of the frontier. 'The differences are surprising,' she says. 'The fish in Spanish Irun is excellent, but more expensive than a few kilometres away in France. In Spain I find the big green sugar melons which are unknown across the border. Also, the Spanish cherries are crisper, with more flavour, and in France cherries are sold with the stalks, but in Spain, without.'

In the summer months, Nicole de Coral is a frequent shopper, for not only do her six children bring their offspring to Urtubie, but she welcomes visitors for the night and dinner *en famille*. The cuisine is simple, and very much of the countryside. The menu might begin with a fish mousse, or a zesty *pipérade* of little green peppers, tomatoes and garlic cooked as a purée with scrambled eggs, then continue on to a farm-raised roast chicken, or tuna steaks baked in the oven and topped with a sauce of peppers, tomato and onion.

The Comtesse de Coral often crosses the frontier to buy special varieties for her authentic Basque dishes, such as Pipérade (below).

The ingredients are typically Basque. Signature of Basque cuisine is the *piment d'Espelette*, a chilli from the village of Espelette close to Urtubie. Whole, moderately hot green *piments d'Espelette* are added to a dish of spring lamb roasted with garlic and olive oil, while ground hot red chillies add an almost Mexican fire to *ttoro*, the local fish soup. To this day, in autumn, the red-tiled roofs of the village of Espelette are festooned with strings of chillies drying in the sun. Each October a weekend festival is held there to celebrate the chilli harvest, with tastings of the food and wine so characteristic of the region.

PIPÉRADE

BASQUE SCRAMBLED EGGS WITH PEPPERS, TOMATOES AND CURED HAM

In the Basque country a mildly hot, finger-sized chilli is used for pipérade. *To recreate the dish in Paris, the Comtesse de Coral takes the special chilli with her from Urtubie. When green peppers are substituted, as here, the* pipérade *is different, but equally delicious.*

2 servings as a light main course

4 tbsp OLIVE OIL
1 ONION, CHOPPED
1 FRESH GREEN CHILLI, CORED, SEEDED AND CHOPPED
2 GREEN PEPPERS, CORED, SEEDED AND CHOPPED
2 CLOVES GARLIC, CHOPPED
4 TOMATOES, SKINNED, SEEDED AND CHOPPED*
SALT
6 EGGS
1 tbsp CHOPPED PARSLEY
2 THIN SLICES OF BAYONNE HAM OR A SIMILAR SALT-CURED, AIR-DRIED HAM

Heat the oil in a frying pan, add the onion and cook over low heat until soft, 3 to 5 minutes. Stir in the chilli, green peppers and garlic and sauté over low heat, stirring often, for 5 minutes. Add the tomatoes and a little salt and cook over moderately low heat, stirring occasionally, until the mixture is very soft and thick, ¾ to 1 hour. Stir often at the end of this time as the mixture thickens. Taste the vegetables for seasoning. (The *pipérade* can be made to this point up to 3 days ahead and refrigerated; reheat the vegetables before proceeding.)

Break the eggs into a bowl, add the parsley and a pinch of salt and whisk to mix them. Add the egg mixture to the vegetables and stir over very low heat until the mixture thickens but still remains soft and moist. Cooking should take at least 15 minutes so it thickens creamily.

Meanwhile, fry the ham slices in a non-stick frying pan or grill them just until the edges begin to brown, about 15 seconds per side.

Taste the *pipérade* for seasoning, then transfer it to warmed plates, top each serving with a slice of ham and serve immediately.

GÂTEAU BASQUE

BUTTERY BASQUE CAKE

At the Coral table, the most popular dessert is gâteau basque. *This must be the purest version of this chewy cake as it is flavoured simply with lemon zest and rum. Many local versions are also filled with black cherry preserves or* crème pâtissière. *If you like, press two-thirds of the dough into the prepared tin, spread with 250g/8oz of preserves or jam and cover with the remaining dough before baking.*

8 servings

425 g/14 oz PLAIN FLOUR
300 g/10 oz CASTER SUGAR
250 g/8 oz BUTTER, CUT INTO PIECES
½ tsp SALT
2 EGGS
3 EGG YOLKS
GRATED ZEST OF 2 LEMONS
2 tbsp RUM
1 EGG, BEATEN WITH ½ tsp SALT TO GLAZE

20 cm/8 in ROUND CAKE TIN

Heat the oven to 190°C/375°F/Gas Mark 5. Butter the cake tin, line the bottom with greaseproof paper and butter the paper also.

Sift the flour on to a work surface and make a large well in the centre. Put the sugar, butter, salt, eggs, egg yolks, lemon zest and rum in the well and work these ingredients together with your fingertips until the mixture is smooth. Gradually incorporate the flour using the fingers and heel of your hand, then work the dough gently until smooth. It will be quite sticky.

Flour your hands and transfer the dough to the prepared tin, smoothing it to an even layer. Brush the top of the dough with the egg glaze and mark a lattice design with a fork.

Bake the cake in the heated oven until firm and golden, 40 to 50 minutes. Turn out on to a rack, turn right side up and leave to cool. Serve at room temperature. The flavour of the cake improves on standing. Store it in an airtight container up to 3 days.

Gâteau Basque – this speciality of the area is easily recognised by the lattice, which is always traced with a fork on the top crust.

26

CHÂTEAU D'ARCANGUES

THE ARCANGUES DYNASTY HAS NOT ONLY LIVED ON THE SAME PROPERTY SINCE 1150, BUT THE DEEDS OF TITLE HAVE ALWAYS PASSED FROM FATHER TO SON. THE PRESENT MARQUIS, GUY D'ARCANGUES, THINKS THIS MUST BE A RECORD IN FRANCE. HOWEVER, NO FEWER THAN FOUR CHÂTEAUX HAVE SUCCEEDED EACH OTHER ON THE SAME SITE, THE LATEST DATING TO 1900 AND FASHIONED IN THE STYLE OF THE SEASIDE PALACES OF NEARBY BIARRITZ.

THE RAMBLING, WISTERIA-COVERED FAÇADE GIVES LITTLE CLUE TO THE GRANDEUR WITHIN. HERE CENTURIES OF FAMILY TREASURES GRACE A GREAT PANELLED LIBRARY, AS WELL AS AN 18TH-CENTURY SALON HUNG WITH MAJESTIC GOBELIN TAPESTRIES. ARCANGUES ALSO BOASTS ONE OF THE MOST SPLENDID DINING ROOMS IN PROVINCIAL FRANCE. IT WAS HERE IN THE 1920S THAT THE SEVENTH MARQUIS D'ARCANGUES, CLOSE FRIEND OF KING ALPHONSE XIII OF SPAIN, RECEIVED LUMINARIES SUCH AS MAURICE RAVEL, STRAVINSKY, HEMINGWAY, ANDRÉ GIDE, JEAN COCTEAU AND SACHA GUITRY. FOLLOWING IN THE STEPS OF HIS FATHER, THE PRESENT MARQUIS HAS MADE HIS MARK ON THE FRENCH ARTISTIC SCENE, AND WISHES TO MAKE THE CHÂTEAU 'A CROSSROADS OF THE CULTURAL WORLD'. RECENT VISITORS HAVE INCLUDED CATHERINE DENEUVE, SYLVIE VARTAN AND PRINCE RAINIER OF MONACO.

A portrait of the first Marquis dominates the splendid dining room at Arcangues. The silver coffee pot on display in the centre of the table was a gift from the Duke of Wellington when he occupied Arcangues in 1814.

This Baccarat crystal glass is etched with the Marquis d'Arcangues' crown and initial (top left and inset above).

Formal menus for a winter lunch party also bear the Arcangues' coat of arms, and unusual shaded candelabra add intimacy to the grand table (middle left).

The Marquis keeps three wine cellars – one for wine bottled on the estate, one for everyday wine, and one for fine vintages such as these (bottom left).

The kitchen at Arcangues boasts a fine array of graduated copper pans (above).

As a prominent landmark on one of the historic routes to Spain, the Château d'Arcangues has always been at the centre of events. The English king, Richard the Lionheart, and later the Black Prince, skirted the property when warring in their province of Aquitaine. The Spaniards destroyed the second Château d'Arcangues in the 1630s. Arcangues was again the scene of fierce battle during the Peninsular Wars, and the Duke of Wellington made it his headquarters for several weeks. He left a silver coffee pot in thanks to Nicolas-François-Xavier, Marquis of the day. The Duke was impressed by French soldiers and the conscription system 'which calls out a share of every class – no matter whether your son or my son – all must march'. British soldiers, on the other hand, 'were the scum of the earth and could not resist wine'.

Today Guy d'Arcangues opens the château for concerts and receptions. Guests dine under the resplendent gaze of the 18th-century portrait of the first Marquis, using the rare ancestral silver and the Baccarat crystal engraved with the Arcangues coat of arms. Downstairs, the surroundings are equally lavish. Arcangues boasts no fewer than three cellars, one for everyday wines, a second for fine wines and a third for the wines that used to be made on the estate. Cooking still takes place in an old Basque-style kitchen with wooden cabinets, open fireplace, and copper pots lining the walls. '*Hurrup eta klik!*' – 'drain your cup' – reads the Basque motto on the chimney beam. Guy d'Arcangues prefers to quote the inscription on the chimney in his dining room which translates as 'A sharp tooth for all set on the table, and a soft tongue for those who sit around it'. He and his forebears have certainly followed this injunction.

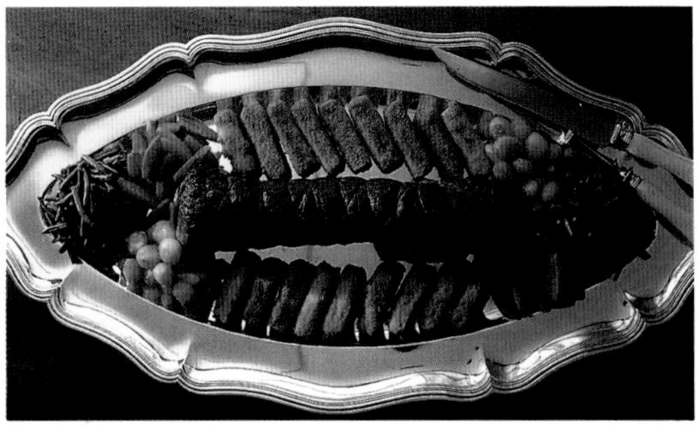

Rôti de Boeuf Jardinière, a traditional dish of roast beef and garden vegetables. The sweetcorn croquettes add a distinctively Basque flavour to the dish. Sweetcorn croquettes are also good as an hors d'oeuvre with drinks.

RÔTI DE BOEUF JARDINIÈRE

ROAST BEEF WITH GARDEN VEGETABLES

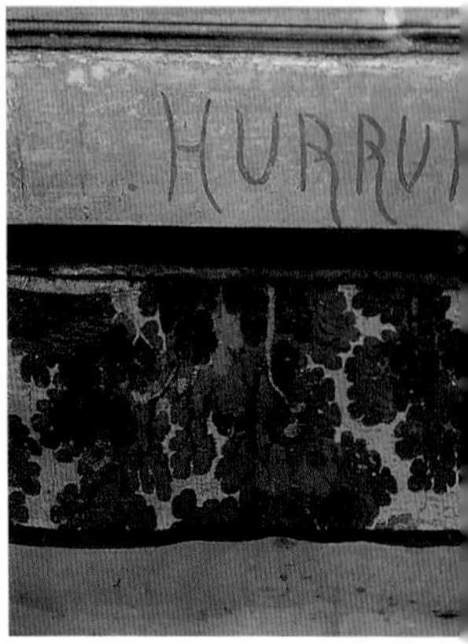

The Basque motto in the kitchen 'Hurrup eta klik' – perhaps best translated as 'cheers!'

Menus at the Château d'Arcangues tend towards the classic – roast beef with garden vegetables and sweetcorn croquettes is a favourite – but oddities creep in like the chicken pie featured at a grand dinner for Yves Saint-Laurent recently.

10 servings

2 tbsp VEGETABLE OIL
1 × 2 kg/4½ lb TRIMMED BEEF FILLET, TIED
SALT AND PEPPER
125 ml/4 fl oz WHITE WINE
250 ml/8 fl oz BEEF STOCK (see page 221)

For the garnish

750 g/1½ lb BABY OR MEDIUM CARROTS
750 g/1½ lb BABY ONIONS
CASTER SUGAR FOR SPRINKLING
500 g/1 lb FRENCH BEANS, TRIMMED AND CUT INTO 5 cm/2 in LENGTHS
60 g/2 oz BUTTER
SWEETCORN CROQUETTES (see opposite)

For the garnish, scrub or peel baby carrots, leaving on a little of the green tops. Peel and quarter medium carrots, trimming the edges to form miniature carrots. Cook the carrots in boiling salted water until tender, 15 to 20 minutes, then drain them.

Blanch* the onions in boiling water for 1 minute, then drain and peel them – the skins will strip away easily. Trim the roots and stalks of the onions carefully so they will not fall apart during cooking. Cook the onions in boiling salted water until tender, 10 to 15 minutes, then drain and sprinkle with a little sugar.

Cook the French beans in boiling salted water until just tender, 8 to 10 minutes, and then drain. Rinse them with cold water and drain

again. (The garnish vegetables can be cooked a day ahead and kept covered and refrigerated.)

Heat the oven to 260°C/500°F/Gas Mark 10. In a roasting tin, heat the oil on top of the stove and brown the meat all over. Sprinkle the meat with salt and pepper. Roast the meat in the heated oven for about 20 minutes, turning it over every 8 to 10 minutes. A skewer inserted in the centre of the meat for 30 seconds should be warm to the touch when withdrawn. For rare meat, a meat thermometer should register 51°C/125°F, for medium-done, 60°C/140°F. Transfer the meat to a carving board with a juice catcher, cover loosely with foil and leave it to rest for 15 minutes.

To make a gravy, pour off the fat from the roasting tin. Add the wine to the tin and bring to the boil, scraping to dissolve the browned roasting juices. Add the stock and simmer for 5 to 10 minutes to concentrate the flavour. Strain the gravy into a small saucepan and season.

To finish the garnish, melt one-third of the butter in each of three saucepans. Add carrots to one pan, onions to another and beans to the third. Add a little salt to each pan and cook over moderate heat, stirring often, until the vegetables are heated through. Taste for seasoning.

To serve, remove the string from the meat and set it on a warmed platter. Stir the juices from the meat into the gravy. Arrange the vegetables in bouquets, or small heaps, and the sweetcorn croquettes around the meat. At the table, carve the meat into thin slices. Pass the gravy separately.

CROQUETTES DE MAÏS

SWEETCORN CROQUETTES

In most parts of France, the sweetcorn or maize you see ripening along departmental lanes goes to animal fodder. But in the cooking of the Basque country, sweetcorn is a venerated staple.

Makes about 25 croquettes

6 COBS FRESH SWEETCORN OR 500 g/1 lb CANNED SWEETCORN KERNELS
2 EGG YOLKS
SALT AND PEPPER
VEGETABLE OIL FOR DEEP-FRYING

For the white sauce

500 ml/16 fl oz MILK
2 SLICES OF ONION
1 BAY LEAF
1 tsp PEPPERCORNS
60 g/2 oz BUTTER
60 g/2 oz PLAIN FLOUR

For the coating

100 g/3¼ oz SEASONED FLOUR
3 EGGS, BEATEN TO MIX WITH ½ tsp SALT AND 1 tbsp VEGETABLE OIL
150 g/5 oz DRY WHITE BREADCRUMBS

If using fresh sweetcorn, cook it in a large pan of boiling salted water until just tender, 5 to 7 minutes. Drain the cobs and cut off the kernels with a sharp knife. Canned sweetcorn is already cooked, so it only needs to be drained.

Make the white sauce (see page 222); it should be fairly thick. Mix in the egg yolks, sweetcorn, salt and pepper and simmer until the mixture is thick but still soft enough to fall from a spoon, about 2 minutes. Taste for seasoning. Spread the mixture in a buttered shallow tin and rub the top with a knob of butter to prevent a skin from forming. Chill until firm, at least 2 hours.

Turn the croquette mixture on to a floured work surface and roll with your hands into a cylinder about 2.5 cm/1 in in diameter. Cut it into 7.5 cm/3 in cork shapes and coat each piece first with the seasoned flour, then the beaten egg and finally with the breadcrumbs. (The croquettes can be kept at this point for up to 24 hours, uncovered, in the refrigerator.)

Heat the oil to 190°C/375°F in a deep fryer. Fry the croquettes a few at a time until golden, 1 to 2 minutes. Remove them and drain on kitchen paper. Keep the first batch of croquettes warm in a low oven, with the door ajar, while you fry the rest. Serve once all are fried.

This fascinating family menu book contains recipes and menus from gala dinners held at the château over 60 years ago.

Domaine de Richemont

When I asked Madame Jonquères d'Oriola if she maintained a vegetable garden, she paused in surprise. 'But of course! Here we live on the property in the old way. My husband's family has been here 200 years. His father was proud that he was able to leave enough land to live off to each of his eight children.' The Domaine de Richemont, inherited by Joseph Jonquères d'Oriola, is a simple brick and tile house with the working buildings attached — barns, stable and, of course, cellars for vinifying and storing wine. Not so long ago, chickens, ducks and guinea fowl used to scratch within the enclosed courtyard. Today pigeons and rare doves, Monsieur Jonquères d'Oriola's pride, still strut on the roofs around the pigeon house.

The vineyard is less active now, but in its day it produced red and amber Rivesaltes aperitif wine, together with a sought-after Muscat de Rivesaltes, a *vin doux naturel* or fortified wine. 'The rules for the production of Muscat de Rivesaltes are strict,' says Monsieur Jonquères d'Oriola, 'and date back to before the Revolution. To obtain the right degree of alcohol, the fermentation of the wine must be arrested at a certain density. This always seems to happen in the middle of the night. I would find myself getting up several times to check, just like a birth.' At one stage it was Madame Jonquères d'Oriola who helped with bottling, then rented a truck with her daughter to tour France, publicizing and selling Richemont's wine.

The old walls and red tiled roofs at the Domaine de Richemont bask in the southern sun. Shutters are closed for coolness during the heat of the day (far right).

The Domaine de Richemont is in Catalonia, with a generous view of the 'magic mountain' of Mont Canigou. Monsieur Jonquères d'Oriola himself is Catalan and speaks and reads the language, which resembles Langue d'Oc (or Provençal), which is even closer to Latin than Castilian Spanish. Christine Jonquères d'Oriola is Basque, from the western end of the Pyrénées, and I asked her about similarities in the cooking. 'Both use a great many peppers,' she says, 'and rely a good deal on fish. In the Basque country, as well as in Catalonia, one finds dishes piquant with anchovies, olives and salty mountain ham. Catalan meals are full of the vegetables and fruits that are the great speciality around here.'

Traditionally, the first *primeurs* or baby spring vegetables in France come from this sheltered corner of Roussillon. The Jonquères d'Oriola table sees tiny artichokes in early spring – the whole head edible – while cherries arrive in May ('the earliest in France', says Madame Jonquères d'Oriola with pride) and the first pears are ripe in August.

'Catalans are great lovers of sweetmeats and dessert,' she adds. In the pastry shops of Perpignan, not far from Richemont, *tourons* of almond paste and honey come in a dozen flavours – dark and light caramel, glacé fruit, triangular hazelnut and pine nut cut in bar shapes. Circular fritters called *bunyols* are a year-round snack, while *bunyetes*, a kind of doughnut for dipping in sweet wine, are an Easter treat. During the wine harvest a curious confection called *rob* is made with grape pressings, sugar and sliced aubergine. As for betrothals, they used to be celebrated with a *croquignolle* – a long biscuit, which each fiancé tackled at one end, meeting in the middle with a kiss.

'Ah, so much of the old life has gone,' sighs Monsieur Jonquères d'Oriola. 'In October, the sunsets behind Mont Canigou are splendid. This is the time when the sheep used to come down from the mountains in the annual transhumance procession. A flock of over 200 would spend the winter with their shepherd in our vineyards. Then one year they did not reappear. We miss them.'

SALADE CATALANE

CURLY ENDIVE WITH PEPPERS, ANCHOVIES AND RED ONION

Here are the flavours of Catalonia packed into a salad bowl.

4 to 6 servings

1 RED PEPPER
500 g/1 lb CURLY ENDIVE (FRISÉE)
2 CLOVES GARLIC, FINELY CHOPPED
2 tbsp CHOPPED PARSLEY
2 HALF-GREEN TOMATOES, QUARTERED
1 SMALL RED ONION, SLICED AND SEPARATED INTO RINGS
½ CUCUMBER, SLICED
1 GREEN PEPPER, CORED, SEEDED AND CUT INTO THIN RINGS
60 g/2 oz OIL-CURED GREEN AND BLACK OLIVES
6 RADISHES, HALVED LENGTHWAYS
4 ANCHOVY FILLETS IN OIL, DRAINED
2 HARD-BOILED EGGS, QUARTERED

For the vinaigrette
2 tbsp VINEGAR
SALT AND PEPPER
2 tbsp DIJON MUSTARD
75 ml/2½ fl oz OLIVE OIL

Roast the red pepper under the grill for 10 to 12 minutes, turning it as needed, until the skin is black and blistered. Cover the pepper with a wet cloth or wrap it in a polythene bag and leave until cool. (The trapped steam helps loosen the skin.) With a small knife, peel off the skin. Rinse the pepper under running water and pat dry. Cut it into thin slices.

Trim the endive, wash it and tear into bite-size pieces. Dry it thoroughly and put in a bowl. Make the vinaigrette (see page 222) and stir in the garlic and parsley. Add the tomatoes, onion, cucumber, red and green peppers, olives, radishes, anchovies and eggs to the bowl. Add the vinaigrette and toss the salad.

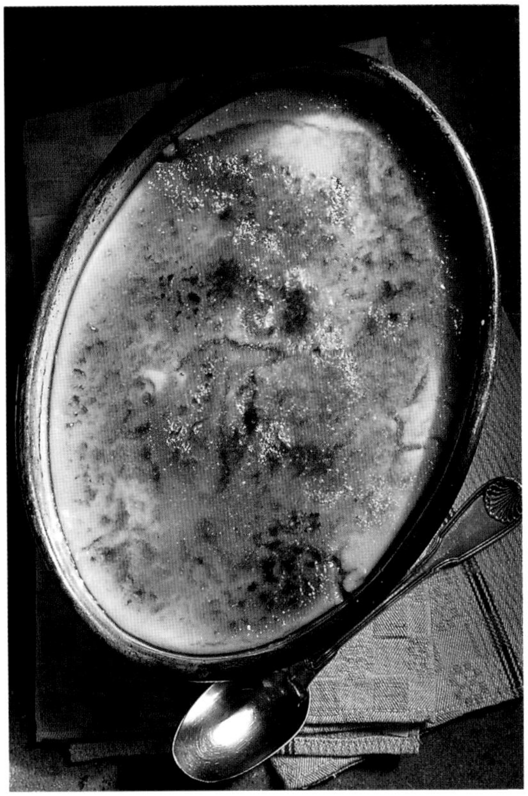

Crème Catalane, a creamy custard enlivened with the spices and fruits of Catalonia.

CRÈME CATALANE

LEMON, CINNAMON AND FENNEL SEED CUSTARD

Madame Jonquères d'Oriola's version of crème brûlée *is spiced in typical Catalan style with fennel, cinnamon and citrus zest. For authenticity it should be baked in an earthenware dish.*

8 servings

1 LITRE/1⅔ PINTS MILK
PARED ZEST OF 1 LEMON
PARED ZEST OF 1 ORANGE
1 tsp FENNEL SEEDS, CRUSHED
1 CINNAMON STICK
2 EGGS
4 EGG YOLKS
20 g/¾ oz PLAIN FLOUR
20 g/¾ oz CORNFLOUR
100 g/3¼ oz DARK SOFT BROWN SUGAR

1.5 LITRE/2½ PINT SHALLOW BAKING DISH

Bring the milk just to the boil. Add the lemon and orange zest, fennel seeds and cinnamon stick, cover the pan and leave over low heat to infuse for 15 minutes.

Meanwhile whisk the eggs and yolks together until thick and light then whisk in the flour and the cornflour.

Strain the milk into the egg mixture and stir it with a whisk until the mixture is smooth. Return it to the pan and bring to the boil, whisking constantly. If lumps form as the custard thickens, take the pan from the heat at once and whisk the custard until smooth. Simmer the custard gently, whisking constantly, for 3 to 5 minutes until it softens slightly, indicating that the flour is completely cooked.

Remove the pan from the heat and transfer the custard to the baking dish; it should form a layer about 2.5 cm/1 in thick. Refrigerate it until cool, at least 1 hour and up to a day.

To finish, heat the grill to high. Sift the brown sugar evenly over the top of the custard and glaze it under the grill for several seconds, until the sugar forms a firm crust, watching carefully so it does not burn.

Prieuré de Monastir del Camp

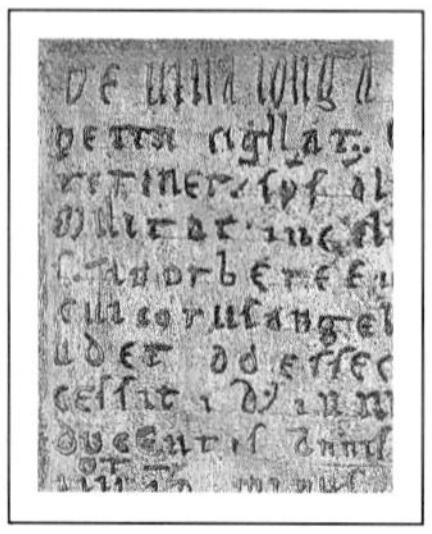

When I talked to Jacques Marceille, he was amongst his vines, supervising the harvest as his family has done ever since they bought the derelict Prieuré de Monastir from the Crown just before the Revolution. Monastir is ancient, evocative, rooted for more than 1000 years in the harsh soil of Roussillon. Legend has it that the first priory was built in the ninth century at the behest of Charlemagne, who passed through on his way to fight the Moors in Spain. His army was exhausted by heat and thirst but, revived by the spring that gushed miraculously from the stones of Monastir, marched on to win their battle. In local dialect the stream still bears the name '*El Rui del Miracle*'.

This part of Roussillon, only 15 kilometres from the Spanish border, is mountainous and wild with some of the ambiance of a frontier culture. In the early 19th century, it attracted the novelist Prosper Mérimée, who knew Monastir's owner, Jaubert de Passa. Passa was himself a noted intellectual and conservationist who wrote about irrigation systems, the Catalan language, archaeology, silkworms and gypsies, but perhaps his most lasting accomplishment was to introduce Mérimée to a gypsy called Pepita. She inspired his novel *Carmen*, which in turn inspired Bizet to write his opera.

The early 14th-century cloister (right) forms an oasis of peace within the walls of Monastir del Camp. In the mid-19th century a cache of gold dinars, struck by the Caliphs of Valencia, was discovered here. The church (far right) has been deserted since Augustinians left in 1786 when Louis XVI sold the whole property to the de Passa family. A memorial plaque dating back to 1196 for Bertrand de Villalonga, an early pilgrim (inset above).

The stone walls of Monastir (above) are timeless, dating back to the 12th century and resembling a crusader fortress – the Templars were active in the region and carved the white entrance to the chapel. Windows in the outer wall are few, originally for safety but kept as protection against the searing sun in this hot corner of France. 'Unlike you in the north, in winter we open wide our windows, but in summer only at night,' observes Jacques Marceille.

Huge casks of red wine in the cellars of Monastir del Camp (below right).

Today at Monastir the harsh landscape is softened by woodland, which grows along the miraculous stream and shelters lush pasture. A passion for horses has remained in Jacques Marceille's family for centuries, and now the national stud – begun in 1665 – brings stallions each year to the region, to cover local mares. But Jacques Marceille's enduring concern is his vineyards, which stretch over 90 hectares, sufficient to produce about 25,000 cases of wine annually. His production includes Côtes du Roussillon red, rivalling a good Côtes-du-Rhône, plus more modest table wines and a sizeable amount of fortified aperitif and dessert wine. Jacques Marceille's pride is a sweet white Muscat de Rivesaltes, golden and rich. 'I've sold this year's production almost before the grapes are gathered!' he says. 'We don't have enough of them!'

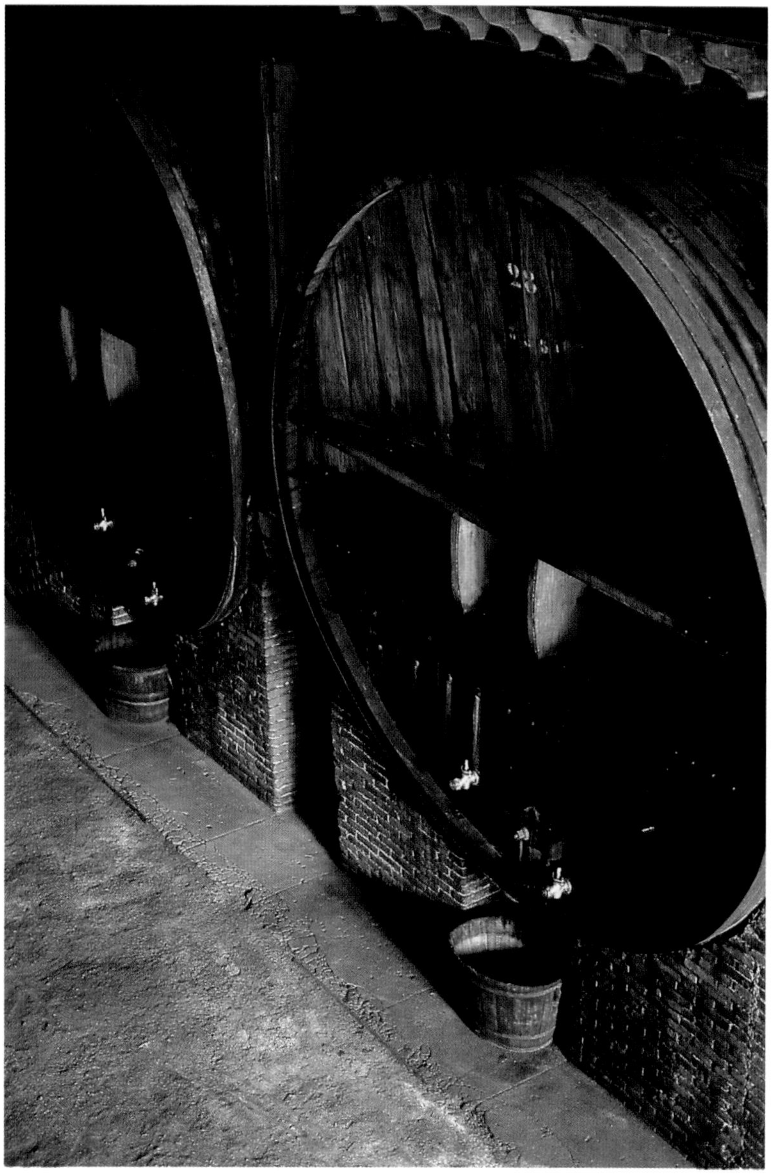

The *vendange* lasts more than three weeks, with some of the two or three dozen pickers coming from as far as Poland to earn the equivalent of four to five months' salary. With only four full-time workers, Jacques Marceille devotes himself to the land year round, leaving the marketing of his wines to a wholesaler. He does, however, find time to cook. He likes to dig into the dog-eared family copy of *La Cuisinière Bourgeoise*, the culinary bible of 18th- and 19th-century households, which claimed to be of use 'to all those who are concerned with the defence of the home'.

BOULES DE PICOLAT

CATALAN MEATBALLS WITH GREEN OLIVES, HAM AND TOMATO SAUCE

Jacques Marceille likes to cook Catalan dishes like crème Catalan (custard flavoured with fennel seeds, see page 211) and these meatballs made of pork and beef served with a rust-coloured sauce rousse *of tomato and green olives. At Monastir, boiled potatoes, peeled or in their skins, are the accompaniment.*

4 to 6 servings

500 g/1 lb LEAN MINCED BEEF
250 g/8 oz MINCED PORK OR SAUSAGEMEAT
3 or 4 CLOVES GARLIC, FINELY CHOPPED
1 EGG
1 EGG YOLK
SALT AND PEPPER
30 g/1 oz PLAIN FLOUR
4 tbsp OLIVE OIL, MORE IF NECESSARY
1 × 100 g/3¼ oz PIECE OF STREAKY BACON, CUT INTO *LARDONS**
2 tbsp CHOPPED PARSLEY

For the sauce rousse
1 ONION, FINELY CHOPPED
1 tbsp PLAIN FLOUR
375 ml/12 fl oz WATER
3 tbsp TOMATO SAUCE (see page 142)
200 g/6½ oz STONED GREEN OLIVES, BLANCHED* IF SALTY
60 g/2 oz SALT-CURED, AIR-DRIED HAM, CUT INTO 1 cm/⅜ in DICE
½ tsp GROUND CINNAMON
¼ tsp CAYENNE PEPPER

Mix together the minced meats, garlic, egg and egg yolk with a little salt and pepper. Beat the mixture in a bowl with a wooden spoon for 2 to 3 minutes until it pulls from the sides of the bowl. Sauté a small piece of the mixture and taste it for seasoning. Shape the mixture into 4 cm/1½ in balls by rolling it in your hands.

Cured ham hanging in Monsieur Montauzer's renowned charcuterie in the nearby town of Guiche. The salty taste of the meat gives an appetizing edge to the tomato sauce in Boules de Picolat.

Spread the flour on a sheet of greaseproof paper and season it with salt and pepper. Roll the meatballs, a few at a time, in the flour until they are well coated.

Heat the oil in a large frying pan. Fry the bacon slowly until the fat runs, then cook until golden, about 5 minutes. Remove it with a slotted spoon.

Add the meatballs, without crowding the pan, and brown them all over for 5 to 8 minutes, then remove them.

To make the sauce, add the onion to the frying pan and cook it until soft, 3 to 5 minutes. Sprinkle the flour over the onion and cook it until foaming, 1 to 2 minutes. Stir in the water and bring to the boil, stirring to dissolve the pan juices. Stir in the tomato sauce, olives, ham, black pepper, cinnamon and cayenne pepper. Taste for seasoning; salt may not be needed.

Reduce the heat to low and replace the meatballs and bacon in the pan. Simmer them, covered, until the meatballs are no longer pink in the centre, 20 to 25 minutes. The sauce should be thick and rich. Serve hot with the chopped parsley sprinkled on top.

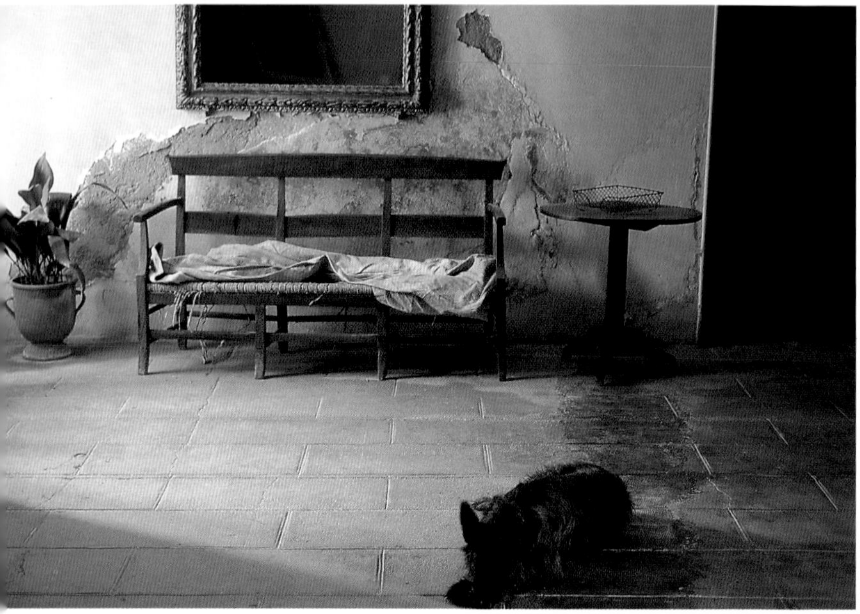

The cool flagstones in the hall provide relief from the midday sun.

Pigeons a la Marianne

Braised Pigeon with Anchovies and Capers

Jacques Marceille also recommends this recipe from La Cuisinière Bourgeoise, *which originally called for cooking the pigeons very, very gently in the ashes of a fireplace. It's no wonder they love this pungent dish at Monastir, with its sauce – almost a relish – flavoured with anchovy, caper and shallot, all local staples. Quail can take the place of pigeon and you will need two per person. 'Serve the birds,' counsels Monsieur Marceille, 'with a Côtes du Roussillon.'*

4 servings

4 OVEN-READY PIGEONS or 8 QUAILS, GIBLETS REMOVED
175 ml/6 fl oz CHICKEN STOCK (see page 221)
2 tbsp VEGETABLE OIL
2 BAY LEAVES
PINCH OF GRATED NUTMEG
SALT AND PEPPER
6 ANCHOVY FILLETS IN OIL, DRAINED AND CHOPPED
3 SHALLOTS, FINELY CHOPPED
1 tbsp CAPERS, DRAINED AND CHOPPED
15 g/½ oz BUTTER
1 tbsp PLAIN FLOUR

KITCHEN STRING

Flatten the pigeons slightly by pressing firmly on the breastbone. Tie the birds with string and put them in a sauté pan or small flameproof casserole in which they fit quite tightly. Add the stock, oil, bay leaves, nutmeg and a little salt and pepper. Cover and simmer over low heat, skimming occasionally, for 35 to 45 minutes until the juice from the centre of the birds runs clear when they are lifted on a two-pronged fork. Quails will take about 30 minutes. Turn the birds twice during cooking. (The birds can be cooked up to a day ahead and refrigerated in the cooking liquid; reheat before proceeding.)

Transfer the birds to a warmed serving dish, cover tightly with foil and keep warm. Skim any fat from the cooking liquid and discard the bay leaves. Add the anchovies, shallots and capers to the pan and bring the sauce to the boil. Cream the butter and, with a fork, work in the flour to a smooth paste. Drop just enough pieces of this *beurre manié* into the boiling sauce, whisking rapidly, until it thickens enough to coat a spoon. Taste it for seasoning.

Remove the string from the birds. Coat the birds with a little sauce and serve immediately, with the remaining sauce.

Chou en Surprise

Sausage and Chestnut Stuffed Cabbage

One 19th-century châtelaine, Madame Jaubert de Passa, was particularly fond of this recipe from La Cuisinière Bourgeoise.

6 to 8 servings

1 MEDIUM SAVOY CABBAGE
(about 1.25kg/2½ to 3 lb)
875 g/1¾ lb FRESH CHESTNUTS, PEELED AND COOKED (see page 89), or 500 g/1 lb CANNED UNSWEETENED CHESTNUTS
500 g/1 lb SAUSAGEMEAT, CRUMBLED
SALT AND PEPPER
1 ONION, CHOPPED
1 CARROT, CHOPPED
A BOUQUET GARNI*
1 LITRE/1¾ PINTS BEEF STOCK (see page 221), MORE IF NEEDED
60 g/2 oz BUTTER
2 tbsp PLAIN FLOUR

Discard any damaged outer leaves from the cabbage and trim the stalk. Immerse it in a large pan of boiling salted water and cook until the outer leaves can easily be bent, 15 to 20 minutes. Refresh* the cabbage with cold water. Peel back the outer leaves to reveal the heart. Carefully cut out the cabbage heart and reserve it, leaving a pocket for stuffing.

Break the chestnuts into two or three pieces. Combine the chestnuts, crumbled sausagemeat, and a little salt and pepper. Fry a small piece of this mixture and taste it. Adjust the seasoning.

Drape a scalded tea towel in a colander. Set the cabbage in the colander, stalk side down. Stuff the cabbage with the chestnut mixture and wrap the leaf ends over to form a parcel. Gather the towel over and tie it with string to make a tight ball. Put it in a large saucepan.

Add the onion, carrot, bouquet garni and a little salt and pepper to the saucepan. Add enough stock to half cover the cabbage. Bring the stock to the boil and simmer, covered, for 1 to 1¼ hours until a skewer inserted in the centre of the cabbage is hot to the touch. Add more stock during cooking if it evaporates rapidly. (The cabbage can be cooked up to a day ahead and refrigerated in the cooking liquid; reheat it before proceeding.)

Shred the reserved cabbage, discarding the core. Melt half the butter in a large frying pan. Add the shredded cabbage with salt and pepper and cook over low heat, stirring often, until tender, 10 to 15 minutes.

Chou en Surprise. The outer leaves of a cabbage are stuffed with sausage and chestnuts and reassembled to look intriguingly like the whole vegetable.

Meanwhile, lift the stuffed cabbage out of the cooking liquid and keep it warm. Boil the cooking liquid until reduced by half. Strain it into a small saucepan and bring again to the boil. Cream the remaining butter and, with a fork, work in the flour to a smooth paste. Drop just enough pieces of this *beurre manié* into the boiling liquid, whisking rapidly, until the sauce thickens enough to lightly coat a spoon.

Arrange a bed of shredded cabbage on a warmed platter. Unwrap the stuffed cabbage and set it on the platter. Pour some of the sauce around the cabbage. Serve the remaining sauce and shredded cabbage separately.

Le Vert-Bois
Lille
Miromesnil
Rouen
Creullet
Canon-les-Bonnes-Gens
Anet
Paris
Dampierre
Saint-Jean-de-Beauregard
Le Bos
Le Marais
Courances
Ittenwiller
Schoppenwihr
Le Feÿ
Vau-de-Quip
La Ferté-Saint-Aubin
Tours
Beauregard
La Verrerie
Nantes
Bastion des Dames
Châteaurenaud
Ainay-le-Vieil
Jozerand
La Roche-Froide
Lyon
Virieu
Anjony
Chassan
Bordeaux
Malle
Caïx
Saint-Vincent
Bonpas
Flaugergues
Toulouse
Arcangues
Urtubie
Marseille
Monastir del Camp
Richemont

Addresses and Opening Times

Many of the châteaux owners featured welcome visitors to their homes. Some offer guided tours, wine tastings, cooking classes, bed and breakfast, annual festivals or other activities.

Châteaux of Leisure

CHÂTEAU DU MARAIS
91530 Saint-Chéron
40 km south of Paris.
Open Sunday and holidays 2 p.m. to 6.30 p.m., 15 March to 15 November. Open to groups year round by written appointment.

CHÂTEAU DE COURANCES
91490 Milly-la-Forêt
Tel: 45 50 34 24.
50 km south of Paris.
Open weekends and holidays 2 p.m. to 6 p.m., 1 April to 1 November. Open weekdays by appointment.

CHÂTEAU DE SAINT-JEAN-DE-BEAUREGARD
91940 Les Ulis
Tel: 60 12 00 01.
28 km south-west of Paris.
Open Sunday and holidays 2 p.m. to 6 p.m., 15 March to 15 November. Open to groups year round by appointment. Plant festival, mid-April. Fruit and vegetable festival, mid-November.

CHÂTEAU D'ANET
28260 Anet
16 km north of Dreux
Open daily 2.30 p.m. to 6.30 p.m., Sunday and holidays 10 a.m. to 11.30 a.m. and 2.30 p.m. to 6.30 p.m., 1 April to 31 October. Closed Tuesday. Open 10 a.m. to 2 p.m., 1 November and 11.30 a.m. to 5 p.m., 31 March.

CHÂTEAU DE DAMPIERRE
78720 Dampierre
35 km south-west of Paris.
Open daily 2 p.m. to 6.30 p.m., 1 April to 15 October. Open to groups in the morning by written appointment.

CHÂTEAU DE LA FERTÉ-SAINT-AUBIN
45240 La Ferté-Saint-Aubin
18 km south of Orléans.
Tel: 38 76 52 72.
Open daily 10 a.m. to 9 p.m., 15 March to 11 November. Open off-season by appointment. Hunting festival, second Sunday in September. Garden festival, first weekend in May.

CHÂTEAU DE BEAUREGARD
Cellettes 41120 Les Montils
6 km south-east of Blois.
Open daily 9.30 a.m. to noon and 2.30 p.m. to 6.30 p.m., 1 April to 1 October. Open daily 9.30 a.m. to 6.30 p.m., 1 July to 31 August. Open daily 2 p.m. to 5 p.m., 1 October to 1 April. Closed January.

Châteaux of Mist and Sea

CHÂTEAU DE CANON-LES-BONNES-GENS
14270 Mézidon-Canon
25 km south-east of Caen.
Open weekends and holidays 2 p.m. to 7 p.m., Easter to 1 July. Open daily 2 p.m. to 7 p.m., 1 July to 1 October. Closed Tuesday.

CHÂTEAU DE MIROMESNIL
Tourville-sur-Arques 76550 Offranville
6 km south of Dieppe.
Open Easter weekend 2 p.m. to 6 p.m. Open daily 2 p.m. to 6 p.m., 1 May to 15 October. Closed Tuesday.

MALOUINIÈRE DU BOS
Quelmer 35400 Saint-Malo
Daily tours 3.30 p.m. and 5 p.m., 1 July to 31 August. Open to groups in May and June by written appointment two months ahead.

MANOIR DE VAU-DE-QUIP
56350 Allaire
10 km west of Redon.
Open to groups 15 July to 31 August by written appointment.

CHÂTEAU DU VERT-BOIS
59910 Bondues
8.5 km north of Lille.
Tel: 20 46 26 37.
Open Sunday and holidays 2.30 p.m. to 6 p.m., 15 March to 15 October. Closed August. Open to groups year round by written appointment.

PARC DE SCHOPPENWIHR
68000 Colmar
Park open daily 10 a.m. to 6 p.m., 15 April to 15 November.

Châteaux of the Heart of France

CHÂTEAU DU FEŸ
89300 Villecien
5 km north of Joigny.
Tel: 86 63 18 34.
Home to La Varenne's gastronomic and culinary programmes. Write or call for information.

BASTION DES DAMES
21190 Meursault
8 km south of Beaune.
Open daily 9.30 a.m. to noon and 2.30 p.m. to 6 p.m., 1 March to 31 November.

CHÂTEAU D'AINAY-LE-VIEIL
18200 Saint-Amand-Montrond
44 km south of Bourges.
Open daily 10 a.m. to noon and 2 p.m. to 7 p.m., 5 February to 30 November. Open 10 a.m. to 7 p.m., July and August. Closed Tuesday February, March and November.

CHÂTEAU DE CAÏX
46140 Luzech
20 km west of Cahors.
Wine cellar open daily for wine tasting and buying 9 a.m. to noon and 2 p.m. to 6 p.m.

CHÂTEAU DE LA VERRERIE
Oizon 18700 Aubigny-sur-Nère
46 km north of Bourges.
Open daily 10 a.m. to noon and 2 p.m. to 7 p.m., 1 March to 15 November.

Châteaux of the Mountains

CHÂTEAU D'ANJONY
Tournemire 15310 Saint-Cernin
22 km north of Aurillac.
Open daily 2 p.m. to 6.30 p.m., Easter to 1 November. Open to groups year round by written appointment.

CHÂTEAU DU CHASSAN
Faverolles 15390 Louaresse
18 km south-east of Saint-Flour.
Open daily 2 p.m. to 6 p.m., 15 June to 15 September. Open 1 April to 15 June and 15 September to 15 October by appointment.

CHÂTEAU DE VIRIEU
38730 Virieu-sur-Bourbre
17 km south-west of La Tour-du-Pin.
Open Sunday 2 p.m. to 6 p.m. June and October. Open daily 2 p.m. to 6 p.m., 1 July to 30 September. Closed Monday.

Châteaux of the Sun

CHARTREUSE DE BONPAS
84150 Caumont-sur-Durance
12 km south of Avignon.
Gardens and wine cellar open daily 9 a.m. to noon and 2 p.m. to 6 p.m. Open to groups by written appointment. Wine cellar closed Sunday.

CHÂTEAU DE SAINT-VINCENT
30300 Jonquières Saint-Vincent
12 km south-east of Nîmes.
Wine cellar open daily for wine tasting and buying.

CHÂTEAU DE FLAUGERGUES
34000 Montpellier
3 km east of Montpellier.
Tel: 67 65 51 72.
Open daily 2.30 p.m. to 6.30 p.m., July and August or by appointment.

CHÂTEAU DE MALLE
33210 Preignac
7 km north-west of Langon.
Open daily 10 a.m. to noon and 2 p.m. to 7 p.m., 21 March to 3 November. Open daily 10 a.m. to 7 p.m., 1 July to 30 September.

CHÂTEAU D'URTUBIE
64122 Urrugne
22 km south of Biarritz.
Open daily 3 p.m. to 7 p.m., 13 July to 2 September. Bed and breakfast available 1 July to 15 September.

CHÂTEAU D'ARCANGUES
Arcangues 64200 Biarritz
Tel: 59 43 04 82.
8 km east of Biarritz.
Open for meetings and seminars of 30 to 120 people by appointment. Eighteen-hole golf course.

PRIEURÉ DE MONASTIR-DEL-CAMP
66300 Thuir
13 km south of Perpignan.
Tel: 68 38 80 71.
Open daily 10 a.m. to noon and 2 p.m. to 6 p.m., October to Easter. Open 9 a.m. to noon and 3 p.m. to 8 p.m., Easter to October. Closed Thursday and 15 to 30 January. Open to groups by appointment.

GLOSSARY

ARROWROOT
Arrowroot is used to thicken sauces lightly at the end of cooking. Mix the arrowroot in a cup with water, allowing about 1 tablespoon of water per teaspoon of arrowroot. It will make a thin, opaque mixture, which separates on standing but can easily be recombined. Whisk this mixture into a boiling liquid, adding just enough to thicken the sauce to the desired consistency. Do not boil the sauce for more than 2 to 3 minutes or it may become thin again.

ARTICHOKE BOTTOMS, PREPARING AND COOKING
Canned or frozen prepared artichoke bottoms can be used to save the time needed to prepare fresh ones. To prepare from fresh, choose large artichokes to make a generous cup shape. Add the juice of $\frac{1}{2}$ lemon to a bowl of cold water. Working with one artichoke at a time, break off the stalk. With a sharp knife held against the side of the artichoke, cut off all large bottom leaves, leaving a cone of small soft leaves in the centre. Trim the cone level with the top of the artichoke bottom. Rub the artichoke well with another cut lemon to prevent discoloration. Cut off the leaves under the bottom and trim it smooth, flattening the base. Rub it again with cut lemon and drop into the cold lemon water. Repeat with the remaining artichokes. To cook the artichoke bottoms, drain them, put them in boiling salted water and cover with a colander or heatproof plate to keep them submerged. Simmer them until tender, 20 to 25 minutes. To serve the artichokes hot, drain them and scoop out the choke with a teaspoon. To serve them cold, leave them to cool to tepid in the cooking liquid, drain and remove the choke.

BAIN-MARIE
A *bain-marie* (water bath) is used both for cooking and for keeping food warm. Water diffuses direct heat and ensures food remains moist and does not become too hot.

To cook in a *bain-marie*, bring a deep roasting tin of water to the boil and set the dish, mould or pan of food in it; the water should come at least halfway up the sides of the dish. Bring the water back to the boil on top of the stove, then transfer to an oven heated to 180°C/350°F/Gas Mark 4 or continue cooking on top of the stove, according to the recipe. Count the cooking time from the moment the water comes to the boil.

To keep foods hot in a *bain-marie*, set the dish or pan in a roasting tin of hot but not boiling water and leave over very low heat. The water should not boil.

BAKING BLIND
Pastry cases are baked blind before a filling is added. This procedure is used if the filling is not to be cooked in the case, or if the filling is especially moist and might soak the pastry during baking. The dried beans or rice for baking blind can be kept and re-used. Heat the oven to 200°C/400°F/Gas Mark 6. Crumple a round of greaseproof or parchment paper and use it to line the chilled pastry case, pressing the paper well into the corners; fill the case with dried beans or rice. Bake for 15 minutes or until the edges of the pastry case are set and lightly browned. Remove the paper and beans or rice and continue baking until the bottom of the pastry case is firm and dry: 4 to 5 minutes if the tart is to be baked again with the filling, or 8 to 10 minutes until well browned, to bake the case completely.

BARDING FAT
Barding fat is thinly sliced pork fat available at most butchers. Barding fat is often wrapped around meat and game when it has little or no natural fat. It is also used for lining terrines, where it is important to enclose meat to maintain a consistent level of moisture. Fat (streaky) bacon can be substituted.

BLANCHING
Blanching is a preliminary to cooking. Generally, the food is put into cold unsalted water, brought slowly to the boil, skimmed, and then simmered for 3 to 5 minutes. The term 'to blanch' is misleading, for as well as whitening, the process also removes salt and other strong flavours, for example from salted nuts, bacon and olives; it cleans and firms meats like calves' feet, sweetbreads and brains; it sets the brilliant colour of green vegetables and herbs, which often do not need further cooking; it loosens the skins of nuts, vegetables and fruits like chestnuts, tomatoes and peaches; and it rids rice and potatoes of excess starch.

BOUQUET GARNI
A bundle of aromatic herbs used for flavouring braises, ragoûts and sauces. It should include a sprig of fresh thyme, a bay leaf and several parsley stalks, tied together with string. Leek greens and celery tops may also be included.

BREAD STICKS, FRIED
Discard crusts of white bread and cut into 1 cm/$\frac{3}{8}$ in sticks. Fry as for *croûtes*.

BROWN STOCK, see Stock, Brown.

BUTTER
Most French butter is unsalted, but *beurre demi-sel* is lightly salted and *beurre salé* has quite a strong salty flavour. You can use either unsalted or lightly salted butter for recipes except where unsalted butter is specified, e.g. for puff pastry.

BUTTER, CLARIFIED
Melt the butter over low heat, skim the froth from the surface and leave it to cool to tepid. Pour the butter into a bowl, leaving the milky sediment at the bottom of the saucepan.

CHANTILLY CREAM
For ingredient measurements, see individual recipes. Put the chilled cream in a bowl set in another bowl containing ice and water and whip until stiff. Note: if the cream is not cold it may curdle before it stiffens. Add sugar to taste, with vanilla essence or other flavouring, if using, and continue whipping until the cream stiffens again. Do not over-beat or the cream will curdle. Chantilly cream can be stored in the refrigerator for an hour or two. It will separate slightly on standing, but will recombine if stirred.

CHICKEN, to joint, see Jointing a raw bird.

CHICKEN STOCK, see Stock, Chicken.

CRÈME FRAÎCHE
This French cream has a slightly tart flavour which is particularly good in sauces. To make 750 ml/$1\frac{1}{4}$ pints of crème fraîche, stir together in a saucepan 500 ml/16 fl oz double cream and 250 ml/8 fl oz buttermilk or soured cream. Heat gently until just below body temperature (25°C/75°F). Pour the cream into a container and partly cover it. Keep it in a warm place at this temperature for 6 to 8 hours or until it thickens and tastes slightly acidic. The cream will thicken faster on a hot day. Stir it and store in the refrigerator; it will keep for up to 2 weeks.

CROÛTES
Croûtes are fried or toasted slices of bread used to add texture or to garnish dishes. If using French bread, cut the loaf into thin diagonal slices; if using sliced white bread, cut the bread into squares, triangles, rounds or hearts, trimming and discarding the crusts.
For toasted *croûtes*: bake the sliced bread in an oven heated to 180°C/350°F/Gas Mark 4 for 10 to 15 minutes, turning the *croûtes* over halfway through so they brown evenly on both sides. For a lightly fried effect, brush the sliced bread on both sides with melted butter before baking in the oven.
For fried *croûtes*: heat enough oil or butter, or a combination of the two, in a frying pan to coat the bottom generously. Add the slices of bread in a single layer, brown them on both sides over a brisk heat and drain them on kitchen paper. *Croûtes* can be made a day ahead and kept in an airtight container. Wrap them in foil and reheat in a low oven if necessary before serving.

DEGLAZING
To deglaze a pan, boil the juices to a glaze that sticks to the bottom of the pan (this may happen naturally during cooking). Pour off any fat, then add liquid and boil, stirring constantly to dissolve the glaze. Continue boiling until the liquid is reduced and has plenty of flavour.

DUCK, to joint, see Jointing a raw bird.

EGG GLAZE
This is made by whisking a whole egg with a large pinch of salt. A glaze of egg yolk, salt and a large tablespoon of water, will give a less shiny, more golden finish.

HERBES DE PROVENCE
A popular commercial mixture of dried herbs including thyme, savory and an anise-flavoured herb such as fennel, perhaps with some sage, rosemary and bay leaf.

HERBS
Quantities given in the recipes are for fresh herbs. The strength of dried herbs varies, but in general they are two to three times as strong as fresh ones.

ICE CREAMS
Vanilla: For 500 ml/$\frac{3}{4}$ pint of ice cream, make vanilla custard (see page 222) using 250 ml/8 fl oz of milk, $\frac{1}{2}$ vanilla pod or few drops vanilla essence, 3 or 4 egg yolks and 60 g/2 oz of caster sugar. Chill the custard until it is very cold. Freeze it in an ice cream machine or freezer until slushy. Add 125 ml/4 fl oz of double cream, lightly whipped, making sure to combine it thoroughly, and continue freezing until the mixture is firm.

Lift out the blade. Pack down the ice cream in the container, or pack it into a chilled freezerproof container, cover it tightly and store in the freezer. If freezing for more than 12 hours, allow the ice cream to soften in the refrigerator for 30 minutes before serving.

Strawberry: For 500 ml/$\frac{3}{4}$ pint of ice cream, purée 250 g/8 oz of fresh strawberries to make 175 ml/6 fl oz of purée; if you like, strain it to remove the pips. Stir it into the chilled vanilla custard (see above for method and ingredient measurements) with 1 tablespoon of kirsch or lemon juice, or to taste. Sweeten the mixture to taste. Continue as for vanilla ice cream.

JOINTING A RAW BIRD INTO SERVING PIECES
With a sharp knife, cut between leg and body, following the outline of the thigh until the leg joint is visible. Locate the 'oyster' piece of meat lying against the backbone, and cut around it so it remains attached to the thigh. Twist the leg sharply outwards to break the thigh joint. Cut forwards to detach each leg from the body, including the oyster meat.

With a knife or poultry shears, cut away and remove the backbone. Cut along the breastbone to halve the carcass. Cut off the wing tips. The bird is now in four pieces.

To cut into eight pieces, divide each breast in half, cutting diagonally through the meat, then through the breast and rib bones so a portion of breast meat is cut off with the wing. Trim the rib bones. Then, cut the legs in half through the joint, using the white line of fat on the underside as a guide. Trim the drumsticks and any protruding bones with poultry shears.

JULIENNE STRIPS
Julienne strips are matchstick length but more finely cut. For root vegetables, trim the sides of the peeled vegetable to a square, then slice into 5 cm/2 in lengths. Cut the lengths into thin vertical slices. Stack the slices and cut into thin strips. For celery, green pepper and similar vegetables, cut lengthways into thin strips measuring 5 cm/2 in.

LARDONS
Lardons are usually cut from a piece of streaky bacon, but other fatty cuts of pork can also be used. To cut the *lardons*, trim the rind from the bacon and slice it 6 mm/¼ in thick, then cut across the slices to make short strips.

LINING A FLAN TIN
Either fluted or plain tins are suitable; flan tins with removable bottoms are easiest to use. Plain pastry should be rolled out to medium thickness (6 mm/¼ in), sweet pastry a little thicker, and puff pastry thinner. Lightly butter the tin. Roll out the dough about 5 cm/2 in larger than the tin. Lift the dough around the rolling pin and unroll it over the tin, being careful not to stretch it. Gently lift the edges and press the dough well into the corners of the tin, using a small ball of excess dough dipped in flour. Roll the pin across the top of the tin to cut off excess dough. With fingers press the dough evenly up the edge of the tin to increase the height of the pastry case. Prick the case every 1.25 cm/½ in with a fork and chill it until firm.

MAYONNAISE
To make 375 ml/12 fl oz of mayonnaise, whisk 2 egg yolks in a small bowl with a little salt, pepper, 2 tbsp white wine vinegar or 1 tbsp lemon juice and 1 tsp Dijon mustard, if using. This will take a minute (or just under). Note: all ingredients should be at room temperature. Set the bowl on a cloth so that it does not move while you are whisking.

Add 300 ml/½ pint of vegetable or olive oil, drop by drop, whisking constantly. After adding 2 tablespoons of oil, the mixture should be quite thick. Add the remaining oil more quickly, a tablespoon at a time, or pour from a jug in a very slow stream, whisking constantly. Stir in another ½ tbsp of vinegar or ½ tsp of lemon juice, and add salt, pepper and mustard to taste.

MERINGUE, SIMPLE
For ingredient measurements, see individual recipes. Whisk egg whites until they are very stiff, then whisk in 1 tablespoon of sugar for every egg white used so that the whites turn glossy, forming characteristic short peaks. Fold in the remaining sugar lightly. (The first batch of sugar stabilizes the egg white foam, but if the second, larger batch is mixed in too vigorously, the egg whites will lose their volume and turn to syrup.) Finally, add any flavouring you are using.

PASTRY DOUGHS
Pâte Brisée (French shortcrust pastry): For ingredient measurements, see individual recipes. Sift the flour on to a work surface and make a large well in the centre. Pound the butter with a rolling pin to soften it. Put the butter, eggs or egg yolks, salt and water in the well with flavourings such as sugar. Work together with your fingertips until partly mixed. Gradually draw in the flour with a pastry scraper or palette knife, pulling the dough into large crumbs using the fingertips of both hands. If the crumbs are dry, sprinkle with another tablespoon of water. Press the dough together – it should be soft but not sticky. Work small portions of dough, pushing away from you on the work surface with the heel of your hand, then gathering it up with a scraper. Continue until the dough is smooth and pliable. Press the dough into a ball, wrap it and chill it for 30 minutes or until firm. *Pâte brisée* dough can be kept in the refrigerator overnight, or frozen.

Pâte Sucrée (Sweet pastry): For ingredient measurements, see individual recipes. Sift the flour on to a work surface and make a large well in the centre. Pound the butter with a rolling pin to soften it. Put the butter, salt, sugar, egg yolks and vanilla essence, if using, into the well and work with your fingertips until they are well mixed and the sugar is partly dissolved. Draw in the flour, then work the dough, wrap it and chill as for *pâte brisée* dough.

Puff Pastry: To make 500 g/1 lb of puff pastry dough, sift 250 g/8 oz of plain flour on to a cold marble slab or board, make a well in the centre and add 1 tsp salt, 125 ml/4 fl oz of cold water and 1 tbsp of melted butter. Work together with your fingertips until well mixed, then gradually work in the flour. If the dough is dry, add more water to form a soft but not sticky dough. Note: do not overwork the dough or it will become elastic. Press the dough into a ball, wrap it and chill for 15 minutes.

Lightly flour 250 g/8 oz of cold butter, put it between two sheets of greaseproof paper and flatten it with a rolling pin. Fold it, replace between the sheets of paper and continue pounding and folding it until it is pliable but not sticky; it should be the same consistency as the dough. Shape the butter into a 15 cm/6 in square and flour it.

Roll out the dough on a floured marble slab or board to a 30 cm/12 in square, thicker in the centre than at the sides. Set the square of butter in the centre and fold the dough around it like an envelope.

Make sure the work surface is well floured. Place the dough seam side down and lightly pound it with a rolling pin to flatten it slightly. Roll it out to a rectangle about 18 cm/7 in wide and 50 cm/20 in long. Fold the rectangle into three, like a business letter. Seal the edges with the rolling pin and turn the dough a quarter turn (90°) to bring the closed seam to your left side so the dough opens like a book. This is called a 'turn'. Roll it out again and fold it in three. Wrap the dough and chill for 15 minutes.

Repeat the rolling process until you have rolled and folded the dough six times, with a 15 minute rest in the refrigerator between every two turns. Chill the puff pastry dough for at least 15 minutes before using it.

PRALINE
Praline is made of caramel and toasted almonds and keeps several weeks in an airtight container at room temperature.

Combine equal amounts of whole unblanched almonds and sugar in a small saucepan. Heat gently until the sugar melts, stirring occasionally. Continue cooking over fairly low heat until the sugar turns a deep golden brown and the almonds make a popping sound, showing they are toasted.

Pour the mixture on to a lightly oiled baking sheet, spread out the praline with an oiled wooden spoon and leave until cool and crisp.

Crack the praline into pieces and grind to a powder in a food processor, blender or rotary grater.

RABBIT, TO JOINT INTO SERVING PIECES
Trim and discard flaps of skin, tips of forelegs and any excess bone. Using a heavy knife or cleaver, divide the rabbit crossways into three sections: back legs, back, and forelegs including rib cage. Cut between the back legs to separate them; trim the end of the backbone. Chop the front of the rabbit into two to separate forelegs. Cut the back crossways into two or three pieces, depending on the size, giving six or seven pieces. Leave the kidneys attached to the ribs. For eight or nine pieces, cut each leg in two crossways.

REFRESHING
After blanching (see above), some foods are rinsed under cold running water to stop the cooking and, if it is a brightly-coloured vegetable, to set the colour. Drain the food well and pat it dry with kitchen paper to rid it of all water.

STERILIZING PRESERVING JARS
It is best to use only special preserving jars with metal or glass tops (check for any cracks or misshapen lids). Some have rubber seals that may be used only once and should be replaced each time. Wash jars and seals and rinse in scalding water. Keep jars in a low oven or submerged in hot water until you are ready to fill them.

Avoid using jars with more than 1 litre/2 pint capacity as the contents tend not to keep in top condition after opening. Small jars are much more satisfactory.

STOCK
Brown: To make about 2.5 litres/4 pints of stock, roast 2.3 kg/5 lb veal bones (you may use half veal bones and half beef bones, if you prefer) in a very hot oven for 20 minutes. Add 2 quartered carrots and 2 quartered onions and continue roasting until very brown, about 30 minutes longer. Transfer the bones and vegetables to a stock pot or large saucepan, discarding any fat. Add a bouquet garni (see above), 1 tsp whole peppercorns, 1 tbsp of tomato purée and about 5 litres/8 pints of water. Bring slowly to the boil, then simmer uncovered for 4 to 5 hours, skimming occasionally. Strain the stock, taste it and, if the flavour is not concentrated, boil it until well reduced. Chill the stock and skim off any fat before using. Stock can be kept in the refrigerator for up to 3 days, or frozen.

Chicken: Duck and other poultry bones can be substituted for the chicken. To make about 2.5 litres/4 pints of stock, combine 1.4 kg/3 lb chicken backs, necks and bones, 1 quartered onion, 1 quartered carrot, 1 stick of celery cut into pieces, a bouquet garni (see above), 1 tsp peppercorns and about 4 litres/6½ pints of water in a large pan. Bring slowly to the boil, skimming often. Simmer uncovered, skimming occasionally, for 2 to 3 hours. Strain, taste and, if the stock is not concentrated, boil it until well reduced. Refrigerate it and, before using, skim off any solidified fat from the surface. Stock can be kept for up to 3 days in the refrigerator, or can be frozen.

White Veal: Proceed as for brown stock, using only veal bones, but do not brown the bones and vegetables and omit the tomato purée. Blanch (see above) the bones, then continue as for brown stock.

SUGAR
In recipes 'sugar' refers to granulated sugar. If another type is needed, such as caster or icing sugar, this is stated.

TOMATOES, TO SKIN, SEED AND CHOP
Bring a large pan of water to the boil. With a small knife, cut the core out of each tomato. Turn the tomatoes over and lightly score a cross on the bottom. Immerse them in the boiling water for 8 to 15 seconds, depending on ripeness, until the skin curls away from the cross. This shows that the skin will peel easily. Lift out each tomato with a slotted spoon, allow it to cool slightly and then peel it. Halve each tomato crossways and squeeze out the seeds; scrape away any remaining seeds with a knife. Cut the tomato halves into slices, then chop them.

TRUSSING A BIRD
Trussing not only keeps in the stuffing, it also holds the bird together so that a sprawling leg does not overcook, and the cooked bird sits neatly for carving. Birds under 500 g/1 lb are simply tied.

Thread the trussing needle. Pull out any pieces of fat located around the tail cavity of the bird.

Fold back the neck skin and remove the wishbone (it prevents the breast from being carved in neat slices), using the point of a sharp knife to cut it out. Remove any fat.

Set the bird breast up, and push the legs well back and down so that the ends sit straight up in the air. Insert the trussing needle into the flesh at the knee joint, and push it through the bird and out through the other knee joint. Push the bird over on to its breast and, if the wing tips have not been trimmed, tuck them under the second joint. Pull the neck skin over the neck cavity, and push the needle through both sections of one wing and into the neck skin. Continue under the backbone of the bird to the other side. Now catch the second wing in the same way as the first, pushing the needle through both wing bones and pulling it out the other side.

Turn the bird on to its side, pull the ends of the string (from the leg and wing) firmly together and tie them securely. Turn the bird breast up.

Tuck the tail into the cavity of the bird and fold the skin over it. Push the needle through the skin. Loop the string around one drumstick and over the other drumstick. Tie the ends of the string firmly together. The bird should sit level on the board.

VANILLA CUSTARD
For ingredient measurements, see individual recipes. Put the milk or milk and cream into a heavy saucepan with the vanilla pod, if using, splitting it to extract the seeds for more flavour. Heat until bubbles appear around the edge of the milk, then remove from the heat, cover and leave to infuse for 10 to 15 minutes. Beat the egg yolks with the caster sugar until thick and pale. Stir in the hot milk and return the mixture to the pan. Heat gently, stirring with a wooden spoon, until the custard thickens enough to leave a clear trail when you draw your finger across the back of the spoon. Note: do not boil or overcook the custard or it will curdle. At once remove the custard from the heat and strain it into a bowl. If using vanilla essence, stir it in now. Rinse the vanilla pod to use again.

Custard can easily be flavoured. For coffee flavour, infuse the milk with coarsely ground coffee beans in place of the vanilla pod, straining the milk before mixing it with the egg yolk and sugar mixture. Or, you can add melted bittersweet chocolate after the custard has thickened and been removed from the heat.

VINAIGRETTE DRESSING
Vinaigrette dressing can be made with neutral vegetable oil, olive oil or nut oil. In France, red wine vinegar is most often used, but sometimes lemon juice is substituted (using roughly half of the quantity called for in vinegar). Other vinegars such as white wine, sherry, balsamic or fruit also make delicious vinaigrette dressings. Flavourings such as chopped onion, shallot, garlic or fresh herbs should only be added to the dressing just before it is used.

For ingredient measurements, see individual recipes. In a small bowl whisk the vinegar with the salt, pepper and any other seasonings (such as Dijon mustard) until the salt dissolves. Gradually add the oil, whisking constantly so that the dressing emulsifies and thickens slightly. Vinaigrette can be made ahead and kept for several days at room temperature; it will separate but will re-emulsify when whisked.

WHITE SAUCE
Proportions of flour and butter to milk vary, giving a thinner or thicker sauce as required.

For ingredient measurements, see individual recipes. Heat the milk in a saucepan until bubbles form around the edge. If using aromatic ingredients such as onion, bay leaf and peppercorns, add them, cover the pan and remove from the heat. Leave to infuse for 5 to 10 minutes. Melt the butter in a heavy saucepan, whisk in the flour and cook until foaming but not brown, 1 to 2 minutes; allow to cool. Strain in the hot milk and bring the sauce to the boil, whisking constantly. Add seasoning and simmer for 3 to 5 minutes. Taste for seasoning.If not using at once smear the surface of the sauce with a knob of butter to prevent a skin from forming over it.

WILD MUSHROOMS, TO CLEAN
All fresh wild mushrooms need the same preparation. Pick them over to remove twigs and grass then lightly trim the stems. Shake and gently brush to remove any earth; morels are the most gritty, so brush each one well, splitting the stem to remove any soil inside. Rinse with cold water, but never soak fresh mushrooms as they quickly soften to a pulp.

Soak dried mushrooms in warm water for 1–2 hours until fairly soft. Morels may need rinsing again, but liquid from other mushrooms adds flavour to a soup or sauce. The flavour of both fresh and dried mushrooms varies very much in strength, but 1 kg/2 lb of fresh mushrooms is the approximate equivalent of 100 g/$3\frac{1}{4}$ oz of dried mushrooms.

YEAST
If using dry yeast, allow half the weight of fresh yeast. Sprinkle dry yeast over the liquid and leave it to dissolve; crumble fresh yeast into the liquid, then stir to dissolve it.

ACKNOWLEDGMENTS

Anne Willan gratefully acknowledges the help of Burks Hamner and Edie Frere in Los Angeles, and Andrew Nurnberg in London, in the planning of this book, and the valuable contributions, as each chapter developed, of La Varenne associates Jackie Bobrow, Elisabeth Evans, Kate Krader, Craig Laban, Kelly McNabb, Cynthia Nims, Stacy Toporoff and Chef Claude Vauguet, whether at the desk, in the test kitchen, or on photographic location.

Princesse Georges-Henri de la Tour d'Auvergne would like to extend her warmest thanks to all those who helped with *Château Cuisine*, and most particularly to Simone Monneron, the organising genius behind the countless on-site visits, meetings and interviews with châteaux owners. It has also been a pleasure to work with Anne Willan and her husband Mark Cherniavsky and their associate Jane Sigal. A special thank you, too, to Christopher Baker for his exceptional photography and to Burks Hamner for suggesting the book.

Conran Octopus would like to thank the following shops for their help in supplying props:
A LA MINE D'ARGENT, 108 rue du Bac, 75007 Paris
ALIETTE TEXIER, 41 quai de l'Horloge, 75001, Paris
ARGENTERIE DES FRANCS BOURGEOIS, 17 rue des Francs Bourgeois, 75004, Paris
ART DOMESTIQUE ANCIEN, 231 rue Saint Honoré, 75001 Paris
AU PUCERON CHINEUR, 23 rue Saint Paul, 75004 Paris
DOMINIQUE PARAMYTHIOTI, 172 galerie de Valois, 75001 Paris
ERIC DUBOIS, 9 rue Saint Paul, 75004 Paris
FANETTE, 1 rue d'Alencon, 75015 Paris
FUCHSIA, 2 rue Ave Maria, 75004 Paris
GEORG JENSEN, 239 rue Saint Honoré, 75001 Paris
HUGUETTE BERTRAND, 22 rue Jacob, 75006 Paris
LA PALFERINE, 43 avenue Bosquet, 75007 Paris

INDEX

INDEX OF RECIPES